Life in West China

You are holding a reproduction of an original work that is in the public domain in the United States of America, and possibly other countries. You may freely copy and distribute this work as no entity (individual or corporate) has a copyright on the body of the work. This book may contain prior copyright references, and library stamps (as most of these works were scanned from library copies). These have been scanned and retained as part of the historical artifact.

This book may have occasional imperfections such as missing or blurred pages, poor pictures, errant marks, etc. that were either part of the original artifact, or were introduced by the scanning process. We believe this work is culturally important, and despite the imperfections, have elected to bring it back into print as part of our continuing commitment to the preservation of printed works worldwide. We appreciate your understanding of the imperfections in the preservation process, and hope you enjoy this valuable book.

LIFE IN WEST CHINA.

THE BOYS' BOARDING SCHOOL, CHUNGKING.

This new building, with Master's residence above, was opened in June, 1905. It is situated on the hills opposite Chungking.

LIFE IN WEST CHINA

DESCRIBED BY TWO RESIDENTS

IN THE PROVINCE OF SZ-CHWAN

BY
ROBERT J. DAVIDSON
AND
ISAAC MASON

WITH INTRODUCTION BY
DR. TIMOTHY RICHARD

LONDON
HEADLEY BROTHERS
14 BISHOPSGATE STREET WITHOUT E.C.
1905

HEADLEY BROTHERS,
PRINTERS,
LONDON; AND ASHFORD, KENT.

PREFACE.

IN passing this book through the press it has not been possible to consult the Authors to any great extent, as both of them are still residing in the Province of Sz-Chwan. Robert J. Davidson (Native name = T'ao Wei-Shin) is living at the capital, Chentu, and Isaac Mason (Native name = Mei I-seng) at the city of Sui-ling. In consequence of their absence, queries which have arisen have been settled without referring to them. For the same reason completeness is not claimed for the book. It is an attempt at an historical sketch of Friends' Mission in China, with details as to the history, religions, customs, etc., of the Chinese, necessary to a clear understanding of the work.

Valuable help has been received from Dr. Timothy Richard, who very kindly ran through the MS. and made a number of practical suggestions. Leonard Wigham, B.A., of Chungking, at present in England, and several other Friends, have rendered great service in the revision of proofs, etc.—a service of love, done with the desire that the book may, in some way, help towards the coming of the Kingdom of Christ in China.

MARSHALL N. FOX.

15, Devonshire Street,
    London, E.C.
        November, 1905.

"I have seen wonderful changes in this land, and there are greater changes at the doors. This is a most interesting period in the history of this great people. China is not only awakening, she is awake. The China that I found fast asleep on my arrival at Shanghai fifty years ago is now all alive, and going to school again, and doing so willingly, gladly, eagerly. What an opportunity is opened up before the Church in this land! There is no reason why China should not be evangelised within this century, so far as China herself is concerned. Everything depends on the Church. A dead Church may prevent it; nothing else can."

DR. GRIFFITH JOHN.[a]

September 17th, 1905.

---

[a] Extract from a letter to Mr. Stephen Massey, reprinted from the *Examiner*, November 16, 1905.

INTRODUCTION.

I HAVE read through this new book on "China" by the Friends' Foreign Mission Association with much interest, especially as I rejoice in knowing some of its devoted missionaries as personal friends.

The conversion of China. How few really comprehend the profound meaning underlying that word conversion and its infinite consequences!

China is the greatest non-Christian nation on earth, in area, number of its people, in quality of character and age. Buddhist Missionaries, with Hindu philosophy and religion, have tried to convert her; Mohammedans have tried and Christians have tried; but though they have been one or two milleniums at it, not one has yet succeeded in getting China wholly converted. Why are all efforts in vain? Is Chinese religion superior to all? Or is there any hope that Christians will now succeed better than in the past?

The comparatively small number of those who were converted during the first few years of this Mission is characteristic of the beginning of all Missionary work in China in modern times. This is largely because it has been the determined policy of the Chinese government and the *literati* to oppose Christian Missions, because they really believed that their seeming charity was to win the hearts of the people in order eventually to win their country. That is the chief explanation of riots, occurring everywhere, whenever new Mission stations were opened in the interior. That is why the advent of medical missionaries did not make any appreciable difference in the number of converts, and why only the poor, and none of the influential classes dared join the Christian Church. It was under a great government ban, that these faithful workers, men and women, toiled on in the face of endless difficulties and disappointments, always ready for service or sacrifice, a sight for angels to admire !

The very same chapters which describe these disappointing toils again and again, speak of a great surprise at last. A wonderful change has come over the people of late, when multitudes seek admission to the Church and when students, who formerly headed opposition to the missionaries, are now seeking for them as for lost friends. This remarkable change has not been without a cause.

On the one hand China has been learning by sad experience, first through the Japanese War in 1895, and then through the Allies in 1900, that violence, riots and massacres of innocent people by a proud despotic government were crimes against humanity, for which she had to suffer the deepest humiliation and penalty. On the other hand, the chief ministers in Peking and the leading students in the provinces had been approached by the missionaries (who had been appointed by the General Conference of Missionaries in Shanghai in 1890, to explain Christianity to them, and that missionaries are not emissaries of their respective governments—as they supposed them to be—but the true friends of China), who pointed out to them that their chief enemy was ignorance and suspicion, and that the best way to get out of this enemy's clutches was to adopt modern education, and to carry out the will of God by friendship with all nations.

These two influences combined, produced a profound effect on the central government. They thanked the missionaries for their suggestions, and shortly after commanded the viceroys and governors to open a modern university in each of the eighteen provinces. Consequently, the attitude of the gentry and students and people in every province changed. This is the explanation of the change far away in Sz-Chwan, and this will justify the important move to have a station in Chentu, the provincial capital, for work among the leaders, for thereby the Mission has an opportunity of converting both high and low.

Converting from what ? From Confucianism ? God forbid ! for the main teachings of Confucianism are benevolence, righteousness, propriety, learning and sincerity. What could the world do without these ?

From Modern Buddhism ? God forbid ! for it teaches the vanity of what is material and temporary as compared with the spiritual and the eternal, the need of repentance, faith in God, service for others and mercy. What could the world do without these ?

From Taoism ? God forbid ! for it teaches that man should have dominion over the forces of nature—material and spiritual. What could the world do without utilizing the forces of nature ?

From Mohammedanism ? God forbid ! for it teaches all men to turn from dead shams to the true God. What could the world do without God to light up lamps for us in the heavens every day ? No man can do it.

What are we to do then ? Follow our Lord's example. He said that He did not come to destroy the law and the prophets, but to fulfil ! that He came to bring us back to God ; that men must be born again ; that the Holy Spirit would be given who would guide to all truth ; that thereby men become partakers of the Divine nature and heirs of immortality. Convert them from sin to holiness, from darkness to light, from hate to love, from death to life !

It is not by attacking long-cherished beliefs but by the presentation of Christ and His salvation, and by doing this as the outcome of our own experience and under the power of the Holy Spirit, that we can lead men into the full light and liberty of the Gospel. It is union with Christ, and not the blind following of even wise precepts, which delivers men from errors of faith and of practice.

Preach and teach such things, then you will find the best Confucianists, the best Buddhists, the best Taoists, the best Mohammedans will soon be ready to drop the non-essentials in their respective religions, and to join with you to establish the Kingdom of God first in human hearts and then in organizations for the salvation of the whole world. Then too, it will be found that where there were hundreds of converts before, there will be thousands now, and where there were thousands before, there will be tens of thousands now, crying "Hallelujah for the Lord God Omnipotent reigneth, King of kings, and Lord of lords, and He shall reign for ever and ever!"

Timothy Richard.

London,
    September, 1905.

CONTENTS.

CHAP.		PAGE.
	INTRODUCTION	vii.
I.	GEOGRAPHY, HISTORY, POLITICAL RELATIONS, GOVERNMENT, AND POPULATION	1
II	FROM SHANGHAI TO SZ-CHWAN	13
III.	THE PROVINCE OF SZ-CHWAN	31
IV.	THE CITY OF CHUNGKING	37
V.	CHENTU, THE PROVINCIAL CAPITAL	43
VI.	THE COMMERCE, BANKING, COINAGE AND POSTAL SYSTEMS	51
VII.	CHARACTER OF THE PEOPLE	65
VIII.	SOCIAL CUSTOMS	77
IX.	THE RELIGIONS OF CHINA	93
X.	LANGUAGE AND LITERATURE	109
XI.	EDUCATION	121
XII.	CHRISTIAN MISSIONS	133
XIII.	CHRISTIAN MISSIONS (*continued*)	145
XIV.	CHRISTIAN MISSIONS (*continued*)	153
XV.	BEGINNING OF FRIENDS' MISSION IN CHINA	161
XVI.	IN THE PROVINCE OF SZ-CHWAN	171
XVII.	FRIENDS' MISSION, CHUNGKING, 1894-1904	179
XVIII.	WORK OF THE LAST DECADE	191
XIX.	R. J. DAVIDSON'S NOTES OF VISITS TO YEN T'ING, 1901	209
XX.	OUR AIMS AND FUTURE PROSPECTS	223
XXI.	APPEAL	235
	APPENDIX	239
	INDEX	243

LIST OF ILLUSTRATIONS.

	PAGE.
The Boys' Boarding School, Chungking	*Frontispiece.*
The Ming Tombs at Nanking	5
Opium Smokers	9
A Group of Chinese Officials	11
House-boat on the Upper Yang Tse	15
Cargo-junk coming Down River	17
Trackers on the Yang Tse	19
The Trackers Taking Their Meals	21
Ascending a Rapid	23
Entrance to Niu Kan Gorge	23
Entrance of the Mi-T'an Gorge	25
The Chin-T'an Rapid	26
The Upper Chin-T'an Rapid	27
A Chinese Gun-boat	29
Area of Sz-Chwan, compared with British Isles	31
Opium Poppy-field	33
Ready for a Journey Inland	35
A Timber Yard on the River-side, near Chungking	38
A Map of Chungking and Neighbourhood	39
River-side Steps, Chungking	41
The Great Examination Hall, Chentu	45
Green Dragon Street, Chentu; Friends' Premises on the Right	50
Types of Coinage : mostly ancient	55
Coins : Past and Present	59
A Bamboo Water-wheel	63
A Way-side Temple and Shrine	67
Rope Suspension Bridge, Sung P'an, N.W. Sz-Chwan	72
A Woman Winding Cotton	75
A Chinese Gentleman	77
A Chinese Student Engaged in Writing	79
Teachers and Students	82

List of Illustrations.

A Chinese " Punch and Judy " Show	85
A Chinese Water-carrier	87
The Barber	89
Gods of Literature and War	91
The Tablet of Confucius, Peking	94
The God of the River	99
The Goddess of Mercy	103
The Great Buddha at Peking	107
The Foolishness of War	112
A Tibetan Family	123
First House for Friends' Mission, Chentu	128
Master's Residence, Boys' Boarding School, Chungking	132
A Mandarin in Full Dress	135
A Group of Chinese Women	139
Masters and Pupil Teachers of the Boys' School, Chungking	152
Men's Side of Chungking Meeting House	155
Map of Sz-Chwan, shewing Division of the Field	160
The First Premises Rented in T'ung Ch'wan	170
The Sanatorium, or " Country House," just outside Chungking	177
A View from Chungking	181
The School for Missionaries' Children	183
The Hill School Children at Drill	185
A Chinese Lifeboat	186
Four Graduates of the Boys' High School, Chungking, 1904	187
Interior of Match Factory at T'a Chi Keo	190
New Schoolroom of the Girls' Boarding School, T'ung Ch'wan	192
The Meeting House at T'ung Ch'wan	195
The Visit of the Deputation to T'ung Ch'wan, 1904	201
The Deputation Travelling from Chungking to Chentu	203
Boys' School Building, T'ung Ch'wan	205
Girls at Drill	206
The Women's Hospital at T'ung Ch'wan	208
I. Mason, and some Chinese Native Helpers	211
A Familiar Road	224
Map of Friends' District in Sz-Chwan	224
One of China's Bridges	226
The Girls' Boarding School Premises at T'ung Ch'wan	228
New Friends' Buildings at Sui-ling	230
Mealtime; during Building Operations at Chentu	231

SOME TERMS EXPLAINED.

FU, a Prefecture, or portion of a province, and its capital; governed by an official (prefect) immediately subordinate to the Provincial Governor (Viceroy). As used in this Book it generally refers to the city—a prefectural city.

T'ING, a division of a province and its capital, smaller than a Fu, governed by an official immediately subordinate to the Provincial Governor (Viceroy) in the case of an independent T'ing, or subordinate to the Fu if a dependent T'ing.

CHOW, a division of a province and its capital, smaller than a T'ing. There are both independent Chow and dependent Chow.

HSIEN, a county, or smaller division, and its capital, dependent either upon a Fu, T'ing, or Chow.

CHEN, a mart.

HO or KIANG, a river.

SHAN, a mountain. LING, a pass or ridge.

PEH, north. NAN, south. TUNG, east. SI, west.

NOTES ON THE

PRONUNCIATION OF ROMANISED CHINESE NAMES.

The vowels are pronounced approximately as in French ; *e.g.* :—
a like a in *half*.   *i* like ee in *seem*.
e like a in *name*.   *u* like oo in *look*.
Modified ï is a very slight sound like e in *the*.
Modified ü is pronounced like French eu in *neuf*.
ai like ai in *aisle*.   *ao* like ou in *house*.

eo (sometimes written *ou*) is a diphthong, the sound of which is approached by saying the English a and o together very quickly.

ui or *wei* is pronounced as English *way*, *e.g.*, Sui-ling pronounced Swayling.

Consonants are mostly pronounced as in English, with the exceptions mentioned below.

Note that the aspirate changes the sound of the consonant, and is marked by an apostrophe, immediately following the consonant it affects. Thus *ch* unaspirated is like English j; aspirated, it is like English ch (soft) or ts, *e.g.*, *chin* is pronounced jin ; while *ch'in* is pronounced chin.

[N.B.—In Chungking and other places the *ch* before a, e, o and u has just the same sound as *ts*.]

k unaspirated is like English g (hard); aspirated, it is like English k.
p ,, ,, ,, b ; ,, ,, ,, p.
t ,, ,, ,, d ; ,, ,, ,, t.
ts ,, ,, ,, dz ; ,, ,, ,, ts.

tsz or *tse* or *tsï* unaspirated is like English ds in *pads*; aspirated, it is like English ts in *hats*.

hs in many places is pronounced like English *sh*.

sh, in a large part of the Friends' Field, is pronounced like a simple *s*. In a few places the h has its force.

WEIGHTS AND MEASURES.

1 Mou = 0·15 acre English.
1 inch Chinese = 1⅜ inches English.
10 inches Chinese = 1 foot Chinese—13¾ inches English.
1 oz. Chinese = 1⅓ oz. English.
16 oz. Chinese = 1 catty—1⅓ lbs. English.
100 catties = 1 picul—133⅓ lbs. English.
TLS. = Taels. An ounce of silver, worth about 2s. 6d.

Sycee, the silver currency of China. It consists of ingots of pure silver, of varying sizes and shapes. The value is ascertained by weighing in balances or steelyards. The unit is the tael, equal to 1⅓ English ounce. In West China, the largest piece in common use, called a *ting*, weighs about 10 taels. In Hankow, the *shoe*, weighing about 50 taels, is also current.[*]

DAYS OF THE WEEK.

The Chinese, in the ordinary way, have no week, but reckon time by the month (or moons). The following names have been given to the days of the week in Missionary circles, and will only be understood by the natives in touch with them.

SUNDAY	Ta li pai (or Li pai rï)
MONDAY	Li pai i
TUESDAY	Li pai er
WEDNESDAY	Li pai san
THURSDAY	Li pai sï
FRIDAY	Li pai wu
SATURDAY	Li pai lu

[*] See illustration on p. 59.

CHAPTER I.

GEOGRAPHY, HISTORY, POLITICAL RELATIONS, GOVERNMENT, AND POPULATION.

GEOGRAPHY.

THE term by which Chinese most commonly designate their country is "Chung Kwoh," *i.e.* "Middle Kingdom." From time immemorial they have been taught to regard the world as a huge flat surface, with China as the one place of importance in the centre, and having other insignificant states on its fringes, and on small islands on the ocean that surround it; which states are given the generic term of "Outside Kingdoms," and the inhabitants are styled "barbarians."

China occupies a position with many natural advantages and, while not realizing the fond dreams of its inhabitants, it is a country of almost unlimited possibilities.

> With a sea-coast upwards of 2,000 miles in length, with a soil of remarkable fertility, open to the ocean winds and watered by noble rivers, with a territory lying almost entirely within the temperate zone, and containing beneath its surface mineral wealth of untold value, China has not only been able to maintain a large population during past milleniums, but in all probability she is destined in the future to be the home of Asia's most numerous and influential inhabitants.*

The area of the Empire, including China proper and its dependencies, is 4,218,401 square miles. This means that it is almost as large as the whole of Europe, and is in itself worthy

---

* "Dawn on the Hills of T'ang," by H. P. Beach, page 3.

of being considered a Continent. The area of China Proper is about 1,312,328 square miles,—about ten times that of the United Kingdom, and more than six times that of France.

In this brief survey, a passing reference only can be made to the physical features, notable among which are the Hwang Ho and Yang Tse Kiang, two immense rivers. The meaning of these names is "Yellow River" and "Son of the Ocean" respectively. While the Yellow River is one of the longest in the world, it is not navigable because of its swift current, and is a source of danger from its floods and the changing of its channel. The Yang Tse may well lay claim to its name, as being a noble and extremely useful river. It abounds with traffic and, at a distance of 1,500 miles from its mouth, it is sometimes nearly 1,000 yards wide. It is navigable for native craft far into the western parts of Sz-Chwan.

In a country so vast, many ranges of mountains are met with, and some peaks attain great altitudes. The lakes and plains of the central region are worthy of more notice than we can give them here.

Two gigantic artificial features, the Great Wall and the Grand Canal, are too famous to need more than a passing mention. The wall is built of bricks and earth, and extends for 1,550 miles, climbing over hill and crag, and running along the Mongolian plateau. It was built about B.C. 214, by the Emperor Ch'in Shih-Huang, to keep out the Tartars of the North. The Grand Canal, about 700 miles long, was made hundreds of years ago to facilitate transmission of grain from the southern provinces to Peking. Though shorn of much of its original splendour, it is still an important waterway.

HISTORY.

The early records of China are shrouded in deceptive haze and myth, a little more definition being assumed when we read of Yao and Shun, two virtuous emperors, who flourished in what the Chinese refer to as "the Golden Days." What many Chinese consider as reliable history begins with the Hsia dynasty, B.C. 2205—1766. Dr. Martin says "The area at that period comprehended within the empire was less than half of China proper. The conquering tribe which formed its nucleus seems to have entered the valley of the Yellow River from the north-west, bringing with them some knowledge of letters and elements of civilization, which enabled them to overcome the savage races by whom the country was then occupied; some they destroyed, others they absorbed, and the process of growth and assimilation went on for ages, until these heterogeneous elements were moulded into one people, the most numerous on the face of the earth." *

The Dynasty of Chow, B.C. 1122-255 produced the famous sages Confucius (551-479) and Mencius (372-289), as also the mystic Lao Tsz, the founder of the system of philosophy which has developed into the Taoism of to-day. The nine centuries covered by the history of the Chows may be regarded as a period of progression, which has left a deep impress on all the subsequent history of the empire.

The Han Dynasty (B.C. 206—A.D. 203) was an exceptionally prosperous period. It so impressed the Chinese themselves that, to this day, they prefer to designate themselves as "Sons of Han." Referring to this famous dynasty, Dr. Martin says:—

The Han period, which stretches over 460 years, is, as might be expected, peculiarly rich in monuments of intellectual activity. It is emphatically an era of reconstruction, when the Chinese people enter on a new career. Two things concur to make it ever memorable—the revival of letters and the introduction of Buddhism. The invention of paper in the second century B.C. contributed greatly to the multiplication of books. It was itself a result of learning, which created a demand for cheaper writing materials. Till then silk or bamboo tablets had been in use. In the year A.D. 67, under the Emperor Ming Ti, the triad of religious creeds was completed by the introduction of Buddhism from India. The apostles of Buddhism had, no doubt, found their way to China at an earlier date and, by this time, they had attracted sufficient

* "A Cycle of Cathay," by W. A. P. Martin, D.D., p. 253.

attention to lead to an embassy in quest of competent teachers. Such an embassy was a natural outcome of the unsettled state of the Chinese mind, agitated by the contentions of rival schools of religious thought. The emperor is said to have been prompted to this measure by a dream, in which he saw an image of gold representing a man with a bow and two arrows. In the Chinese name for Buddha the radical is man and the phonetic a bow and arrows. It is evident that the analysis of the character gave birth to this legend.*

Following the Hans, came a period when the empire was divided into the Three Kingdoms, one of which was the present province of Sz-Chwan. This was an age of martial prowess, which produced the heroes so often represented in the Chinese drama.

The T'ang Dynasty (A.D. 618-905) is famed as the period when poetry attained its highest pitch of perfection, and also for the art of printing from wooden blocks, the introduction of paper money, and the issue of the *Court Circular* now known as the *Peking Gazette*. The highly objectionable custom of foot-binding also probably belongs to about the end of this dynasty.

The Sung Dynasty (A.D. 960-1278) was marked by three things:— (1) by the rise of speculative philosophy, the thinkers of that period being both acute and profound ; (2) by expositions of Chinese texts, the most noted expositor being Chu Fu Tsz, from whom it is heresy to dissent ; (3) by the re-organization of the civil service examinations, which then received their final form.

The Yuen, or Mongol, dynasty (A.D. 1260-1341) is celebrated as the first dynasty of Tartar origin which succeeded in subjugating the whole of China, though for two centuries previously the northern provinces had been under the sway of the Tartars, in spite of the Great Wall erected to keep them out. The dominions of Kublai Khan were probably more extensive than those of any monarch of ancient or modern times.

The intellectual character of the Ming dynasty (A.D. 1368-1644) is chiefly marked by the formation of encyclopædic collections and the codification of the laws. During the troubles which preceded the overthrow of the Mings, the Manchus, an insignificant tribe of Tartars, made themselves masters of the region to the north-west of the Great

* "A Cycle of Cathay," p. 260.

Wall. Called in as auxiliaries by a general in charge of the pass, who, under the pretence of avenging the death of his sovereign, veiled a private ambition, they seized the throne, and in seven years saw the whole empire at their feet. The celerity of their conquest was equalled by the wisdom of their government. By adopting the institutions of the conquered they minimized the odium inseparable from a domination, and prolonged their tenure much beyond the average of Chinese dynasties.*

THE MING TOMBS AT NANKING.

They inflicted a badge of servitude on the Chinese men in the shape of the pigtail, or queue, but their efforts to abolish foot-binding among the women were unsuccessful. Professor Giles, in speaking of the present Manchu or Ch'ing dynasty says:—

Eight emperors of this line have already occupied the throne. Of these eight, the second in every way fills the largest place in Chinese history. K'ang Hsi reigned for sixty-one years, thus completing his cycle, or term of sixty years, a division of time which has been in vogue

* "A Cycle of Cathay," p. 262.

among the Chinese for many centuries past. He was essentially a wise and great ruler. He treated the early Catholic priests with kindness and distinction, and availed himself in many ways of their scientific knowledge. He promulgated sixteen moral maxims, collectively known as the Sacred Edict, forming a complete code of rules for the guidance of everyday life, and presented in such terse, yet intelligible, terms that they at once took firm hold of the public mind, and have retained their position ever since. K'ang Hsi was the most eminent patron of literature the world has ever seen. He caused to be published under his own personal supervision the following compilations known as the four great works of the present dynasty:—

1. A huge thesaurus of extracts, in 110 thick volumes.
2. An encyclopædia in 450 books, usually bound up in 160 volumes.
3. An enlarged and improved edition of a herbarium, in 100 books.
4. A complete collection of the important philosophical writings of Chu Hsi, in 69 books.

In addition to these, the Emperor K'ang Hsi designed and gave his name to the great modern lexicon of the Chinese language, which contains over 40,000 characters, under separate entries, accompanied in each case by appropriate citations from the works of authors of every age and of every style.*

Fifty years ago the Manchu dynasty came near being overthrown by the T'ai P'ing rebels. This rebellion originated in 1852 by the revolt of native Christians, goaded to it by official persecution. The movement spread rapidly and gained force until a large tract of territory was in possession of the rebels, who destroyed cities and devastated the land with murder and pillage. They at last made Nanking their headquarters, and the leader was styled " King of Peace." A degenerate form of Christianity was practised, which culminated in blasphemy. The rebellion was finally crushed in 1864, by the aid of Colonel (afterwards General) Gordon, who entered the service of the Imperial Government.

During the past forty years, there have been many internal rebellions. It would not be easy to point to a time when there

* "Historic China," by H. A. Giles, p. 113.

was not rebellion or riot in some part of the empire. In addition to these active outbursts of the internal discontent, there have been periodical uprisings, of late years, against foreigners residing or travelling in the interior. These culminated in the Boxer scenes of horror of 1900, which impressed themselves too deeply upon the world to need reviving here.

POLITICAL RELATIONS.

Perhaps a glance at the political relations of China with other powers may help us to understand recent events and also the problems of the present and future.

The history of the past hundred years is a tale of the humiliation of China. In the early part of the 18th century, Opium smoking was strictly prohibited in China, and edicts were issued condemning it.*

The drug was at first imported in small quantities. This was gradually increased until in the year 1800, this contraband trade from India amounted to 2,000 chests per annum; in 1820 it had risen to 5,000; and in 1834 to over 17,000 chests.

The Chinese authorities continued to oppose the trade, and in 1839, after repeatedly warning the English merchants who were engaged in it, Commissioner Lin seized the whole quantity of Opium then lying in ships in Chinese waters. This, valued at over £2,000,000, he utterly destroyed. War followed, which resulted in opening the five ports, Canton, Amoy, Fuchau, Ningpo, and Shanghai to foreign trade. China was compelled to pay £2,000,000 for the destroyed Opium and £4,000,000 for the expenses of the war.

England lost a grand opportunity at the close of that war, as is well pointed out by Dr. Martin :—

> Not a word was inserted in the treaty in favour of the trade in opium: yet the result was as foreseen, a complete immunity from interference; the traffic flourished beyond measure, the traders having nothing to fear and no duties to pay. Had England, after exacting due

* See Royal Commission Report, Vol. i., pp. 156 and 157.

reparation, introduced a prohibition clause, there can be no doubt that China might have been freed from a terrible scourge. What a contrast between her opium policy, and her anti-slavery legislation ! *

In 1857 another war, known as the "Arrow" war, took place. The Taku forts and Tientsin were taken and, in 1860, Peking was entered by the allied French and British forces. More ports were opened and the trade in Opium was legalised. The treaties made at the close of this war contain an important religiou toleration clause. It reads as follows :—

"Art. 29. The principles of the Christian religion, as professed by the Protestant and Roman Catholic churches, are recognized as teaching men to do good, and to do to others as they would have others do to them. Hereafter those who quietly teach and profess these doctrines shall not be harassed or persecuted on account of their faith. Any person, whether a citizen of the United States or a Chinese convert, who, according to these tenets, peaceably teaches and practises the principles of Christianity, shall in no wise be interfered with or molested." The phraseology of the British treaty, signed the following week, was on this point conformed to that of the American.†

In 1869, on the revision of the Treaty of Tientsin, the Chinese Government again attempted to save its people from the inroads of the Opium habit, BUT their plea was REJECTED by England in the interests of the Indian revenue.

Then China, in order to secure as much of the revenue from the drug as she could for herself, and also hoping by this means to get the trade into her own hands, permitted the general growth of the poppy. It has now spread throughout the Empire.

There can, therefore, be no doubt that an immense responsibility rests upon the Christian nation that has not sought to help the heathen one to throw off the deadly incubus which its own Emperor was endeavouring to remove from his people. As a nation England continues to reap a large revenue for her

* " A Cycle of Cathay," p. 23.   † Ibid, p. 182.

Indian possessions from the opium trade with China, whilst the Chinese as a nation have no more deadly enemy, destroying the mind and body of its people, than the same opium drug. It is to be found in every corner of the empire in increasing quantity, now mostly native grown.

The Chinese are born traders, and yet the main article of British trade has been the source of endless strife and poverty. They are naturally tolerant of religions, and yet the religion of love has roused

OPIUM SMOKERS.
When smoking opium the Chinese recline, as shown above. On the floor, in front, is one of the water-pipes used for tobacco smoking.

their extremes of ferocity. . . . The linking of the religion of Jesus of Nazareth with the British opium trade is as bitter an irony as professing Christians have ever brought on themselves, which is saying much. To the Chinese, they came together, spread together, have been fought for together, and finally legalised together. Nor can the natives know that the humiliation of the combination is felt by many on Western shores as keenly as it is in their own land.*

But poverty is the least of the ills it has helped to fasten upon China. It has enervated her people, corrupted her officials, undermined the authority of her Government, embittered the advent of the English and of a nobler faith and violated the moral sense of the Chinese.†

* " The Imperial Drug Trade," by Joshua Rowntree, p. 242.   † Ibid, p. 274.

Since the opening of the Treaty Ports, foreigners have penetrated into all parts of the Empire, and have, unfortunately, been the cause of a long series of disturbances and riots, often ending in bloodshed. Many of these riots were doubtless connived at, if not actually instigated, by those in authority, and a game of retaliation has been played by the Powers concerned. The nations whose subjects suffered have become increasingly peremptory in their demands, and the Chinese have made yet more desperate attempts to free their country from the foreigner.

England led the way by taking Hong Kong in 1842, and this has been followed by France in the South, Russia in the North, Japan in Formosa, Germany at Kiao Chou and England again at Wei Hai Wei. More ports have been opened and, nominally at least, the extensive waterways are now open to trade. The war between Japan and China in 1895, in which the former won an easy victory, exposed the weakness of China, and since that time she has been the sport of the first-class powers. Partition of the Empire has been freely discussed and, possibly, mutual jealousy has been a large factor in postponing that event for so long.

The British Government has clogged the progress of Christianity by associating it in the popular mind with the ruinous spread of the "foreign smoke!" The Governments of France and Germany have made it repugnant, the one by insisting on unjust privileges, the other by territorial aggrandisement. It is to be wished that the missionaries may yet be able to atone largely to the Chinese for the sins of their respective countries.[*]

A few years ago a party arose in China which realized that the national safety lay in general reform, and in coming into line with the other great powers. Foremost in this new party was the Emperor Kwang Hsü, but it will be remembered that his well-meant efforts were thwarted by the conservative element, which hastened the country to the disaster of 1900.

GOVERNMENT.

While nominally an absolute monarch, the Emperor is very much in the hands of his ministers and members of various

[*] "The Imperial Drug Trade," p. 252.

"Boards," and at the head of all is now the Empress-Dowager.*
Speaking of the form of government, Professor Giles says:—

Roughly speaking, all Chinese society may be divided into two classes—rulers and ruled. An official career, including all the highest and most lucrative posts, is open to every man who can pass successfully through the ordeal of the great public competitions. This fact, taken as a set-off against the practically democratic spirit of the Chinese

A GROUP OF CHINESE OFFICIALS.
The photograph of above was taken at the opening of the Women's Hospital, T'ung Ch'wan, in July, 1905.

people, goes far to reconcile them with their form of government, which in all outward form is essentially despotic. The Chinese as a nation recognise the necessity of being governed, and they believe in the divine right of their emperors. They throw open the public service to competition, and agree to regard successful competitors as their masters

* The Government has announced that the people may expect the grant of a free constitution in twelve years, and that from this time forward a certain measure of local self-government is to be conceded as a preparation for Parliamentary representation.—Dr. W. A. P. Martin in *The East and the West*, October, 1905.

rather than their servants. Hence, they think it right to put up with a good deal that would not be tolerated in the extreme west.*

The more important provinces have a Viceroy each, and others are in charge of Governors or are grouped under a Viceroy. This important post may be filled by either Chinese or Manchus. At each provincial capital, there is also a Tartar General, and a garrison of Manchus. This latter arrangement is a survival from the conquest of over 200 years ago. As the Manchus are not trained in arms and are forbidden to engage in business they appear to be the drones of society.

The provinces are divided into circuits, of some twenty or thirty counties each; the circuits into prefectures, of some ten counties more or less; and prefectures into counties ("hsiens," "cheos," or "t'ings," sometimes called "departments") which are the smallest units of government through mandarins, all with their respective officials. H. P. Beach says :—

Officials are civic fathers and mothers, while the emperor, Son of Heaven, prays and sacrifices to the heavenly powers when his children suffer from great calamities. That this government should have long survived is quite natural; for it supports by its strong sanction the authority of rulers on the one hand, while on the other it authorizes resistance to glaring evil in high places. As every family has in its membership some noted official, Chinese clan-spirit supports the system.†

POPULATION AND LANGUAGE.

As no reliable census is taken, it is impossible to arrive at exact figures as to the population of China. The commonly accepted estimate is about 400,000,000, and of these, 380,000,000 live in China proper. The province of Sz-Chwan, in which the Friends' Foreign Mission Association is at work, is credited with 60,000,000 of these; but Consul-General Hosie, after careful investigation, estimates it at 45,000,000.

The people are remarkably homogeneous, differing but little in habits of life and thought, and, while dialects differ, the written characters of the language are the same throughout China, and this fact has doubtless exercised a powerful influence in welding together the component parts of this numerous race.

* "Historic China," p. 122.   † "Dawn on the Hills of T'ang," p. 29.

CHAPTER II.

FROM SHANGHAI TO SZ-CHWAN.

HAVING glanced at China as a whole, our aim now is to invite attention to that special part of the "Flowery Kingdom" which for members of the Society of Friends has of late years been the centre of much interest and work.

While many of the statements made with reference to Sz-Chwan apply with equal accuracy to other Provinces, the geographical, commercial and agricultural details given, and industries mentioned, are those of our "promised land," which by many travellers, whose personal observations give them the right to speak, has been considered as a "*good* land and a *large*," " a land flowing with milk and honey," compared with the waste and poverty-stricken districts found in many of the other Provinces.

Considering the prominent part which the journey from the coast occupies in the life of the foreign resident in this far western Province of Sz-Chwan, it seems necessary to give some account of how it is approached from the east.

How far inland is Sz-Chwan ? This question is better answered by describing the time and effort taken to get there, than by any statement of the miles to be covered; although, as a matter of fact, it may be said to be one thousand five hundred miles from Shanghai to the port of Chungking, the city in which Friends have been longest at work. It is situated just inside the eastern borders of Sz-Chwan.

Perhaps the best impression can be gathered by tracing the journey inland, noting, in passing, the most important places.

SHANGHAI.

The feeling on arriving here is one of surprise that so many up-to-date foreign appliances are in full use. True, the jinrickshas and wheelbarrows, pulled or pushed by the veritable Chinaman with his inseparable "pigtail," may seem to contradict the statement, yet the Mexican dollar and other silver coins, telegraph and telephone poles and wires, gas lamps and electric lights, imposing buildings in broad, well-paved streets, policemen guiding the traffic in the busy thoroughfares, fire stations, horses and carriages, gardens laid out in good taste and variety, all confirm the impression that foreigners have the management of the "model settlement" of the far East. The English, American and French Concessions occupy the long river foreground called the Bund, the Chinese city being some distance in the rear.

THE LOWER YANG TSE.

At Shanghai the river is about three-quarters of a mile wide. On the banks, on both sides, for a great distance, are business premises of one kind and another, and a great trade is done there. Leaving this port, to start on the long journey westward, fine steamers ply some six hundred miles up the Yang Tse. The old southern capital, Nanking, is passed, and Hankow reached in about three days.

HANKOW.

Hankow, which has long been an important centre for the tea trade of China, is one of three large cities which form a group at the mouth of the river Han, where it flows into the Yang Tse. These three cities together have a population of some five hundred thousand people. Hankow is commercially the most important of the three, but Wuchang, on the opposite side of the Yang Tse is the official capital of the province of Hupeh. There the great Chinese statesman, Chang Chih Tung, the well-known, progressive and patriotic Viceroy of Central China, has been in authority for many years. He has large iron works in Hanyang, the third city of the group, on the banks of the Han. Hankow is also the terminus of the Lu Han Railway, the great Trunk line connecting Northern and Central China, just completed.

HANKOW TO ICHANG.

From Hankow, steamers of lesser draught run a distance of some 350 miles as far as Ichang, passing Sha-sï and other cities on the way. The river itself extends to a great width, but the channel in some parts is very narrow and shallow.

HOUSE-BOAT ON THE UPPER YANG TSE.
The boat shown above is ready to go up the river. Hence the mast is in upright position.

Navigation, therefore, requires skilful pilots, and the best sometimes fail to avoid running their craft aground. Delays from this cause are no uncommon occurrence at certain seasons of the year. This stage of the journey ought, nevertheless, to be completed in five or six days.

The scenery thus far, with little exception, is flat and uninteresting the whole way from Shanghai. Near Kiukiang, which is the port for a district where much fine porcelain and pottery are produced, there is one exception, where Kuling rises in the background and forms a bold relief to the otherwise flat picture.

On this mountain, some three thousand feet high, is now established a summer resort for foreigners, where a large number of bungalows have been erected. These have proved a great boon to the residents in the adjacent cities of Hankow, Nanking and Chinkiang.

At Ichang steam navigation ends and the traveller, bound further west, must prepare for slower and more difficult progress.

Ichang itself is nine hundred and fifty miles west of Shanghai, and was opened in 1887 as a Treaty Port to foreign trade. It remained the last open port up the Yang Tse for several years, and is a great rendezvous for merchandise from the west. At almost any time of the year, large numbers of native junks and house-boats may be found there, lying closely packed together along the shore for a distance of over a mile.

The Sz-Chwan junks are strongly built for ascending the rapids, and the cypress wood-work, stained and oiled, looks like varnished pine. They are often as much as one hundred and fifty feet long, and capable of carrying over one hundred tons burden.

The house-boats usually contain three or four rooms. In place of the native paper windows, small glazed ones can be fitted with little trouble and expense. If curtains are provided to cover the cracks between the boards of the partitions, the separate rooms can be made comfortable and even cosy. A party wishing to start on this journey must be prepared to fit up the boat with all travelling requisites in the way of furniture, bedding and food. J. Endicott, of the Canadian Methodist Mission, Chentu, describes, very clearly, the boat and its working, as follows:—

The boat we have is above the average size, but is built similarly to all others. Picture then a long, flat-bottomed boat, eighty-five feet long, with a square bow, and a high projecting stern. Its hull has an average depth of about three feet from the floor to the deck. The deck is composed of hatches about eighteen inches long, and reaching across the boat. The hull is divided into compartments of varying width, in which we stow away some five tons of baggage, etc.

From the bow, going aft about two-fifths of the length of the boat, the deck is open. Near the centre of this part is the cook's galley, where he works from early morn till late at night, in a manner somewhat startling to our minds.

At the end of this open space stands the mast (the peculiarity of which is that it has no rigging), rising about forty feet from the deck; on it is spread the sail. Immediately behind the mast the house part begins and runs for another two-fifths of the boat. It occupies the entire width of the boat (about eleven feet). The ceiling is about eight feet high in the centre, and six feet and a half at the sides.

Behind the house is another open space of about ten feet, in which stands the steersman. Back of this open space is a very tiny room,

CARGO-JUNK COMING DOWN-RIVER.
It will be noted that the mast is taken down, and is lashed to the side of the boat.

occupied by the captain, his wife, and four children. Above the door leading into this room is a little niche, in which is placed a small, gold-covered idol.

On each side of the boat is an immense oar, or yalou, each requiring from five to eight men to work it. Then, projecting over the bow about twenty-five feet, is a round piece of timber, which is used as a sweep to direct the bow of the boat in different directions. This sweep is of great value, especially in the rapids. As you know the boats are pulled up the river for the most part by men; the winds, of course, sometimes assisting them. These men are called "trackers," and are usually considered the "hardest" class in China. They run along the banks of the river, now clambering over boulders, and again along the sides of steep cliffs, where the footing is often very difficult. For hundreds of miles the rocks are worn smooth by the constant tread of their bare feet or straw sandals.

The ropes used to pull the boat are made of bamboo, and are of remarkable strength. It has been a revelation to us to see the strain they stand in the rapids. Sometimes the men are over two hundred yards away, and at others but forty or fifty. All along, the rocks are marked by ruts, cut by the constant passage of ropes over them. The men pull the ropes by means of long sashes worn across the shoulder like a bandolier.*

These trackers usually present a miserable appearance. They are piteously poor and work hard for a bare living. When their work for the day is done, they seem to have no other resource in life than to smoke their opium pipes and sleep till the earliest gleam of dawn calls them to commence another day of toil. For a voyage from Ichang to Chungking, occupying from thirty to fifty days, these trackers get about four shillings for wages and their food, for the return journey about one and sixpence and their food. Badly paid as they are, their work is, as Consul Bourne remarked when he made the journey, " inhumanely hard."

The largest house-boats on the river Yang Tse are usually manned by a captain, a pilot, a steersman, a cook, and some fifty or sixty boatmen and trackers. Extra trackers are engaged, as required, at the various rapids, and sometimes from one hundred to one hundred and fifty men will be added to the regular crew

One very important duty must not be omitted at Ichang. This is the passing of all cargo through the Imperial Customs. Even the stores, which will be consumed on the journey, must be declared.

When everything is supposed to be ready to leave Ichang, some delay is usually caused by the captain's failure to collect the full number of men stipulated for in the agreement. If you are short-sighted enough to allow him to proceed before he has produced the proper number, you will certainly repent it, arriving at one rapid after another with too few men to manage the pulling properly.

* "The Heart of Sz-Chwan," p. 44.

TRACKERS ON THE YANG TSE.

The start from Ichang is frequently made toward evening, and the first stage consists in simply crossing the river. The boat is fastened up for the night, close to a number of big junks about to leave on the same perilous trip. The noise all night is deafening. The shouting and quarrelling between the crews of the different boats effectually prevents sleep.

THE TRACKERS TAKING THEIR MEALS.

Mrs. Bird Bishop thus describes her experience at this spot :—

I was up at daybreak not to lose anything, but hour after hour passed, and no *lao pan* (captain) appeared; at ten we started without him, to meet him on the bank a few miles higher, when there was a tremendous row between him and the men. We were then in what looked like a mountain lake. No outlet was visible, mountains rose clear and grim against a dull gray sky. We cast off from the shore, the oars were plied to a wild chorus; what looked like a cleft in the rock appeared, and making an abrupt turn round a high rocky point, in all the thrill of novelty and expectation, we were in the Ichang gorge, the first and one of the grandest clefts through which this great river, at times a mile in width, there compressed into a limit of from four to five hundred yards, has carved a passage through the mountains.

The change from such a lake stretch, with its light movement, to a dark, narrow gorge, black with the shadows of nearly perpendicular limestone cliffs, broken up into buttresses and fantastic towers of curiously splintered and weathered rock, culminating in the " Pillar of Heaven," a limestone pinnacle rising sheer from the water to a height of one hundred and eighty feet, is so rapid as to bewilder the senses. The expression "lost in admiration" is a literally correct one. At once I saw the reason why the best descriptions, which are those of Captain Blakiston and Mr. A. J. Little, have a certain amount of " fuzziness " and fail to convey a definite picture.

In the Ichang gorge the water is from fifty to one hundred feet deep, of a striking bottle-green colour, and flows along without swirl or ripple in a grand full volume. The stillness is profound, enlivened only by the passing now and again of some big cargo junk, with lowered mast, gliding past at great speed, with fifty or sixty men at the sweeps, raising a wild chant in keeping with their movements.

The Ichang gorge is about twelve miles long, and ends at the village of Nan T'o, where stands the " Needle " or " Pillar of Heaven."

Then comes the Niu Kan Ma Fei (ox liver and horse lungs) gorge, so named from a stone high up in the cliff said to resemble them. Captain Blakiston well describes it thus :—

> The Niu Kan gorge suddenly opened to view, a huge split in the mountain mass ahead of us by which the river escapes as through a funnel. As we entered, the gloom was very impressive, huge walls of rock rise vertically on either hand to a prodigious height, with great table-shaped slabs standing out from the face of the cliff, for all the world like the sounding boards of pulpits, hanging from which are long stalactites; and on the upper surface are some trees looking like diminutive bushes, whose roots droop in festoons from their edges. This is not a long gorge, but it is more impressive than the first one!

At the mouth of the Niu Kan gorge is the fatal rock on which the German steamer *Sui Hsiang* foundered in 1900. In less than fifteen minutes after striking the rock, the steamer was totally lost, sunk out of sight in the waters below.

A few years previously, Mr. A. J. Little had succeeded in getting a small steam yacht, the *Li Chwan*, up to Chungking, and later on the *Pioneer* accomplished the trip, with some manual help at the rapids. It was hoped that these might herald

ASCENDING A RAPID.
To the right can be seen a boat going down-river.

ENTRANCE TO NIU KAN GORGE.
The scene of the wreck of the "Sui Hsiang."

the advent of passenger steamers, but the signal failure of the *Sui Hsiang* has discouraged enterprise in that direction, though small gun boats belonging to England and France have been taken up.

The third gorge is the Mi-T'an, only about four miles in length, and then comes the longest one, the Wu Shan, stretching a distance of some thirty miles. Writing a letter to *The Friend* in this gorge, on December 8th, 1903, Albert J. Crosfield said :—

We passed the boundary between the two provinces of Hupeh and Sz-Chwan this afternoon. It is marked by a small gorge on the right, and a big cave on the left; also by the sudden ending of a road wide enough for two men to walk abreast, which has been made up to the Sz-Chwan border, and which comes to a sudden end some way up the mountain side. This gorge, thirty miles in length, is very fine, but we get on slowly. We have only made good about ten miles to-day. In many places tracking is impossible, as the cliffs are too steep and slope downwards, giving no possible foothold. In the absence of an up-river wind we are dependent on rowing; and when we could track the ground was so rough the men got on but slowly. The river is very deep, and quiet, most of the way, through the gorge. We had most charming sunshine yesterday and this morning; both have been like fresh summer days.

December 9th. We had a little wind, that helped us this morning, but it soon died away. We were near the end of the Wu Shan gorge, and we have had two fairly stiff rapids to-day, and saw a junk break away at each of them, though we got safely over. This afternoon we had a couple of hours' walk along the path some way up the mountain on the south side of the river. It was a very stiff climb. It reminded me of walks along Lake Como, but in place of olives we had the candle nut tree, which bears a white berry which is melted down for vegetable tallow. Every available scrap of hillside is cultivated. We passed masses of cliffs to-day, in which the rocks were most marvellously contorted. All the rocks in the gorge appear to be igneous. In places the perpendicular precipice must be about one thousand feet. In other places the rocks slope down to the water's edge, giving no foothold at all.

Following the Wu Shan gorge is that known by the name of the " Wind Box," from having a number of holes in the side of a cliff through which the wind whistles, as through a Chinese wind box or bellows. In ancient times it was called the " Gate of Tsu," the gate of Sz-Chwan. The appropriateness of the title is clear as one passes through its narrow north end, with perpendicular cliffs rising over one thousand feet high. It is perhaps the grandest and most imposing of all the gorges, especially when approached from the west, and the river, after flowing swiftly and steadily on between the well cultivated hills of Sz-Chwan, suddenly takes a remarkable turn at right angles, and enters the narrow chasm, where the channel is narrowed so much that the water must be an enormous depth. It is described as the most dangerous spot in the whole Empire. The Chinese have a saying regarding it :—

> When the flood beacon's seen of an elephant's size
> The ascent of the river all prudence descries :
> When the flood beacon's seen as the size of a horse,
> The attempt to descend is fraught with remorse.

ENTRANCE OF THE MI-T'AN GORGE.

Between and within these gorges are the rapids which render the navigation of the Upper Yang Tse so dangerous and uncertain. Their number and size vary considerably with the rise and fall of the water. The Ch'in, Yeh, and Hsin t'àn (*t'àn* is Chinese for *rapid*) are the largest and most formidable. These alternate in their condition according to the state of the river, for in high water there is practically " Yeh " and no " Ch'in," and in low water, " Ch'in " and no " Yeh," so at no season of the year can the traveller avoid both of them. The " Hsin t'àn " is of very recent formation. In 1896 there was a great landslip, which carried with it huge boulders and rocks, and

THE CHIN-T'AN RAPID.
From a photograph by Dr. Wilson, C.I.M.

deposited them in the bed of the Yang Tse, thus almost stopping the navigation of large boats for a time. Some improvement was effected by the blasting of rock and widening the channel, but the *Hsin t'àn* nevertheless remains an object of dread to all owners of boats and to their passengers.

Dr. William Wilson, Secretary of the Friends' Foreign Mission Association, thus describes his experience of some rapids on his recent journey in China:—

It is often dangerous work stemming the full force of the current round projecting points, as, if the rope breaks, or the trackers are too feeble or too few to sustain the heavy strain as they pull steadily inch by inch, your craft is left at the mercy of an eight to ten knot current with unpleasant looking rocks on all sides. For about an hour we went quietly forward, and then we again put out the trackers on the right bank to haul us round what is known now as Roller Point.

In most places where the rope drags along the stones and boulders deep ruts are worn, but here at Roller Point the angle to be pulled is so sharp that a couple of wooden rollers have been set up in a frame and fastened securely in the rock. The river takes a rather sharp bend at

THE UPPER CHIN-T'AN RAPID.
From a photograph by Montague Beauchamp.

this point, and the path for the trackers, cut out of the solid rock in places and carefully built up in others, is completely out of sight of the boat. The rope is paid out for about five hundred yards, and dragged round into position so as to pass round the rollers and on to the main towing path. When the trackers are ready and have got the rope fairly taut, the chief tracker, standing where he can see both the trackers and the boat, gives a signal and the boat is thrust out into the current. For a moment or two the rope tightens and stretches, the vessel swings as if she were going down stream, but the steady pull on shore tells in time, as inch by inch the trackers, all bent down to pull to the greatest advantage, steadily haul. If you watch the boat you can scarcely see any progress at all, and it is worse still if you are on board, for the cracking and stretching of the rope give the impression that it will part every minute. Evidently from what we have already seen China is no place for nerves!

A day later he adds :—

Our men were astir at daybreak as usual, and before we were dressed we had crept up to a position in line with the boats waiting their turn (to ascend the Yeh t'àn). The river narrows considerably and is not more than 400 to 450 feet broad, and the angle of the water glide is quite perceptible. The down-stream boats shoot down at a great rate, and look as if it might be dangerous unless skilfully managed. Before the actual rapid is reached the boats creep up in the back-wash, and are fastened with their sterns out in the current, and anything attempting to pass at the back of them is in danger of being carried away. The prospect of having to wait for a couple of days for our turn is not pleasant and we are trying to arrange to pass some of the boats ahead. About four o'clock we were told that the pilot and boatman were going to try and pass, the owners of the other boats being willing for us to do so. We went on shore, and our house-boat moved slowly out and crept up. She had got up to the stern of the second boat when she began to go back. We saw her swing right out into the stream, where the current caught her and away she went. As we watched her we did not know to where she would drift. We could only hope that the men would keep their heads and guide her into one of the bays. After a struggle they managed to clear some nasty rocks and a bank of shingle, and by an energetic use of the bow-sweep she was just got into the current of the back-wash again, and brought up about 100 yards below the place where she moored last night.

The next day they made a second attempt.

While it was still dusk the men were up and had put away their sleeping gear, and had begun to loosen the ropes. We got off in a small boat and went ashore. The men worked quietly on the back-wash and crept up to our old place of yesterday. They secured the services of five other men from boats which will be stationary all day so that in case of any extra strain they may have plenty of hands to work the ropes. We watched anxiously from some boulders. Slowly and quietly she crept up at the back and, without attempting too much, waited for an opening between the boats near the top end. Most of the junks lying at their moorings were not yet astir, but directly they found us in their rear they began loosing and slackening their ropes fastened to the shore, and so allowed their junks to swing further out into the stream. This was done with the intention of pushing us out into the stream. Once there they knew pretty well that we could not hold. Still they reckoned without their host this time. Our men were more cautious after their failure yesterday, and already had a rope out on the shore besides another which was hitched on to the junk above. So her broad prow was put in, and by pulling steadily and persistently a place opened for her and a short line was brought in and made fast. We are now tenth on the line instead of thirty-sixth, and a whole day will be saved.

A later traveller gives another side of boat life as follows:—

Quite late last evening, when it was really time to tie up, our men were unable to pull the boat up round a difficult corner, so after several vain and wearying attempts they sought help from another boat crew, and the two crews succeeded. When all was safely up our boatman in a frank, open way turned to the other men and thanked them for their help, saying, "We have troubled you," in true Chinese polite language; and as politely came the response immediately, "Not at all, not at all." It was *fine, grand*, to see that group of about the most ragged and deplorable set of humanity that you can imagine—such as these trackers usually are—standing there addressing one another in refined, gentlemanly words; and that at the end of a long, hard day's work, which many might have considered sufficient excuse for refusing to spend any more of their strength.

A CHINESE GUN-BOAT.
By kind permission of the " FOREIGN FIELD.*"*

In writing of the voyage between Ichang and Chungking Mrs. Bird Bishop says :—

The perils of the journey fully warrant the worst descriptions which have been given of them. The risks are many and serious, and cannot be provided against by any forethought. The slightest error on the part of the pilot, any hampering of the bow-sweep, a tow-rope breaking, the position of a submerged rock altering with the rise or fall of the water, and many other possibilities, and life and property are all at the mercy of a raging flood, tearing down at the rate of from seven to eleven miles an hour.

CHAPTER III.

THE PROVINCE OF SZ-CHWAN.

SZ-CHWAN being reached, it will be found to have attractions second to no other in the whole eighteen provinces. Indeed, Consul-General Hosie, a reliable authority on the subject, asserts that " Western China is the most interesting part of the Empire."

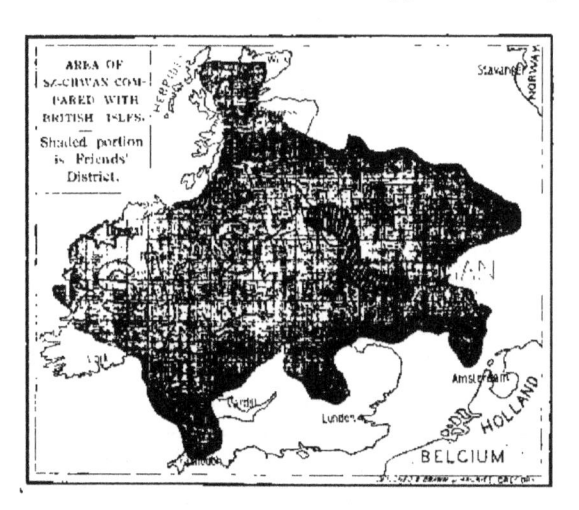

As its name implies, it is the province of the Four Streams, which flow through it and are tributaries of the Yang Tse. Its area is about equal to that of France, being greater, by 33,800 square miles, than the whole of Great Britain and Ireland; while its population, as stated before, is at least 45,000,000.

It is bounded on the north by Kokonor, and the two provinces of Kan-suh and Shen-si, which are separated from it by the Chin Ling range. These mountains, extending to the valley of the Yang Tse also, form the eastern boundary between Sz-Chwan and Hupeh. Kwei-chau and Yun-nan are on the south, with a mountain range there also; while the high table land of Tibet extends along the whole western frontier. Thus it will be seen how completely Sz-Chwan is hedged in on every side by high mountain ranges, some of which rise to the snow level, while all of them are difficult to cross, so that the great water-way of the river Yang Tse is really the only main thoroughfare in the province.

Sz-Chwan naturally divides itself into two sections, eastern and western. The western is practically part of the mountain range stretching towards Tibet, is almost uncultivated, inhabited by aboriginal tribes, and sparsely populated. With it we shall have little to do in this present volume. The eastern section is fertile, swarming with life and industry, and forms one of the most productive regions in the whole of China. It is known as the " Red Basin," being a large triangular basin of red sandstone, dotted with hills everywhere, except in the large plains of Chentu and Sui-ling. Owing to the softness of the rock throughout this district, the numerous rivers and streams cut deep channels for the floods of water which are poured into the basin by the heavy rains and melting snows.

Though as a whole this section of Sz-Chwan is exceedingly fertile and productive, dry seasons now and again cause small crops, with attendant high prices, which soon impoverish the large population dependent, in country districts, upon the produce of the ground for a scanty living.

The province is also rich in mineral produce, though its resources are by no means properly worked. Good coal abounds in some parts, in others it is poor. The coal of one mine not very far from Chungking has been said by experts to be equal to the best Cardiff.

Its Industries. 33

Around Chentu, Kia-ting, and T'ung Ch'wan are large silk producing districts, while insect wax is another staple article in the Kia-ting neighbourhood. The eggs of the insect are produced on one kind of tree, and are then removed with the utmost care and pains to an altogether different kind of tree. The people will travel by day and night to accomplish this. When

OPIUM POPPY-FIELD.
This field is passed through on the way to the School for Missionaries' Children, on the Hills opposite Chungking. The rice-fields are seen beyond.

hatched, the insects feed upon the leaves of the latter tree and in turn secrete the white wax. Opium, unfortunately, is also increasingly cultivated in the first harvest in the spring. Being ripe in April or May, it is cleared from the ground in time for rice, maize or millet to follow in the greater summer heat, for gathering in the second harvest about August or September.

Extensive and apparently exhaustless Salt wells in the centre of the province are worked by primitive machinery.

Small holes are bored to a great depth into which long bamboo buckets are let down. These are raised to the surface by treadwheels, thus bringing from the depths below, the brine from which salt is then produced by evaporation. The quality varies a great deal, that coming from the neighbourhood of T'ai Ho Chen and T'ung Ch'wan being specially white and good, but the great salt wells are in the district of Tsï Liu Chin.

The chief rivers, which have already been mentioned as passing through and giving the name to the province, are as follows :—

In the east, rising in the hills bordering on Shen-si, is the Chia Ling, flowing through Kwan-yuan, Pao-ning, and Ho-cheo to the Yang Tse at Chungking.

At Ho-cheo it is joined by the Fu from Mien-cheo and T'ung Ch'wan. This also is navigable most of the year as far as these cities,—at any rate for craft of a small kind.

Another large river, the T'o Chiang, passing through the important cities of Chien-cheo, Tsi-cheo, and Lui-chiang, flows through the centre of the province, and joins the Yang Tse at Lu-cheo.

The Min is really a large arm of the Yang Tse, which rises in the hills north of Kwan-hsien, where are the great irrigation works for the Chentu plain; it then flows down past Chentu and joins the other branch of the Yang Tse at Sui-fu.

Besides these main arteries, there are numerous small rivers and streams which flow into them. These are of considerable size and use in the flood season, although they may be almost or quite dry at another time of the year.

Passing from the river ways, one naturally turns to the roads, especially when remembering that though fairly good speed can be ensured for down-river traffic, the *ascent* of any of these streams is always exceedingly slow, and often dangerous to life and cargo. The Sz-Chwanese have not been slow to meet this difficulty, and the whole of the province is supplied with main roads between the chief centres, and smaller ones to all the towns, villages, and markets. These are paved with stone, of which there is plenty in the province. But you must not picture wide roads, with pavements for foot passengers on each side, as in our Western cities. Remember there are no carriages, other than the sedan chairs carried by men in tandem style. These chairs are mostly only about two feet* wide, though the official chair of the magistrates may be two and a half. Neither must you imagine straight roads. Most of the Sz-Chwan

READY FOR A JOURNEY INLAND.
To the left are seen the coolies with their loads, containing food, bedding, etc.

roads would be better described as "paved paths" up and down hill, round rice fields, and between narrow rows of houses, whose occupants on either side would often be within touch of each other if their hands were stretched out. Nevertheless they are roads, exceedingly useful, and well worn by the thousands who travel long distances, and the tens of thousands who ply hither and thither in pursuit of a living.

Three main roads may be specially mentioned:—one starting at Wan-hsien, on the river Yang Tse, passes through Shu-ting,

* A Chinese foot is equal to 13¼ English inches.

and T'ai Ho Chen, and across the country to the capital of the province, which can be thus reached in thirteen days from Wan-hsien.

Another even more frequented is from Chungking to Chentu, and consists of ten stages, so that these cities can thus be considered as only ten days' journey apart, though goods conveyed up-river from Chungking are frequently ten or more *weeks* in reaching the capital.

Then there still remains, in good repair, part of the great highway from Chentu to Peking, along the north of the province. It dates back to the third century. In many places passages have been cut through the solid rock and steps hewn on both sides of mountains from summit to base, evidences of a work worthy of great engineers.

"Among the inhabitants of the eighteen provinces, the people of Sz-Chwan are said to be most gentle and amiable in character, and most refined in manner. They are also more cleanly and orderly in dress and habits than the Chinese in general. They meet you with civility and a show of respect, and are not in the least shy, they answer frankly and without hesitation." Such at least is the character given them by one who had travelled and seen enough to give him the right to offer an opinion.

There are no less than twelve Prefectures in Sz-Chwan, one hundred and forty cities, many of them large and important, and almost innumerable villages.

CHAPTER IV.

THE CITY OF CHUNGKING.

THE name of Chungking represents not only the city itself, but also the Prefecture which it governs. It is locally spoken of as Pa Hsien, or the county of Pa, the town being the chief city both in the county and the prefecture. It is also known as Yu Ch'eng, or the city Yu, this being one of its ancient names.

Various histories of both the county and the prefecture have been written at different periods, but the only one extant dates from 1760.

The city, as it now stands, was built by Hung Wau, the founder of the Ming dynasty, but it was occupied in the reign of Ching Cheng, the last Emperor of the same dynasty, by the rebel Chang Hsien Cheng, who devastated the greater part of the province.

Chungking is built on a high hill, and is surrounded by a substantial wall which was rebuilt in 1761, after the rebellion. The wall is now in good condition, with battlements and parapets complete, having seventeen gates, nine of which are open daily from dawn to sunset. All of these gates, save one, lead down to the river side, where the constant activity of the populace is sufficient to warrant the title given to this busy port,—" the Liverpool of West China." The banks and quays are always crowded with boats engaged in the trade with cities still further inland, and from which wax, bristles, hemp, medicines, hides, musk, opium, wool, silk, etc., are sent down to this centre.

The city, lying in lat. 29°33′ 50″ N. and long. 107.2, E., is hemmed in on two sides by the rivers Yang Tse and Chia Ling, while the narrow neck of land, which saves the city from becoming an island, is so covered with the graves of the ancients that there is no room for expansion.

In 1890, Chungking was made an open port, and some idea of its business and commerce may be gathered from the returns of the Commissioner of the Chinese Imperial Customs there. To quote from his report for 1902, we find, " the total revenue

A TIMBER YARD ON THE RIVER-SIDE, NEAR CHUNGKING.

collected by the customs for the previous year amounted to Tls. 364,639=£45,580 ; Native exports, not including opium, being Tls. 5,880,730=£735,090, and the Foreign imports Tls. 12,598,741 =£1,574,842, the highest figures on record for any year."

Chungking is the distributing centre for Tibet, Yunnan, Kwei-chau, Kan-suh and Shen-si, as well as the whole province of Sz-Chwan, of which it is justly called the commercial capital.

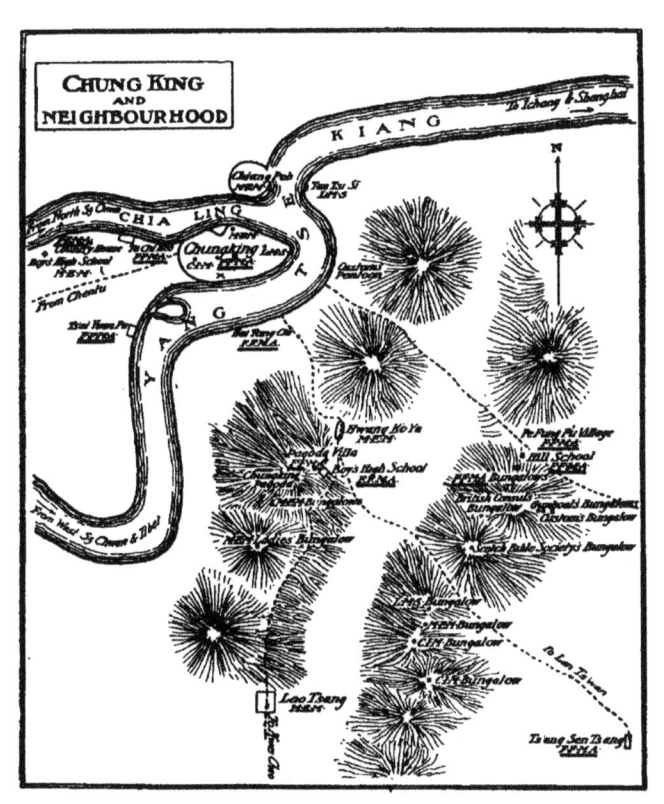

A MAP OF CHUNGKING AND NEIGHBOURHOOD.

The above shows position of Chungking at the junction of two rivers, the Yang Tse and the Chia Ling. It also shows relative positions of the new Boys' High School, the Hill School for Missionaries' Children, etc., on the South side of the Yang Tse.

But, while the city cannot make any permanent extension in its size, the most is made of all the narrow banks between the city walls and the edge of the river. Shanties of the meanest description are erected here and serve as homes to the thousands who scramble for a miserable living amongst the river craft. When the river rises in summer, they are liable to be washed

RIVER-SIDE STEPS, CHUNGKING.

out of their homes at a few hours' notice. The water, which comes rushing down the two rivers, reaches a level forty to ninety feet above the lowest water mark.*

From the city gates, irregular flights of stone steps are ascended to long and busy streets. Well-stocked shops bespeak the prosperity of the merchants and tradesmen, and the amount

* In August, 1905, the rise in the river was abnormally high—some 107 feet above low-water mark. Several villages were flooded, resulting in much distress and loss of life, and premises rented by Friends in T'a Chi Keo and Ts'ai Yuen Pa were completely destroyed.

of foreign goods exposed for sale is continually increasing. The streets are almost always wet from the dripping of the water carriers. The whole of the city, with its 350,000 inhabitants, is supplied with water from the river, carried in buckets suspended on a pole across men's shoulders. The sum of eight to fourteen cash ($\frac{1}{4}$d. to $\frac{1}{2}$d.) is paid for what one man can carry in two buckets. The water-carriers alone, in this one city, number some thousands.

Most of the streets are narrow and dirty, and smell offensively. The streets are irregularly built, and the city itself is of such irregular shape that it is not easy to find one's way about. In summer it is certainly hot and oppressive in the city. This must of necessity be the case, where the houses are so crowded together, and when the shade-temperature is between 90 and 100° Fahrenheit. In winter, it is frequently damp and depressing, but in spring and autumn there is often beautiful weather. Foreigners now have free access to the delightful pine-dotted hills on the south side of the river, within two hours from the most distant part of the city, and are able to have bungalows on or near their summits, to which they resort in summer.

Temples abound within and without the city walls, as do also shops for the sale of the candles, paper, and incense used in worshipping at the temples, homes, shops, and graves.

Chungking stands at an elevation of 1,050 feet above the sea level, and is 1,500 miles inland, yet even there at low water the river Yang Tse is about 800 yards wide, while at high water, when the torrents rush down from the mountainous regions beyond and fill up the broad expanse, it stretches to two thirds of a mile. Then it is often dangerous to cross, owing to the swiftness of the current and sudden gusts of wind. It is hardly possible to have a true conception of this mighty volume of water until one has, slowly and painfully, crawled along its banks for weeks and, arriving at last at Chungking, has seen its size at such a distance from the sea, and realised that it is still navigable some hundreds of miles further west.

CHAPTER V.

CHENTU, THE PROVINCIAL CAPITAL.

AS early as the thirteenth century we find authentic record of Chentu as a great city. How much longer it has existed it would be hard to say, but about the year 1270, Marco Polo thus describes the city: —

Chentu was in former days a rich and noble city, and the kings who reigned there were very great and wealthy. It is a good twenty miles in compass; but it is divided in the way that I shall tell you. You see the king of this province, in the days of old, when he found himself drawing near to death, leaving three sons behind him, commanded that the city should be divided into three parts, and that each of his sons should have one; so each of these parts is separately walled about, though all three are surrounded by the common wall of the city. Each of the three sons was king, having his own part of the city and his own share of the kingdom, and each of them was in fact a great and wealthy king. But the great Khan conquered the kingdom of these three kings, and stripped them of their inheritance.

Through the midst of this city runs a large river, in which they catch a great quantity of fish. It is a good half mile wide, and very deep withal, all so long that it reaches all the way to the Ocean Sea—a very long way, equal to eighty or a hundred days' journey—and the name of the river is Kian-Suy. The multitude of vessels that navigate this river is so vast that no one who should read or hear the tale would believe it. The quantities of merchandise also which merchants carry up and down this river are past all belief. In fact it is so big that it seems more like a sea than a river. Let us now speak of a great bridge which crosses this river within the city. This bridge is of stone; it is seven paces in width, and half a mile in length (the river being that much in width as I told you), and along its length, on either side, there are columns of marble to bear the roof, for the bridge is roofed over from end to end with timber, and that all richly painted; and on this bridge there are houses, in which a great deal of trade and industry is carried on. But these houses are all of wood only, and they are put up in the morning and taken down in the evening. Also there stands upon this bridge the great Khan's Comerque, that is to say, his custom-house, where his toll and tax are levied; and I can tell you that the dues taken on this bridge bring to the lord a thousand pieces of fine gold every day and more. The people are all idolators.

Coming down to later times, Baron F. von Richthofen and Captain Gill both speak in high praise of it. The former, a traveller of large experience, asserts " I do not hesitate to say that Chentu is the finest Chinese city I have seen " ; while Captain Gill, who travelled through China in 1877, affirms that " Marco Polo's description of it as a ' great and noble city ' is still true."

The plain in which Chentu is situated is about one hundred miles long, and the city stands enclosed by a massive wall, which is kept in good repair. The latter is not so imposing in *height* as it is in *width*, being about forty-four feet wide. It is built of stone with no less than eight bastions, through four of which are the city gates, called North, South, East, and West. Chentu is now about three and a half miles long, by two and a half broad, the length of the wall encompassing it being over nine miles. The approach by any of the four main roads is somewhat disappointing. There are no high or imposing buildings to be seen, and the foliage of large trees abounding gives it rather the appearance of an enclosed park than a busy city. Yet the traffic on all the four roads outside the gates dispels such an idea, and gives good evidence of busy life within, although the city cannot compare with Chungking for commercial importance. The Blackburn Commission formed a correct estimate of Chentu and Chungking, and no one disputes their opinion that for a business centre, and for influence on the commercial life of the whole of West China, Chungking stands first.

But this fact admitted, another fact is equally true ; for intellectual, official and social influence over as wide an area, the great western capital of Chentu stands alone in its glory.

A Centre of Political Influence.

Its influence may in some measure be imagined by the following facts. There are always at least fifty mandarins of high rank resident in the city, while it is estimated that there are generally as many as one thousand five hundred more of the same class, awaiting appointment there or to some other part of the province. In addition, every third year, there are held the great examinations when no less than fifteen thousand students,

THE GREAT EXAMINATION HALL, CHENTU.
Students reside in small cells during the Examination, lasting several days.
Several rows of these are shown above.

who have already obtained their first or Hsiu Ts'ai (B.A.) degree, come up from all parts of the province to compete for the second or Chü Ren (M.A.) degree. Students also come up from the various Prefectures to the Provincial College and Civil and Military Academies. All these, returning to their scattered homes, cannot fail to carry with them the influence of the capital on matters of education and politics, and thus there is no portion of the whole province unaffected by what takes place there.

Chentu was the imperial city of the short-lived dynasty of Shu or Posterior Han, from which the province takes one of its classical names. The present Examination Hall is in the enclosure where the imperial residence stood, surrounded by a moat and city wall.

In the western part of Chentu is also another walled city, the Manchu quarter, which is thus quite separate from the Chinese portion of the capital, and in it reside a considerable population of Tartars. The streets in the Manchu city are straight and broad, but look lifeless and deserted, practically no business being carried on by either Manchus or Chinese within its borders. Here is the residence of the Tartar General of the province, who is equal in rank with the Viceroy, and who has control of the military of the province.

Little difference can be distinguished between Chinese and Manchu men, either in dress or features, but the women maintain a peculiar selectness in the style of their dress which marks them off at once from the Chinese. They wear long gowns, very large hair pins, and their feet are of natural size. It is a noticeable fact how tall they are as a race and doubtless this is due in good measure to the absence of the custom of foot-binding.

Turning to the appearance of Chentu itself, the city is almost perfectly flat, one small hill in the N.W. corner being the only exception. The streets are wide for a Chinese city, as a rule run at right angles to each other, and are so straight that anyone passing along them gets a good idea of their importance. They are mostly paved with stone and of late years have been better lighted than Chinese cities often are, owing to the introduction of western shaped lamps, where glass now takes the place of the thin semi-opaque paper of the past. The lamp posts are short and gaudily painted, many of them are bright green, with the lamp frame above them a pronounced blue. The light does not yet compete with that of Western street lamps, it is produced still from a tiny pith wick in native vegetable oil.

The houses are of one storey, but many are large and grand nevertheless. Such are called "*kung kwans*," or official residences, from the fact that they are frequently the private homes of temporary or permanent officials. The rooms are built round the four sides of courts, which open one out of the other, the innermost one containing the chief rooms, while the outer courts are occupied by attendants or servants.

The shops are well stocked with all the usual merchandise of a Chinese city, while there is a special trade in silk, embroidery, lacquered goods, and filigree silver work. There are now at least three large shops which advertise that they supply foreign articles for sale, and the stocks they hold certainly would astonish many people. The prices asked are really not exorbitant considering the distance the goods are brought, and the time it takes to get them two thousand miles from the coast, with, all the way, the risk of shipwreck and loss. Good brass hinges, for instance, from threepence halfpenny each, and brass screws at the rate of five a penny can hardly be called expensive. Many foreign articles—lamps, umbrellas, watches, unbreakable ware, Berlin wool, and other things—are to be found now on almost any street, as regular stock-in-trade.

The temples in the city and suburbs are well kept up, and the paved courts swept clean and tidy. The gods, decked in gorgeous paint, look as if only lately in the workmen's hands, and order seems to reign in the forms of worship performed at stated hours daily. Some of the temples are richly endowed, and have large numbers of priests in residence.

Anyone passing frequently through the streets will be impressed by the evidences of religion among the people. Candles, paper, and incense, are frequently burned at the doors of the shops and houses. Little children have been seen playing at worshipping the sun, one teaching the other how low to bow, etc. Little boys of two or three years are led out into the street to worship the new moon, and old men may be observed morning after morning prostrating themselves in the open thoroughfares in the attitude of worship ; while the spirits of the dying or recently dead are carefully helped on their exit from this present life by rows of lighted candles placed along the public road for long distances !

Another feature, common throughout the province, but especially prominent in Chentu, is the frequent gathering of the people, in or near the public tea shops and " *kung kwans,*" to hear some teacher or scholar narrate stories illustrative of filial piety, or discourse on the Sacred Edict or similar books ; this seems a usual evening occupation in both summer and winter.

Owing to the enterprise and energy of a recent Viceroy, a city police has been established, and the men are conspicuously on 'guard at the corners of most of the streets. True, they do not quite equal in appearance the Western policeman, but they make a good show of official importance, with their foreign-shaped straw hats, and short jackets. Each man is duly numbered on the hat and shoulder, carries a substantial walking stick, and has a penny English whistle tied round his neck. So far the pigtail and straw sandals are still worn by the police, and the fan is also well to the front on hot summer days. That they stand ready for work, as well as show, was fairly demonstrated recently. One of our missionaries was riding through a busy street, and the chair-bearers, who are often very rough, encountered a beggar, somehow got entangled with him, and broke his staff. A gentleman, passing by, suggested a " few cash " as compensation for the loss, but, before any arrangement could be considered, a policeman was on the spot, and quickly managed the business, to the satisfaction of the beggar and the offenders.

Another noticeable instance of modern advance is the loud horn which is blown several times a day to mark the hours for meals and work at the city arsenal, where large numbers of men, who turn out some very creditable iron work, are regularly employed.

In another part of the city is an extensive parade ground and large barracks for the Chinese soldiers, who are drilled daily, according to Western methods. It is a curious sight to watch these Chinese, wearing short jackets, with their queues twisted round their heads, going through various gymnastic exercises on the horizontal bars, poles, etc. which are also provided on the drill ground. The officers are now mostly instructed by Japanese, specially appointed for the purpose.

Another effort marking the advance of Western influence, is that being made to introduce into the city a regular silver and copper coinage in place of the *sycee* and ancient cash. Silver dollars, about equal in value to the Mexican, are now being coined in the Imperial Mint, with ten and twenty cent pieces in copper. It takes time to make radical changes in an ancient country like China, and this last attempt cannot yet be said to have been crowned with success. Only a limited number of dollars can be obtained at one time at the Public Treasury for the lump silver which is still required for use in all the country round. The long waiting and much scrambling necessary to obtain the dollars is not enticing to a people who have no desire for innovations.

The Anti-footbinding movement, started in accordance with recent edicts of the Empress-Dowager, is making rapid strides in Chentu. There are many unmistakable signs that public opinion in this matter is at last yielding to the enlightening influence of the twentieth century.

But perhaps the most radical change, and the most important one, is in the education of the *literati*, and in the evident intention to encourage the study of Western learning.* Three classes of Public Schools are now being generally established, the

---

* The following, the substance of a telegram from Peking, is quoted from the *Times*, Sept. 8th, 1905 : " An edict has been issued in reply to a memorial from Yuan Shih Kai and other prominent men abolishing the whole system of examination for degrees, under which candidates for official positions were required to be proficient in the writings of Confucius and other Classics. In future, officials will be recruited from the ranks of those educated under a modern system in schools established throughout the country. Examinations will be held in the various schools and not in the central towns as formerly. This edict offers the strongest inducement to a Chinaman to acquaint himself with Western learning."

highest class or Provincial College, the Prefectural and the Hsien. The city of Chentu, being divided into two Hsiens, has two schools of this latter class, one of them in the same street as our own Mission premises.

In Chentu a Consul-General of the British Government and a French Consul are in residence. Many official visitors pass through, presumably, though not avowedly, on business connected with railway enterprises. So far, indeed, has the idea of railways taken hold of the Chinese

GREEN DRAGON STREET, CHENTU; FRIENDS' PREMISES ON THE RIGHT.

mind that a missionary in Chentu was quite recently shown a map, which had been printed by a native in the city, giving the details of prospective routes, running through all the chief centres of activity in the whole province. It was interesting and hopeful to find herein the promise of a direct line from Chungking to both Chentu and T'ung Ch'wan, through the district set apart for the work of Friends' Mission.

CHAPTER VI.

THE COMMERCE, BANKING, COINAGE AND POSTAL SYSTEMS.

THE waterways of China are a ready means of communication between the provinces, and have tended to promote the large internal commerce met with. Medicines, silk and wool find their way from the extreme West to Shanghai, while sea delicacies, best pottery and fans, besides the foreign imports, go from the sea-board provinces throughout the empire. A long list might be made of the commodities of internal trade, and would be found to include practically everything needed by the Chinese as essentials. Their long period of seclusion has taught them to regulate their requirements by their actual productions, and in this they have succeeded to a remarkable degree. The internal trade seems fairly well regulated, though one is struck with the annoying multiplicity of the local customs barriers and illegal squeezes to which it is obliged to submit.

Commercial relations with foreign nations—at least to any considerable extent—are of comparatively recent date. The Portuguese and Dutch seem to have been first in trading by sea, the British East India Company finding its way there later. In those early days commerce was restricted and greatly hampered by regulations. One of the results of the wars, of which mention has already been made, has been the gradual opening of China to all comers, and there is now an immense import and export trade, for which Shanghai and Hong Kong are the chief ports. Of this trade, at least sixty per cent. is British.

The Imperial Customs Service of China is an unique institution, having been, for about fifty years, in the hands of a foreign staff, and a well-known British subject, Sir Robert Hart, has been Inspector-General for over forty years. The foreign staff, of perhaps 1,000 men, is cosmopolitan, having probably more nationalities represented than has any other public service. The Chinese staff is a very large one, and should ultimately dominate the Service, but thus far the honesty of foreigners has resulted in returns so satisfactory to the Government that they are content to pay higher salaries to them rather than employ Chinese in the highest posts. This excellent service has done much to promote and consolidate commerce.

At Hong Kong and Shanghai may be seen first-class banking houses with European assistants. These are, of course, of comparatively recent growth and, speaking properly, are not Chinese banks, but banks in China.

There can be no doubt, however, that a system of banking has been known for a very long time, and the use of paper money goes back 1,000 years, though it has been discontinued at times. In a treatise dealing with the subject, written nearly fifty years ago, Mr. A. Wylie said :—

> The invention and priority in the use of paper money by the Chinese is now generally admitted. Klaproth and others have given details to some extent, regarding the history of the currency. From native records we learn that it was first used by the imperial government in the ninth century, and was continued with intervals till near the close of the fifteenth ; from which, down to recent times, no attempt has been made to revive the practice. The extensive use of promissory notes, however, in various parts of the empire, and the exhausted state of the imperial treasury, has suggested the desirability of another attempt, by this means, to relieve the state from the financial pressure, and after a cessation of four hundred years, government banks have again been opened in the large cities for the issue of a new paper currency. The success that has attended the experiment is not such as to promise a long continuance of this expedient.

Of the government banks referred to in the above extract, we now know nothing in Sz-Chwan. The native banks are not under government control ; any individual or company—with funds sufficient—may open a bank and issue bills as they choose. These banks, speaking generally, maintain a good reputation for honesty, and their bills circulate widely in the transaction of business. Bills are safeguarded in such a way as to make counterfeiting practically impossible. The description given by Doolittle, of the practice in a coast province, is true in the main of Sz-Chwan.

The outline of the bill, with various devices to make counterfeiting difficult, is engraved neatly on a solid block of brass or wood. The value of the bill and the day of issue are filled in with the pen, and one or two more words to facilitate detection of a counterfeit. Various stamps, large or small, round or square or oblong, some of which are very curiously and elaborately engraved, are impressed on different parts of the bill, using red or blue ink. These add very much to the neat and pretty appearance of the note, and are believed usually to have some secret or private mark, and are very difficult to imitate with precision and exactness.

But perhaps the use which is made of the wide right-hand margin furnishes the greatest security against counterfeiting. On this margin are stamped or written various words, phrases or sentences, before the bill is cut off or put in circulation. When everything is ready, these stamped or written sentences are cut through by a sharp knife, leaving the right-hand margin of the bill about the same width as the left-hand, though it presents a very different appearance. Of course the edge of the right-hand margin of the bill, and the edge of the paper which was cut from it will precisely match each other : but as the sentences have been cut into two parts, part of the words and stamps will be on the bill and part on the slip of paper cut off. These slips are all carefully kept in a book form ready for reference, each slip containing the value, date, and private marks of the bill corresponding to it. On the presentation of the bill, if there is the least doubt of its genuineness, reference is made to the corresponding proof-slip, and the banker or his clerks know immediately whether it is genuine or counterfeit. A successful imitation of the written sentences and words, the blue and red stamps, which are found on the right margin of a bank-bill, and which have been cut through on a line parallel with the left-hand margin, it is almost impossible to make so exact, precise, and minute as to fit the preserved proof-slip.*

In large cities like Chentu and Chungking, though so far inland, it is easy to find bankers or merchants who will cash the

* " Social Life of the Chinese," vol. ii. p. 140.

cheques drawn on the foreign banks at the coast, as the security of those banks is well known in the interior. In smaller places where regular banks may not exist, some well-established business firms,—with visible stock-in-trade as additional security,—will act in that capacity. The officials deal largely with such firms, and items of local expenditure are paid in promissory notes payable at certain dates. There are also the "cash shops" or exchanges, where the strings of copper cash are arrayed, and large and small amounts of money change hands.

Before entering upon the present currency and money values, it may be of interest to glance briefly at the interesting past of China's *Coinage.* In no country in the world can the current coinage claim to be so interesting as in China. While to a casual observer the little round "cash," with the square hole, are all similar, the careful observer will discover differences of dynasty, of emperor, and peculiarities of minting, in startling variety. It is not uncommon in daily use to handle coins of over a thousand years old, and very many that were coined several hundreds of years ago.

The bulk of present day coinage is composed of "cash" coined during the present dynasty, which commenced A.D. 1644, and one can scarcely take ten cash at random without finding among them one or more of about the time of Cromwell. Coins of the present dynasty are distinguished by having two Manchu characters on the reverse side, where previously most were blank.

The earliest coins of China lead back to the days of primitive barter. They are copper facsimiles of common objects, the first kind representing the spade, some with, and others without, holes. The earliest recorded specimen is of B.C. 2356, and must be exceedingly rare. For shape (not inscription) see Fig. 1. Next came the "Knife" or "Sword" cash, so-called from their resemblance to that instrument, (Fig. 3.) These all date from long before the Christian era.

There are of course many forgeries, and some of them are of such great age as to possess an interest of their own, and to be

TYPES OF COINAGE; MOSTLY ANCIENT.

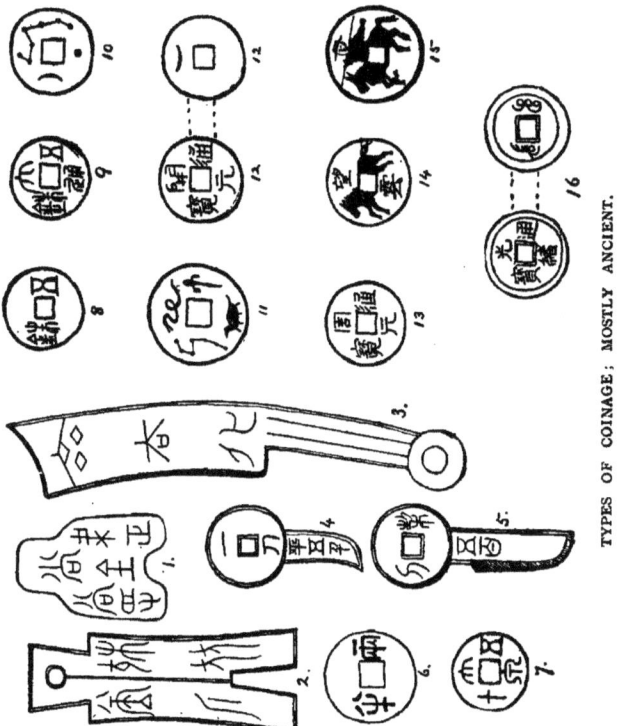

almost, if not quite, indistinguishable from originals. That people possess, apart from imitations, many genuine coins of antiquity, is explained by the fact that among the Chinese for many centuries there have been keen curio-hunters and collectors of coins. Since the Sung dynasty (A.D. 960-1278) there have been works on the coinage. In 1830 was published a standard work, the title of which, translated, is "Chronicles of Cash." In this book full particulars are given of the coins dealt with, their weight (which must, however, be an uncertain guide), their dimensions, and every little peculiarity, besides woodcuts for identification. Over 300 kinds are given, not including those of the present dynasty, which adds nine more emperors, with about 200 varieties of mintings.

It is not known exactly when the round coin with the square hole was introduced, but it was probably about B.C. 300. Some opinions give the reign of Emperor Chin Wang (B.C. 554-520) as the time when circular money came into use. The distinguished Emperor, Chin-Shih-Hwang B.C. 221, builder of the Great Wall, (and from the title of whose dynasty we derive the name "China" for the country) instituted the circular "Pan Liang" (half-ounce) shown (Fig. 6). The first few years of the Christian era produced several interesting coins, specimens of which may often be met with still (Figs. 4, 5, 7, 8). Fig. 5 was an attempt to re-introduce the "Sword" pattern, while compromising largely with the new round ones, which by that time had doubtless become very popular (A.D. 20). It was worth 500 of smaller cash. The denomination of Fig. 7 was 50 cash.

About A.D. 230 a coin was issued with a value of 1,000 ordinary cash. The year 502 saw the first iron coins used in China. These are plentiful with curio-dealers. A few years later a curiously small and light cash, known as the "goose eye" from its size, was circulated. The book tells us that it did not sink in water. Figs. 10 and 11 belong to about the middle of the 6th century, in the former are seen the sun, moon, and seven stars, and in the latter similar stars, with tortoise, snake and sword.

Fig. 12 of A.D. 620 has a romantic interest as it is said the crescent on the reverse was made by an empress, perhaps in playful mood, impressing the wax of the mould with her fingernail. This coin was also the first to have on it "T'ung Pao" *i.e.*, "Universal current value," which has ever since been found on Chinese coins.

Burning questions of past history may occasionally be traced through the coinage. For instance, those of the years 841 and 954, were made out of bells and images from suppressed Buddhist temples (Fig. 13). More than 3,300 temples were thus suppressed in A.D. 954 by the Chinese "Henry VIII."

The numbers of cash coined, of course, varied widely, but a record coinage of about A.D. 1000 is given at 1,830,000 strings of 1,000 each, in one year.

Figs. 14 and 15 are types of a large class known as "horse cash," the times and values of which are uncertain. Other figures occur on coins or charms and "lucky-pennies" in great variety.

Fig. 16 represents a cash of the present Emperor, Kwang Hsü, on the reverse of which are Manchu characters. It may become historical as the last of the long list of cast coins, for contact with Western nations is beginning to affect the currency, and already mints are being established which are producing coins, without the holes, of the denominations of 10 and 20 cash. These mints are also putting out silver dollars and fractions thereof. While the innovation is being sullenly contested in Sz-Chwan, by those who gain by keeping things as they are, it has doubtless come to stay, and will be a boon to business men.

The best one can say of the present system is that it is on the common-sense decimal plan, and is thus far ahead of the British coinage, the irregularities of which are so troublesome to foreigners. But the inconveniences and perplexities of the way of actually using money in China need only be mentioned to be appreciated. While at various times there have been coins of different values, such as those representing 1,000, 500, 100 or 10 of the ordinary cash, yet by far the greater number in the

COINS: PAST AND PRESENT.

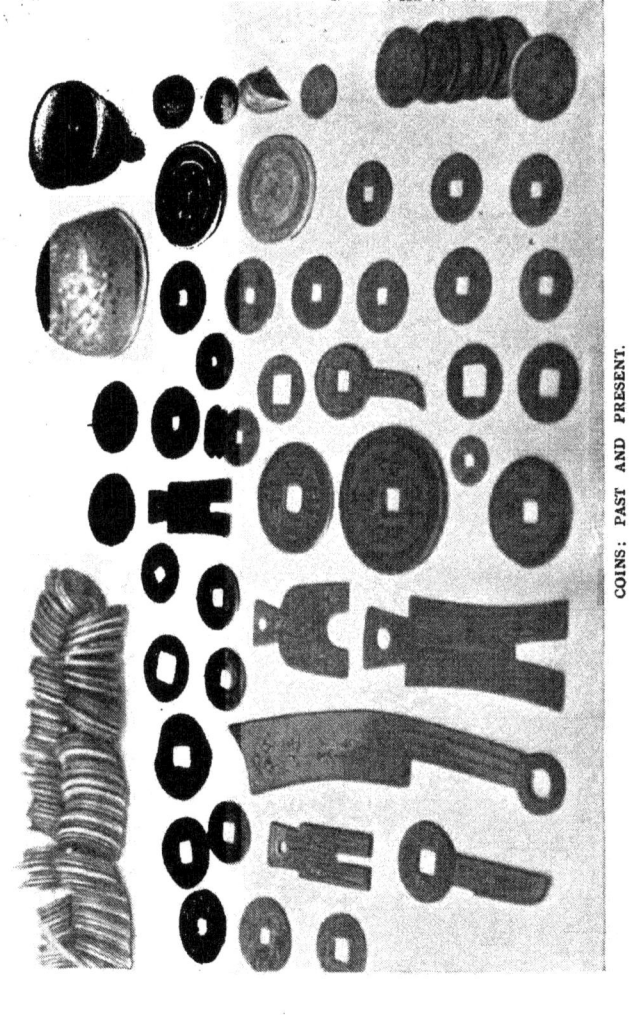

Lump silver and the new silver dollar and copper 10-cash piece may be seen above in right-hand top corner.

past, and practically all now in use, are of the denomination of one cash. These are strung up together by means of the holes. Two strings are used and are crossed after putting on each hundred, so that, when the 1,000 is reached, they look something like a string of sausages of a particularly indigestible kind. But even these numbers are nominal; a hundred cash are not a hundred, and a thousand are not a thousand, nor is the shortage sure to be the same on each string. Nothing short of a tedious count will declare the actual number, and the foreigner has neither time nor patience for that, though the Chinese would tenderly handle every coin. Again, in some places, one cash counts for two, but not in Sz-Chwan. The local abatement varies at almost every city. One has the rule of 99 being equal to 100, another 98 or 84, while some proudly proclaim " man ch'ien," the full number, less six however, for the labour of stringing them.

The difficulty of number having been disposed of, a still more formidable trouble arises from the admixture of small or spurious cash. There is no standard size or weight of the coin, so the vendor inserts as many bad cash as his hundred will reasonably stand, the reason being that he can buy those at a lower cost, or perhaps he has had them passed to him, and must get rid of them in his turn. The receiver faithfully sorts the bad cash out, perhaps a dozen from a hundred, and demands replacement; then a harangue ensues, and after both sides have waxed warm and cool again, it ends as they knew it would, in a compromise. The bad cash are used for beggars, who are in reality "demanders," who will not leave the door without the customary cash, so the shopkeeper gets even by making him wait a long time, and then giving a bad cash, and these the beggar sells when he gets sufficient; so they find their way back to the givers, ready for another trip round—nobody is deceived, and everybody seems satisfied.

No money deserves to be called " filthy lucre " more than Chinese. In bulk it is thrown about on the mud floors;

when scattered, it passes through hands, pockets and houses better imagined than described, or is brought forth from reposing in a man's ear, if he has no purse. The strings often break and scatter the cash on the street, and, at the best, they are weighty and unwieldy. One invariably seeks water after handling such cash. A string of 1,000 good cash weighs about eight pounds, and is at present worth perhaps 2s. 3d. Such is China's only coin, and a great many of the people never handle any other money in a lifetime than these curious pieces of copper, of which it takes over thirty to equal our penny.

Happily for business men and travellers,—and missionaries,—silver is used throughout the empire. Many have heard of the Chinese "Tael," and may have remarked upon its scarcity among curios at home. The reason is a simple one, namely that there is no such coin. The word is used to denote an ounce of silver, but very rarely would any piece weigh exactly an ounce; pieces may be of any size, but the most convenient are ingots of about ten ounces, but so uncertain as to always need weighing. The patriarchal practice of weighing out the silver, which we read of so often in the Scriptures, is better understood after living in China where the same practice is observed. Perhaps Abraham found his transactions less perplexing than we do, when, as a foreigner, he bought land from natives. (Gen. xxiii. 16). The weights vary in every city, 100 taels from Chungking, for instance, weighing only 98.50 at Sui-ling, or 98.85 at T'ung Ch'wan. Besides this, there is another standard, largely used in official payments, which makes Tls. 100 something different; and yet another, which is known as the Hai Kwan or Customs Tael.

The quality of the silver is also a fruitful source of discussion, and abatements have to be made for questionable pieces which may have been adulterated. As nobody trusts another person's scales, the buyer and seller, where silver is concerned, must go together to a "public" scale, where a small payment is made to have the silver weighed by impartial scales.

It would seem as though no real business could be transacted under these conditions, and yet there is an immense amount of internal trading. The Chinaman accommodates himself to circumstances, and with remarkably little grumbling. If an inconvenience has only the saving grace of age, he will put up with

A BAMBOO WATER-WHEEL.
As seen on the road from Chungking to Chentu, for raising water to the level of the rice-fields.

it, in the same spirit of the Scot who said, " Ye ken what ye hae, but ye dinna ken what ye may get."

POSTAL SYSTEMS.

Up to a few short years ago, the needs of the Empire were met by a multitude of courier posts, foot and horse, and the most important documents, as well as the letters of the people, had to reach their destination along circuitous routes and after weary days or months of travel. Some of these posts, however, attained a considerable degree of speed, the charges were moderate, and the service comparatively trustworthy.

For some years past the telegraph has linked together the provincial capitals and some other centres, and Imperial Edicts from Peking can reach Chentu in a few hours instead of weeks as was formerly the case by special couriers. Official dispatches still travel by a "Dispatch Bureau," of which there is a branch in every Hsien (county) city, where men are ready to depart, day or night, so that official messages get round in very quick time.

Within the last decade the Chinese Imperial Post has come into existence and, while at first confining its operations to treaty ports and similar places, it is now reaching far into the interior, has branches at some hundreds of cities, and will soon form a complete network over the whole empire. Begun as a branch of the Imperial Customs Service, it now employs a considerable staff of Europeans, and a large number of Chinese. At first, the charges were very moderate, local letters being carried, from say one part of Shanghai to another, for one half cent, the cent of a Mexican dollar being equal to one farthing. A letter weighing $\frac{1}{2}$oz. could be sent from Chentu to Peking, over 2,000 miles, by road, river, and sea, for one cent. The carriage of newspapers and parcels was correspondingly cheap, and, in consequence, quite a demand for the former—in Chinese—sprang up in the interior, while much business has been done with the coast ports by parcels post. It was discovered that these rates resulted in loss to the revenue, and they have accordingly been increased.

While speaking of the Postal service, it is a pleasure to mention the generous and loving act of the Christian Postal Employees of Great Britain, who have recently made a presentation of a handsome New Testament to every Chinese Postal servant. Letters of greeting, in English and Chinese, were inserted. This act has been much appreciated, and may result in great good. The Testaments were supplied by the British and Foreign Bible Society, whose Agent superintended their distribution.

CHAPTER VII.

CHARACTER OF THE PEOPLE.

IN his interesting work entitled "Chinese Characteristics," Dr. Arthur H. Smith has succeeded in giving a life-like pourtrayal of the Chinese, and fills nearly 300 pages in doing so. It will be at once manifest that we have here a subject of which, in a few pages, we can give only an outline, and we would commend the above-mentioned book to those who wish to pursue the subject further.

Physically the Chinese are much the same as Europeans in build; their colour is a pale yellow, but amongst them are many similar to the inhabitants of southern Europe, and occasionally women or girls will be as fair as a brunette of England. The hair is black and coarse. They have little or no beard, and that little not grown until past forty years of age, eyes aslant, cheek-bones prominent, and lips thicker than amongst Europeans. In physical endurance the Chinese rank high. They are in the main an industrious people and extremely economical. In habits they are temperate, so that seldom will a man be seen drunk. The opium vice is increasing lamentably, and is unmistakeably sapping the vigour of the nation, as well as breeding other vices.

While conservatism and hide-bound tradition conspire to prevent much display of originality or genius, it must be conceded that the Chinese have considerable power of intellect. Those who in recent times have been fortunate enough to secure a Western education have done honour to their nation by their attainments. Perhaps no nation can surpass the Chinese in feats of memory.

So homogeneous are the people that most of their characteristics may well be called national ones, yet in these pages we speak chiefly of the Chinese amongst whom we live and work in Sz-Chwan.

They do not appear to have the finer emotions to the same extent as Europeans. Love, sympathy and altruism are not prominent features, and religious feeling does not seem to be what we call spiritual. On the other hand, anger and hatred appear ungovernable when aroused, and are the source of many crimes and much sickness.

While not sensitive on the nice points of honour, there is a mysterious quality known as "face," about which they are extremely sensitive. It is seldom that one will make a plain straightforward statement, from a fear that somebody's "face" will be involved. To acknowledge a fault is to lose "face," and any amount of falsehood will be justified if "face" can thereby be saved. The idea may be likened to our sense of shame, but it seems more comprehensive; and cannot be fathomed because of its inconsistencies, which sanction greater evils in order to cover the loss of "face" that might be involved in a matter. A man considering himself injured will lightly commit suicide to "save his face," and when the Emperor makes the suggestive present of a silken cord to a minister who is in disgrace, the recipient and his family take consolation in the fact that though by its use the life will be lost, yet the "*Face will be saved!*"

The educated Chinese is a marvel of politeness, ranking second to none in this grace. The result of Confucian teaching and of long-settled habit has been that, from the highest to the lowest, all seem to know exactly what is the proper thing to do at the proper time. That the politeness is often the merest veneer detracts nothing from it in the eyes of the Chinese. Though a man may be dealing with one whom he positively dislikes, or whom he is taking advantage of, yet he would despise himself if he omitted the punctilious observance of such details as offering tea and tobacco, or omitted a bow at the right time. Even when showering the vilest abuse upon one, politeness forbids personal reference, and the abuse must be of a man's ancestors more or less remote. It is fortunate for the missionary that his hearers are too polite to sneer at his early blunders ; on the contrary they will put all misunderstanding down to their own stupidity. Politeness is especially manifest in terms of address

A WAY-SIDE TEMPLE AND SHRINE.

and in matters of precedence, and in many other ways it oils the social machinery to such an extent as to reduce friction to a minimum.

In travelling or living amongst the Chinese one cannot fail to be impressed with their industry and economy. The former is often more apparent than real ; everybody *seems* to be doing something, but closer acquaintance often reveals that motion and progress are not synonymous terms. There are a considerable number of idlers and of those who live by their wits at the expense of others, but after making allowance for these the fact remains that the large body of the people are industrious. The intensity of their labour varies considerably according to circumstances. On some occasions we have been persuaded that probably no man could get through less work in a given time than a Chinese, but on the other hand we have seen that in their homes and shops, and on the farms, they plod away steadily from sunrise to sunset, or even far into the night. We do not find that absorption in their work that Westerners display, nor have we noticed that feverish hurry we know too well at home. The Chinese are at all times ready for a rest and a smoke, and dearly love to gossip.

Competition has reached such a point among China's millions that hard toil is generally rewarded with a bare existence only, hence the virtue of economy is a practical necessity. Unfortunately the greatest economy cannot save large numbers from the pinch of poverty or starvation when the crops fail or other untoward circumstances occur. The land is made to produce to its utmost extent, and practically every available foot of soil, including the steep slopes and peaks of hills, is requisitioned.

In the matter of food there seems no waste, and cooking is accomplished with the minimum of utensils and fuel. For the daily ablutions of the average Chinese, less than a pint of water will suffice, and a towel the size of a handkerchief will possibly do duty for a whole family.

Living so continually from hand to mouth, it is not surprising that the claims of extraordinary events such as weddings and funerals involve people in debt. It seems, in consequence, that but few of the Chinese are absolutely free from financial embarrassment. Many people seem perpetually to be collecting, or trying to collect, debts one from another, as a means of livelihood. The pawnshop, which is a very old and well regulated institution in China, is much patronised, besides which people with a little capital lend it out at exorbitant interest, with the result that "loan oft loses both itself and friend."

Gambling is a deep-seated passion with the Chinese. This is shown when the little child, who can scarcely toddle, takes his one " cash " to the itinerant sweet-vendor, and has a spin at the wheel for " double or quits," and by the grey-beards who sit solemnly round the gaming table. Card-playing for stakes is exceedingly common, but betting is not a noticeable feature of their gambling.

From of old the words " Licentiousness and Gambling " have been used to describe vice generally, but now a third is added, viz. : " Opium-smoking." With regard to the first named of these, a stranger might be struck with the absence of open indications of immorality ; but closer acquaintance compels us to acknowledge that there is a lamentable amount of it, notwithstanding early marriages. Adultery may be punished as in the Mosaic law, by immediate death of both parties, and yet it is far from uncommon. Other forms of uncleanness and depravity are painfully prominent.

The natives of Sz-Chwan are true to Oriental type in their love of exaggeration and disregard of accuracy. Imagination is very fertile, and from the slenderest thread of fact can be woven remarkable stories, abounding in circumstantial details. The wild stories about foreigners are examples of how exaggeration runs riot, and equally wild statements are made about local places and people. Even when speaking with no intent to deceive, the language employed gives considerable latitude. A man who is asked his age may reply, " Fifty or Sixty," or if he wishes to be more exact " Fifty odd." A distance is " several tens " or " several hundreds " of miles. The population of a city is stated quite nearly enough as " Several tens of thousands." The Chinese never seem able to understand our desire for accuracy, and wonder whatever can prompt us to want to know more nearly than a few years in time, or a few miles in distance. One of the most constantly recurring phrases is " ch' a pu toa," *i.e.*, " not much different," and if the foreigner is annoyed at the delay of a few hours in an appointment, or at the short payment of an account, or a day's journey instead of a promised couple of hours, or if work which he has given careful instructions about is patchy and inaccurate, or perhaps he discovers that statements he has accepted in good faith have been dreadfully warped from the truth, he is met with the smile that is " childlike and bland," and the answer to all his remonstrances is that it is " not much different," therefore practically correct, and there is no occasion whatever for any fuss.

But when a Chinese *intends* to deceive, which is not seldom, he goes the whole length and lies in the most bare-faced manner without wincing. There is no shame noticeable, except when the deception happens to be found out, and then not because of the immorality of the action, but because the lie was not smart enough effectively to escape detection.

It often happens that the Chinese prefer to imply their meaning rather than actually state it, and when such is their purpose, the Drumtochty people could not be more cautious in their speech. What a Chinese says is frequently not the same thing as what he means, and as a rule he prefers to leave something to be inferred, rather than say all that is on his mind. Confucius long ago said that in giving instruction he only mentioned one corner of a subject and expected the listener to have wit enough to infer the other three corners, otherwise he was not an apt pupil ! The Chinese of the present day follow the sage closely in this, and will seldom say all they *could* say on a matter, or say it in the plain outspoken way of the Westerner. The Chinese are adepts at " whipping one man over another man's shoulders," and there is almost an art in the way they will refer to " somebody," and make it quite plain whom they mean without mentioning, or even glancing at, the person. They can convey profound meaning by simply sticking out the lips, without saying a word. The omission of some little act, easily unnoticed by a foreigner, or some slight irregularity in the mode of address, may mean much to Chinese observers.

Another prominent feature of the people now under review has been well described by one writer as the " Absence of nerves." This is not to imply that the nervous system of the Chinese differs materially from that of others; yet it is certain that he seems a stranger to much of the nervousness and sensitiveness with which we are so well acquainted. Sights, sounds and smells which the foreigner finds trying, the Chinese not only endures, but seems to take a pleasure in. The screeching wheelbarrow never gets the needed drop of oil,—not altogether because of economy—but because the noise is counted an agreeable part of the work, and is enjoyed as such.

The Chinese opera often lasts for days, and the accompaniment throughout consists of shrill-sounding instruments, with gongs and drums, so dearly loved by the people.

Filthy open drains and cesspools, and the carrying of manure through crowded streets, are not only tolerated but are looked upon as a perfectly natural state of things, and it is a remarkable fact that notwithstanding the daily defiance of the laws of hygiene, millions of people thrive and appear to be happy in their surroundings. The damp mud floors, draughty windows and doors, the leaking roofs and the absence of chimneys, do not seem to act much on Chinese nerves and, a Chinaman, after he has eaten his coarse meal, can lie down with a brick for a pillow—or with no pillow at all—and sleep on a bed of no comfort, oblivious of the terrors of the night which abound. He will sleep as soundly as the proverbial " top " on a five-inch form; in fact we have yet to discover the place and position in which a Chinese cannot sleep, if permitted!

Deformities and the hideous effects of disease are far too common to cause much remark or excite pity, and are more often made the subject of jest. Physical pain is borne with fortitude; when death approaches, it is met in a stoical manner, the sufferer being often left alone while relatives call in priests or exorcists who make a great noise to drive away evil spirits, while, all the time, preparations are going forward for the expected decease. We remember one filial son who showed his devotion to his dying mother by having carpenters in the house to make a coffin, that she might die happy in the knowledge that she would be decently buried.

While we must describe the Chinese as unsympathetic, we must not omit to mention that there is considerable almsgiving among them and other works of charity. Building bridges, making roads and providing ferries are common ways of showing benevo-

ROPE SUSPENSION BRIDGE, SUNG P'AN, N.W. SZ-CHWAN.
The bridge is suspended from bamboo ropes, requiring renewal periodically.

lence, and there are in some places orphanages and almshouses, also shelters for the destitute. These last-named institutions are of the most primitive description, and are wholly inadequate for the needs of the people. There are often free distributions of rice to the poor, and of medicines to the sick. But the motive underlying these efforts is often not so much sympathy as a desire to accumulate merit. It may be said that the Chinese seldom give anything without expecting or hoping to receive more in return, either in this world or the next. Even the importunate beggar knows this, and adds to his plea for alms the assurance that every copper given to him will return as gold to the benefactor.

It may be that ages of keen competition and of struggle for existence have largely contributed to the cause, but certain it is that a large amount of selfishness exists. The weakest are pushed to the wall, and no one hesitates to take advantage of another, even under conditions which rightly call for sympathy. It is notorious that in distributions during famine, or after calamities, a large part of the money never reaches the needy. One night we found a man apparently dying on the street, and two passers-by busying themselves around with exclamations of pity; but when, after a little attention, the man recovered from what was only a fit, his sympathisers had disappeared with his hat and shoes. In Chungking, it is by no means an uncommon thing to find a dying man lying in the street, who will be allowed to remain there until the end comes, while the crowds pass by and the shopmen ply their trades a few yards off and without apparent concern.

In view of their social conditions it is well that the Chinese possess in large measure the admirable virtue of patience. Notwithstanding periodical rebellions and riots, the Chinese must be called a peace-loving people. They are naturally patient and willing rather to endure the ills they have than fly to others that they know not of. When flood and famine overtake them there is seldom serious revolt but, rather, patient suffering, starving to death, or emigrating to distant places and enduring cruel hardships. At the best of times the average Chinaman knows little of comfort, and is seldom free from hunger, yet he does not often complain of his lot. His horizon is very limited, and he is content to live one day at a time, step by step patiently plodding his way through life.

Foreigners are soon impressed with the results of excessive patience, in the absence of hurry and the disregard of time. The Chinese usually saunter along at a slow pace and in single file, with an air which plainly says "What is not done to-day may be done to-morrow." If we make an appointment with a Chinaman, he may turn up half-a-day before the time, or a day behind, and in either case without showing much embarrassment. The people of Sz-Chwan know practically nothing of clocks, their guide being the sun by day and the watchman's gong by night. Time is divided into periods of two hours each, and the name of a period covers any part of the two hours, so that an appointment for the " Wei " period for instance, may mean any time between one and three p.m.—an arrangement which leaves nothing to be desired in its possibilities for wasting time. It is difficult to keep regular times for meetings and classes, as attenders may come two hours before we are ready, or may walk in as the service is concluding. As the meetings are becoming more understood and appreciated, rather than miss the hour, many of the attenders devote the whole Sunday morning to the purpose.

When advocating railways and other time-saving methods of travel, we describe to the Chinese how quickly we can get about at home. They may be astonished, but their expressions seem to imply that they cannot understand why we should want to be flying around in such a ridiculous fashion instead of at a reasonable three or four miles an hour. Most of us try at some time or other to get the Chinese to " hustle " a little, but such attempts usually end in ignominious failure. Rudyard Kipling shows deep acquaintance with Eastern character in his poem beginning :

> It is not good for the Christian's health
> To try to hustle the East—

and concluding :—

> And the end of the fight, is a tombstone white,
> With the name of the " late deceased : "
> And the epitaph drear, " a fool lies here,
> Who tried to hustle the East."

This inadequate list of prominent features in the character of the people of Sz-Chwan may fitly close with the mention of Filial Piety, which is at once the strength and the weakness of the Chinese nation. It is sometimes said that the continuity of the Empire is the result of the steady observance of the spirit of the fifth commandment. According to the Confucian standard, there is much " filial piety," but it should be remembered that the standard thus set is principally one of " ceremony " and punctilious observance of outward shows. Confucius said that the son who for three years after his father's death did not depart

A WOMAN WINDING COTTON.
Women can be seen outside many of the houses in Sz-Chwan engaged in this way.

from the ways of his father, could be called a filial son, a standard which in these days will scarcely be considered adequate.

As true filial piety is based on love, we should hesitate to give that name to much that we see too plainly has its motive in custom or pride, or the fear of what others may think. It is the "correct thing" to show outward honour to parents, hence some sons will spend large sums, especially at funerals, and otherwise make great demonstrations, but always, as we should say, "playing to the gallery." In real life the aged often suffer severely, and are reminded that they are burdens. It is after they are dead that they are most honoured, and then, principally, that the performance may reflect credit on the living and, while helping the soul on its way, also secure benefits from the spirits of the departed.

One of the evils of this "filial piety" is the thraldom of the son even to a wicked father. The father of the famous emperor Shun tried again and again to kill his son, yet the son dare not complain. When a father commits murder, it is considered filial of the son to carry him away into security, and thus defeat justice. Boys may steal if it be for their parents. A father may kill his child if he is unable to support both his parents and his children. The wife is set aside in favour of parents, as the husband is bound first to consider their wishes. Ancestral worship is also intimately connected with "filial piety." There exists in this virtue the base of a noble and enduring structure, but it is covered with weeds and rubbish, and is waiting the day of better things, when the words shall have a truer meaning, and "filial piety" in its best sense shall be a blessing to the nation.

Enough has been said of the character of the people amongst whom we live and work to show that, while possessing an interest of their own, they are not fundamentally different from ourselves. Left to themselves and their imperfect systems, they develop the vices and failings common to humanity, but when touched by the love of Christ, they become valiant soldiers of the Cross. Some of them have already proved their devotion by suffering hardship and persecution, even unto death.

CHAPTER VIII.

SOCIAL CUSTOMS.

SO much has been written and spoken of late years about this interesting nation that the children of to-day have the opportunity of knowing more about the social customs of the Chinese than had the wise men of two generations ago; and yet the average Englishman in thinking of the Chinese probably remembers only a few prominent features, such as the wearing of a "pig-tail," binding of women's feet, the growth of tea and consumption of opium. It is the purpose of this chapter to show that on closer acquaintance there is much of interest, and some things to admire in the customs of a people so ancient as the Chinese.

Seeing that large volumes are available which deal minutely with the subject, notably Doolittle's "Social Life of the Chinese," the present writer need but briefly refer to the more prominent features, and this with reference chiefly to things as observed in Sz-Chwan.

We find the usual gradations of society, from the rich to the poor, but there is an absence of the caste system of India, and a

A CHINESE GENTLEMAN.

democratic spirit is noticeable in the way that masters, servants, rulers and ruled mingle together. The Chinese have themselves divided society under four general headings as, Scholars, Farmers, Craftsmen, and Merchants. As official position is nominally gained by examination, the first heading is meant to include the official class, and the greatest deference is usually paid to members of it. Agriculture has always had an honourable position in China, the Emperor himself handling a plough once a year as an example to his subjects. Most of the people delight to claim some connection with the land, even those who have long lived in cities think of some country home as their proper place. The craftsmen are many and varied, pursuing, with hand labour, much the same industries as are found in England. Merchants and tradesmen, while a large and influential part of the population, are placed last on the list as they are not producers, but simply distribute what others have made. There are of course very many people who cannot be placed under any of the headings given, such as soldiers, clerks, boatmen, barbers, actors, etc.

The Chinese are highly amused at the dress and habits of foreigners, and we are equally amused and interested in theirs. In many things their customs are the opposite of our own. In dress the men wear the gowns, and the women the trousers. Apart from an overcoat, the last article a man puts on is a waistcoat over his other garments. A man's hair is mostly shaven off, the remainder making a plait about a yard long. The small feet of the women are pitiable to see, being often four inches, or even less, in length. Often have our hearts ached as we heard the cries of the little girls undergoing the cruel footbinding process. If a person tries to walk on his heels, he will realise the gait of these crippled Chinese women. Another strange custom is that of allowing the nails of the fingers to grow to a great length; these may frequently be seen two or three inches in length, while one of our inquirers boasted nine inches!

A man's shoes are made of cloth, their paper soles having a thin facing of leather. His socks are of calico, always white, but he wraps his feet in a remnant before putting on his socks. If he wears a watch it must be on his breast like a medal, and in nine cases out of ten it is either not working or gives no clue to the time of day. Walking sticks are not used, but pipes of a yard long are common. Another kind of pipe, rejoicing in the name of "hubble-bubble," is made of brass, with a reservoir for water through which the smoke is drawn.

A CHINESE STUDENT ENGAGED IN WRITING.
By kind permission of the "Foreign Field."

The usual way of taking meals is for the people to sit at a square table, when each person has a separate basin for rice, but everyone dips into a common basin for vegetables or meat. Chopsticks are universally used, and it is considered an act of politeness to select some dainty morsel and place it with your chopsticks in your neighbour's basin for him to eat.

We might mention more of the customs which are the opposite of ours. White is worn for mourning, and red for weddings and festivities. When attending a funeral, old clothes are worn. Instead of shaking hands with his friend, the Chinese clasps his own hands, and makes a bow. Shoes are whitened instead of being blacked; red is the colour for visiting cards, the larger these cards the better; writing is done with a brush; the words read downwards in perpendicular columns, and from right to left; the beginning of a book is what we should call the end. In eating, both chopsticks are held in one hand; at a feast the dessert comes first, and the guests disperse immediately after the meal, the social time being previous to and during the eating. In rowing a boat, the oarsman looks in the direction he is going and pushes away from him; a tailor also pushes the needle away from him. A carpenter holds the wood he is sawing with his foot instead of his knee. The roof of a house is put on before its foundations are finished, and a haystack is tied round a tree without touching the ground at all. The Chinese say that the magnetic needle points to the South; and in speaking of the cardinal points they invariably begin with the East.

While differing from us in so many details, it is to be noted that, in the important matters of the human relationship and of the constant virtues, they have a standard of which any nation might be proud and, considering the lax system of government, it is remarkable how little friction exists in the social machinery. Ancestral worship has produced strong clan relationships, so that in some districts, hundreds, or thousands of descendants will live near the old homestead and, when official employment, business, or stress of circumstances, compel some to go afield, there always remains the longing to return, if not during life, then after death, to their native place. Sons take their wives to the paternal home and occupy a room or rooms there, instead of having separate establishments of their own. It is regarded as a calamity when the number of descendants becomes so large or unmanageable as to necessitate dividing off.

The law against intermarriage with those of the same surname is no doubt wholesome, and yet, with charming inconsistency, it will allow first cousins to marry, whilst absolutely preventing total strangers, perhaps from different provinces, marrying, if their names happen to be the same. Similarity of name is very common, as there are only about 200 surnames in general use and, according to an analysis by an eminent authority, twenty of these cover half the people, while the five most common ones are owned by one quarter, that is to say about 100,000,000 people.

Marriages are arranged by " go betweens " who are responsible for seeing that the stars and other circumstances connected with the births of the parties are harmonious and favourable to the union. Betrothals often take place very early in life, especially as regards the girl. Frequently the prospective bride is taken to her future home when quite a child, and kept there as a daughter and drudge for several years before actual marriage. A wedding is an occasion of great festivity to all except the bride! She must lament aloud at leaving her parents' home, and is expected to be so overcome with grief as to touch little or no food during the first days of the ceremony. She is carried off in a closed and stuffy sedan chair with no windows, being taken along with the wedding presents, which are openly displayed so as to make a good impression. After the ceremony, during which the bride joins the bridegroom in worship of his ancestors, the veil is removed from her face by her husband, who probably sees her then for the first time. There may be great disappointment, but it is too late to retreat. Friends then scrutinise the bride, and pass all kinds of remarks about her in her presence, as might be done in buying cattle.

A young wife is of very little account in the house so long as her mother-in-law is living. Confucianism does not pay honour to women until they have sons who owe them filial piety. A shrewish old woman will often assume the government of all the females, and make life so unbearable to young daughters-in-law that they prefer suicide; and those who struggle through are doubtless supported by the hope that their own turn for such power will come in due time.

Births are naturally great events, but the amount of rejoicing is dependent upon the sex of the child. An infant girl is rarely welcomed, and in some parts infanticide is by no means uncommon, though it is not a noticeable feature of Sz-Chwan. The crime results not so much from heartlessness as from disappointment and poverty. As ancestral worship depends on the male succession, the birth of a son is welcomed with great rejoicings : presents and feasts abound, and in middle-class families the son is decidedly a person to be reckoned with from his very entry into the world. While still a tiny infant his head will be shaved, and some-

TEACHERS AND STUDENTS.
A group taken at the Girls' Boarding School, T'ung Ch'wan.

what later he will be found with bristling tufts of hair at various parts of his head, all giving promise of that ultimate glory of the Chinese—the queue.

For a few years boys and girls play happily together, largely at games of " make-believe," or with such toys as they have ; but all too soon begins the cruel footbinding for the girls, which makes their lives miserable.

About the time the little girls' woes begin, a boy will be sent to school, and this is a most important event. The Chinese have a profound respect for letters, and every scholar is supposed in some way to reflect the accumulated wisdom and honour of ages. The teacher may have his school of twenty or thirty boys in some temple. All the elementary native schools we have seen have had but one teacher each, with no divisions into classes, and the children are bathed at wisdom's font amid a babel of each other's voices, the sole object, at first, being to memorise the set pile of classics, regardless of whether the meaning is or is not understood. The explanation of the classics comes later on.

The boy on entering school is generally confronted by a huge pair of goggles (the badge of learning), behind which looms the teacher's head, which might be well described by Goldsmith's lines :—

> And still the wonder grew
> That one small head could carry all he knew;

for is it not said that "the man of the 'budding talent' degree without needing to travel, knows all the philosophy of heaven and earth!" Albeit he will assert the earth is flat, that eclipses are caused by a celestial dog trying to swallow the orb, that there is a country where the people have a hole through their chests so that they can be carried on a pole, that foreigners can see three feet beneath the surface of the ground, and that they make medicine of children's eyes. Such details of information as these, he is ready to impart to the gaping youths around him.

The successive steps of education are referred to in an earlier chapter. The pupil may develop into a useful member of society, perhaps with official position, but, unless he drifts off to work other than study, he far too often becomes a drone, living an idle life supported by others. Having once made himself illustrious by the study of literature, it is not expected that he shall afterwards descend to ordinary avocations. Hence we have the class of *literati*, mostly proud and selfish, and the bitterest enemies of the foreigner. Since 1900 a welcome change has begun to steal over this class, leading, as we have already said, to more inquiry after Western education, with consequently a greater respect for people from the West.

Notwithstanding the large city populations, the Chinese are essentially an agricultural people, and it is in country life that they may be studied to advantage. With very primitive methods the ground is made to yield abundantly, several crops per year being secured. This means hard toil for the men, women, and children, who must all help in the support of the family. Occasionally one comes across a well-plenished farmstead, surrounded by trees or a wall, and giving the idea of prosperity, but far more often the houses are wretchedly built of mud or wattle, with earth floors and no windows or chimney; fowls and pigs share the same roof with human beings, and cesspools abound in which manure is conserved for the fields. Children are usually numerous, and share the gutters with the swine and dogs; in summer time the boys' clothing amounts to even less than Professor Drummond's minimum of " a helmet and three mosquitoes," as they have no helmet and often no hair!

The round of life is very hum-drum, the monotony being relieved by a wedding or a funeral, or a " Punch and Judy," or such simple entertainment. A great many women never travel more than a few miles from their home all their lives, and here lies an important claim for more women missionaries, and also such " home missionaries" as native Bible-women. The men find change at the markets held very frequently at the towns. Thither the thousands of countrymen gather with their produce, and in the forepart of the day there is keen bargaining. Afterwards wine-drinking and gossip, with occasionally a quarrel or a fight, will fill up the day, or perhaps a theatrical performance will attract the crowds. These performances take place in temple court-yards, and are free to all, the expenses being paid by various clubs and societies, or a local rate. A fact worth noting about the Chinese theatres is that there are no women actors. Men impersonate women, but it would be utterly opposed to Chinese sense of decency to see a woman on the stage. Actors form a special class of society, and share with barbers the disability of not being permitted to compete at literary examinations. The Chinese play is invariably in opera.

The country people are not intellectual, and their horizon is a very contracted one; yet we have found them polite and reasonable as a whole, and it is from amongst them that the Christian Church is now gathering many adherents. City life

A CHINESE "PUNCH AND JUDY" SHOW.

is proverbially more difficult to influence, but the large populations offer splendid scope for our efforts.

Chinese cities must be seen to be properly appreciated. They consist of houses and shops of all shapes and sizes crowded together, with the least possible space left for streets, which may be anything up to ten feet wide, but seldom wider in actual thoroughfares. As there is no cart or carriage traffic in Sz-Chwan, the middle of the street is for passengers, and the sides are well encroached upon by the shopmen with their wares. There is considerable variety in the goods displayed, such as silks and satins, cloth, yarn and cotton, silverware, ironmongery and copper, crockery and earthenware, pens, ink and paper, boots, shoes, and all kinds of clothing, sauces and soys, and abundance of eatables. On the street, too, will be seen tailors, barbers, medicine vendors and general hawkers, and beggars everywhere. There are also restaurants and tea-drinking saloons open to the street. The latter take the place of the public-houses in England, and are a great deal less harmful. Friends meet there for social chat, and a large proportion of the business is also done there. When quarrels arise there is seldom any real fighting, but, after the principals have emptied themselves of all the abuse they can deliver, they are hurried off to a tea-shop or perhaps invite each other to go, and there the grievances are gone into before a crowd of people who sip tea while listening, and, in the end, the one who is in the wrong must pay the score.

Of late years the opium den has become a painfully prominent institution. Within the memory of men we know, opium-smoking was an offence punishable by banishment. But now the dens are numbered by tens of thousands, and it is asserted with regard to Sz-Chwan, "that in cities 50 per cent. of the males and 20 per cent. of the females smoke opium, that in the country the percentage is not less than 15 and 5 per cent. respectively." [*]

While the British connection with the trade is still indicated by the use of the term "foreign smoke," practically no foreign opium is used in this province; on the contrary, vast quantities are exported to other parts of the Empire. The trade with India will continue to diminish, even if our Government refuse to prohibit it. While it is our duty as Englishmen to spare no pains until the British Government is absolutely free from all connection with the sale of opium, we feel continually that the time has come to grapple with the evil from the other side, and lessen the results of our sinful

---

[*] "Report by Consul-General Hosie on the Province of Ssuch'uan." China. No. 5 (1904), p. 28.

policy by saving the victims. Opium refuges have been very successful in some places. Without established refuges we have

A CHINESE WATER-CARRIER.
By kind permission of the "FOREIGN FIELD."

helped to deliver some by quinine and other medicines and a little oversight ; and such benevolent work might be increased if some of the anti-opium funds could be so used.

To return to our description of a city. Signboards are generally hung perpendicularly, reading from top to bottom. These will boast that the "goods are genuine and the prices fixed," and that there are "no two prices;" and yet it is extremely rare that anything is bought or sold without considerable bargaining, and, during this, tea and tobacco are indulged in with an utter disregard of time. Accounts are kept literally by the yard, being written in perpendicular columns, reading from right to left and looking "like stockings on a clothes-line." Calculations are made mechanically by the abacus, resembling a child's counting frame, or, if that be wanting, then a few loose cash or small stones may be used; at such counting some of the people are extremely clever, but, as every move obliterates the previous one, there is no check for correction, so a mistake means that the whole must be gone over again.

The absence of factories and large workshops may be noticed. With a few exceptions of recent growth, the system is for workers to work at home and sell their produce to shops, or else to be hired for the day or month or longer. Considering the primitive nature of their tools, workmen in the various trades turn out some good work. Their silks, carving, lacquer, crockery, and the like, are world-famous. In our building operations we necessarily see a good deal of the builders, and have found them often skilful and hard-working men, who cheerfully endure a lot which would be unbearable to a Westerner. Work begins at daybreak and continues until sunset, with brief intervals for rest and meals. No sabbath is observed, but at the three main feasts of the year holidays are taken, two being brief, the feast of the New Year lasting about a fortnight. The food of the people consists of rice and a little vegetable, with, twice a month, an addition of pork—the fatter the better, and preferably only half-cooked, as it "goes further." Wages are paid at the rate of about 2d. per day besides the food given; but the equivalent of a penny has the purchasing power in China of a shilling, or even more, in England. It will, however, be seen that wages are very low, and, with a wife and family, it means a keen struggle for existence. Notwithstanding their hardships, the working-classes seem generally cheerful and are so used to their condition as to appear contented.

Reference has just been made to the Chinese New Year, and so important an occasion demands more than a passing mention. The Chinese Year does not coincide with ours, nor is their time reckoned from Anno Domini, but from the reign of the Emperor for the time being. Usually the Chinese year begins in our February, and, as the date approaches, much bustle and excitement prevails. Accounts are settled up and stocks taken, and there

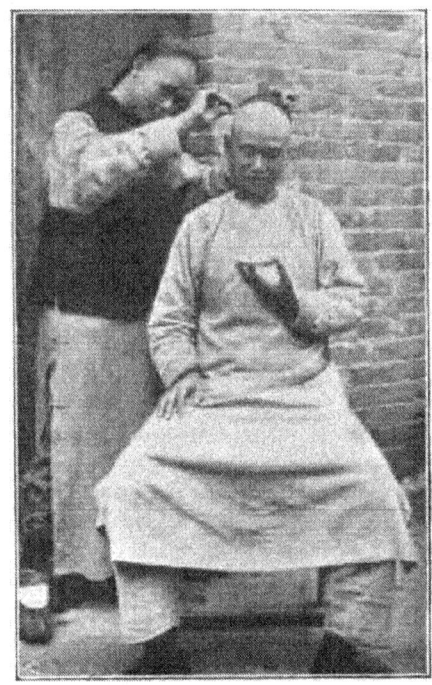

THE BARBER.
The operation pictured above, is performed by the road-side, in the street, or at home, to suit the customer's convenience.
By kind permission of the "FOREIGN FIELD."

is a general collecting of debts. The now-dirty paper representations of gods on the street doors, which have done duty for a year, are replaced with new and highly coloured successors; new mottoes are pasted on doors and shutters, with such wishes as " On opening the door let there be great joy,"

"May the five happinesses enter our door," and across the street will be "May he who is opposite me beget riches," supposed to be the good wish of a neighbour, but in reality put up by the one to whom it refers. When things are satisfactorily arranged, a volley of fire-crackers announces the fact, after which the next few days are given up to pleasure and hospitality. New Year's morning is more like an English Sunday than any other day of the year. For a time the streets are deserted, but presently men and boys appear dressed in their best, the men ostentatiously carrying their huge visiting cards and paying calls, during which tea and sweets are indulged in. Friends meeting on the streets are very ceremonious in their bows and wishes for the New Year. Later on the women issue forth on similar errands, and altogether there is an air of peace and goodwill reminding one much of Christmas at home.

The year is not considered properly entered upon until after the Feast of Lanterns on the 15th day of the first month of the Chinese year. On the evening of that day there are processions with lighted lanterns of many shapes and forms, the dragon being in most general favour.

There are other feasts and set times, such as the month for visiting the ancestral graves; and the night for floating paper boats with lights to give peace to the spirits of the departed who have been forgotten, or who have no descendants to give them their due; also the fifth month Dragon boat, when paddled canoes are raced; and the eighth moon when it is asserted that the gates of the moon may be seen to open. We once heard a man stoutly declare that he had witnessed this wonder!

Little space remains to tell of the many other customs which interest those who live in this land. Geomancy, fortune-telling, selecting days, "wind and water" influences, demon possession, and exorcism, all have their bearing upon the customs of these people.

Perhaps the most important ceremony of all is the final one of death and burial. Very often a coffin will have been among the household treasures for years awaiting this event. Perhaps no people are so anxious to be well taken care of at death as the Chinese. The corpse is dressed in three or four suits of clothes,

GODS OF LITERATURE AND WAR.
A translation of the Characters on the tablet above them, is "The virtue of the Lords shines brightly far and wide."

and is placed in a coffin made of solid wood, eight inches thick, or more. It is so heavy that when taken to burial, it will require eight or sixteen men to carry it. A lucky day must be chosen for the funeral, and while this is usually not long delayed, it is not uncommon to see coffins unburied for months or even years. The choosing of a proper ground is also a matter of importance. When all is ready, the mourners are dressed in white sackcloth, the chief mourner, son or wife perhaps, is enveloped in white and is led along and supported, as presumably incapable from grief. If there are no spectators, the grief is considerably reduced, and opportunity may be taken for a smoke, but that is outside the programme. But though there is so much make-believe, we have at times witnessed obviously genuine grief, which could not fail to evoke one's sympathy for the bereaved. A special chair is carried empty, for the use of the spirit of the departed. Gongs are beaten, with a screeching accompaniment of music on an instrument sounding like a bagpipe.

Coffins are not buried one above the other as in England. Indeed, the graves are very shallow, seldom being deep enough to receive the coffin entirely, so that the top is usually above the surface of the earth ; but a tumulus is raised over the coffin ; and around a city may be seen tens of thousands of these mounds, the dead taking up many times more space than the living.

These observations refer to the death of a middle-class person. The poor are given less ceremony, and the destitute are treated more shabbily still. We have seen a rough box used, the end being knocked out to make room for the feet, and also burials with no covering but a bamboo mat.

No proper religious ceremony takes place at a graveside ; crackers are used to scare off the devils, and one witnesses the scene with a feeling of melancholy, and an intense longing that the sure and certain hope of the glorious resurrection might take possession of these multitudes, brightening their lives, purifying and ennobling their manners and customs, and cheering them in death.

CHAPTER IX.

THE RELIGIONS OF CHINA.

THE three systems of religion met with everywhere in China are Confucianism, Taoism and Buddhism, and in these days the three are so interwoven with each other in the daily life of the people, that it is not easy to draw a line of demarcation.

Standing on a hill not far from one of our out-stations, is a temple dedicated to the " Three Religions," and within it the devout may distribute their worship impartially to shrines representing all. This is an apt figure of what is found throughout China, the line of argument to the Chinese apparently being that since it is good to call upon spirits and ancient worthies, the *more* one can invoke the better, especially if it can be arranged that one payment or one visit shall compass the goodwill of all the three great sects.

And yet the Taoist and Buddhist priests have their own temples and their distinctive creeds and dresses, and the fanes of Confucius are jealously guarded by the officers specially appointed to that duty, so that we must speak of them as three distinct systems.

CONFUCIANISM.

Confucianism is the name given to the system propagated by K'ung Fu Tsz (the Master K'ung)—who was born B.C. 551, in North China. He was a statesman, student, scribe and historian rather than a prophet or poet and, in his own words, was " a ransmitter, not an author." He edited the Historical Books, and rescued from threatened oblivion the memory of great and good kings and sages who flourished long before his time. He sighed for the " good old days," and did not spare the vices and follies of his contemporaries. While unquestionably exercising a good influence he failed to accomplish much of a practical nature during his brief periods of office, though his claims on behalf of his system of morality and government were high in the extreme. After his death his influence grew to such an extent that few men in the world's history have been more reverenced or by greater multitudes.

It will enable readers better to understand Confucianism if, in this brief sketch, we follow the threefold division of the subject, made by the late Dr. E. Faber.* We scarcely could have a better authority. He contrasts Confucian and Christian teaching as follows :—

THE TABLET OF CONFUCIUS, PEKING.
This Tablet of the great Philosopher, in the Confucian Temple at Peking, is an object of worship for Chinese people generally.

---

* " China Mission Handbook," article " Confucianism," abridged.

I. Points of similarity between Confucianism and Christianity.
II. Points of antagonism.
III. Points of deficiency in Confucianism which are perfect in Christianity.

I.—POINTS OF SIMILARITY.

1. Divine Providence over human affairs and visitation of human sin are acknowledged. A plain and frequent teaching of the classics is that calamities visit a country, and ruin overcomes a dynasty through the displeasure of heaven.
2. An invisible world is firmly believed in.
3. A moral law is positively set forth as binding equally on men and spirits.
4. Prayer is offered in public calamities as well as for private needs, in the belief that it is heard and answered by the spiritual powers.
5. Sacrifices are regarded as necessary to come into close contact with the spiritual world. Even its deeper meanings of self-sacrifice and of a vicarious sacrifice are touched upon.
6. Miracles are believed in as the natural *efficacy of spirits*. This is a fruitful source of superstition among the people.
7. Moral duty is taught, and its obligations in the five human relations—sovereign and minister, father and son, husband and wife, elder brother and younger, friend and friend. We may say that it is the quintessence of Confucian education.
8. Cultivation of the personal moral character is regarded as the basis for the successful carrying out of the social duties. That self-control should not be abandoned in private when no mortal being is near to observe it, is repeatedly emphasised.
9. Virtue is valued above riches and honour.
10. In case of failure in political or social life, the moral self-culture and the practice of humanity are to be attended to even more carefully than before, according to opportunities.
11. Sincerity and truth are shown to be the only basis for self-culture and the reform of the world.
12. The Golden Rule is proclaimed as the principle of moral conduct among our fellow-men.
13. Every ruler should carry out a benevolent government for the benefit of the people.

II.—POINTS OF ANTAGONISM.

1. God, though dimly known, is not the only object of religious worship. This cannot be regarded as only a deficiency, it is a fatal error. Polytheism is taught in the classics. Idolatry is the natural consequence.
2. The worship of spiritual beings is not done in spirit and in truth, but by punctilious observance of prescribed ceremonies to the minutest details.
3. The worship of ancestral spirits, tablets and graves, we have to regard as a *sin*, for it takes the place of the worship of God. It is an *error* so far as it rests on wrong notions in regard to the departed in the other world. It is an *evil*, because selfish considerations take the place of moral and religious motives. The superstitions of geomancy, spiritualism, exorcism and all kinds of deceit practised by Taoist and Buddhist priests, have their origin in it. Confucianism is responsible for all this religious corruption, for sacrificing to the dead is taught as the highest filial duty in the classics, and Mencius sanctions polygamy on its account.
4. The erection of temples to great warriors and other men of eminence in which sacrifices are offered and incense is burned to their shades. There are certainly over a HUNDRED THOUSAND such temples in China.
5. The memorial arches erected to persons that committed *suicide*, especially to widows, throw a sad light on the morality of a community where such *crimes* are necessitated.
6. Oracles, by stalks and the tortoise shell, are declared necessary to the right conduct of human affairs.
7. Choosing lucky days.
8. Polygamy is not only wrong; it has ever been a curse in Chinese history. Confucianism has not only no censure for it, but sanctions it in the classics.
9. Rebellion. The dethroning and even murder of a bad ruler is justified.
10. Confucianism attaches too high authority to the emperor. He is called the Son of Heaven, the only supreme authority on earth.
11. Parental power. A father may kill his offspring, may sell even grown sons and daughters into slavery. Their property belongs to him.
12. Blood revenge. It is a strict demand of Confucius in the classics that a son should lose no time in revenging the death of his father or of a near relative.
13. Absolute subordination of sons to their fathers and of younger brothers to their eldest brother during lifetime.

14. Official corruption receives its sanction from the classics, and Confucius himself carried presents with him on his journeys.
15. Confucius broke a solemn oath and excused it, and the lying and deceitfulness so highly developed in China probably owe much to this cause.

III.—POINTS OF DEFICIENCY IN CONFUCIANISM WHICH ARE PERFECT IN CHRISTIANITY.

1. The God of Confucianism is the majestic Ruler on High, inaccessible to the people. The emperor of China is the only person privileged to approach Him. God is not known in His nature of love as our Heavenly Father.
2. The Confucian Divine Providence appears in conflict with the Confucian notion of fate. Providence presupposes a personal God, a God who can feel compassion with living creatures, as in Christianity.
3. Confucianism acknowledges a revelation of God in nature and in human history, but a revelation of God's nature, will and intentions for the salvation and education of the human race remains unknown.
4. There is no conviction of an unconditioned responsibility to God, who will judge in righteousness. Therefore a deep sense of sin and sinfulness is absent.
5. The necessity of an atonement is not conceived, because neither the holiness of God, nor the depth of human sin are taught in the classics.
6. The need of a Saviour is not felt. Salvation is sought in external performances.
7. Confucianism has never anticipated the perfect union of the divine and human as it has been realised in the person of Christ.
8. As every man has to save himself, there cannot be a universality of salvation in Confucianism.
9. Confucianists remain, in spite of their best efforts, estranged from God. They do not come into communion with the Spirit of God, for strength to holy living, and for peace and hope in death.
10. Confucianism teaches the immortality of the soul, but in a disembodied state, dependent for all its needs on the goodwill of living men. Resurrection in a spiritual body for eternal happiness in God's glory is unknown.
11. The highest ideal of Confucianism is political, the government and state of China. Christ shows us another ideal, the Kingdom of God.
12. Self-examination, one of the excellent fundamental principles of Confucianism, has a deeper meaning in Christianity.

13. Self-culture also has a deeper sense in Christianity. It implies purity in every way. Sexual impurity is tolerated by Confucianism to a shocking extent.

Confucianism has no sabbath day or regular day of rest. It has nothing approaching the Lord's prayer, nor the apostolic blessing, " the grace of our Lord Jesus Christ, the love of God, and the communion of the Holy Spirit be with you." What Confucianism needs is the Divine Life. May God's spirit move the field of dry bones!

The officials throughout China are required to appear at the local Confucian temples twice a year—spring and autumn—to kneel before the tablet of the Sage, and bow the head nine times to the ground, and to offer sacrifices, the animals being killed previously and laid whole before the shrine, and afterwards eaten. In the colleges and schools recently instituted officially, with the professed object of imparting Western education, the attempt is made to bolster up the state religion by compelling Confucian worship, on the first and fifteenth of every moon, with the result that many worthy and conscientious students are debarred the privileges of education unless they get it by other means. Happily there are Christian colleges available, and it is to be hoped that very soon the government will change its attitude and allow religious liberty to its subjects.

TAOISM.

Taoism is at once associated in the mind with Lao Tsz, its famous exponent, who was a contemporary of Confucius, but the principles of the system are obscure. It seems to deal largely with the laws of nature, and incidentally may be credited with alchemy and some discoveries of elementary chemistry. It recognises with awe that mysterious and eternal powers are working throughout nature and man, which powers are called Tao. To participate in this power is to become immortal. The following are extracts from two Prize Essays written by Chinese for the Parliament of Religions, held at Chicago in 1893.

THE GOD OF THE RIVER.

The TAO bounds space as with a cord, and is the root of all life. During the chaotic period there was a Prince of Heaven, the Nameless One. He was the supreme Mystery of mysteries. After that period there was produced another Prince of Heaven, the Originator and Creator, the First of all things. He was not without existence though as without existence; invisible, yet not empty space; of endless age, without beginning and without end. He is the King of kings, and says, "I with the TAO have created all the universe from period to period, and brought all things to pass in the fulness of times."

To understand the mystery of Taoism is to be able to draw cheques on divinity! When the poor and ignorant get and practise it, the earth on which they stand becomes holy ground, and they become children of the gods.

Generally speaking the art of obtaining immortality is obtained in three ways:—1. By copying nature's ways—the acting and re-acting of Yin and Yang on each other. 2. By copying the reproductive processes of nature. 3. By nourishing the vital force which is partly material and partly non-material. Fire and water are wisdom and quietness. The outward pill of immortality has reference to the body: the inward pill has reference to the soul.

The result of this study of Tao, the mystery of the universe, has been the worship of many things as gods, such as Hien Yuen the thunderer, who often smites evil doers dead: Wen Ti, the literary spirit: Kwan Shing, the martial spirit, etc.

While these definitions are being inwardly digested we may add a word as to the Taoism of the present as met in China. There is a recognised "Pope" who lives on the Lung Hu mountain in Kiang-si province, in a palace of imperial splendour. He is said to have charge of all evil spirits, and sealed jars containing some of these are shown to visitors. The position has been held for very many generations by members of a family named Chang, and the "Pope" is supported and consulted by the Emperor and his government.

The Taoist temples swarm with idols and signs of mystery. The priests may be either celibate or married. Those wearing the distinctive dress have their long hair coiled up on top of the head, and showing through a hat without a crown. The travelling or mendicant priests often carry curious looking staves or wands, and gourds containing medicines for which they claim marvellous powers. We once heard of a man being persuaded to swallow a literal "golden pill" of immortality, with the result that he has swallowed nothing else since!

BUDDHISM.

While Taoism and Confucianism are native to China, Buddhism is entirely a foreign introduction. Its doctrines and claims are so fully dealt with in works relating to India—its birthplace—that we do not propose to say much of them here.

The Chinese Emperor Ming Ti, having heard (A.D. 67) of a new religion in the West, sent ambassadors to procure information and books. The footing thus gained has never been lost, despite several vigorous attempts in after years to oust it, and at the present time the land is covered with evidences of Buddhism, and not only is there practically a shrine under every green tree, but also in every street and house. The temples are innumerable, and the priests constitute quite a formidable class in point of numbers, though they seem mostly ignorant and indolent. Some however are industrious, and work the land around the temples, and we knew one so thrifty as to take advantage of the fall of a cliff to build a stone into a grave for himself, with epitaph complete, only lacking the date of his death!

The Buddhist priesthood is celibate; there are also nuns to be found in convents. The dress of both sexes is similar, the head being shaven and, as the feet of the women are not bound, it is not easy to avoid making ludicrous mistakes sometimes on meeting them.

Worship consists largely in chanting prayers and making prostrations before idols, together with burning of candles and incense. When petitions are presented, resort is had to tallies made of wood, one side round and the other flat, and the way in which they fall gives the answer yes, no, or neutral. Consolation comes in being able to repeat the process as often as may be necessary to secure just the answer one wants.

THE GODDESS OF MERCY.

The characters on the tablet over the central figure signify "Cloudy Portal of Compassion."
Prayers are offered to this goddess by women desiring a son.

The laity will spend considerable sums of money and go to great inconvenience to attend various "Hui" or festivals to pay their vows or seek the favour of the gods. The city of Sui-ling where we have now a station, has a famous "Goddess of Mercy" to which great crowds go every year; groups of men, women and boys, with cords of scarlet upon them, and carrying huge candles and bundles of incense. Sometimes a devotee with a special vow may be seen performing a toilsome journey by walking three or four steps, prostrating the body, then rising and going as many more steps and repeating the whole, with wearying monotony. Others come cheerily chanting over hill and dale "O mi t'o Fu" the name given to Amitta Buddha, which name it is the duty of priests to repeat thousands or even tens of thousands of times *daily*.

Many of the idols are repulsive in form, and to add to the terrors of evildoers there are realistic and horrible representations of punishments in hell. So far from having the effect hoped for, we have generally been shown those particular scenes with a good deal of hilarity on the part of bystanders. Report says that among the priests themselves the vices so threatened, as gambling, drinking, opium smoking and immorality, are far from uncommon.

Referring to Chinese Buddhism Dr. W. A. P. Martin says :—

The acme of attainment nearest to Nirvana, a state of unconscious felicity, is to think nothing and feel nothing, in which state the soul will of course enjoy perfect tranquillity. With such a discipline a highly intellectual clergy could hardly be expected. In general, the priests have stolid faces and eyes fixed on vacancy. Most of them are unable to read, the recitation of prayers being their sole duty. No longer doing anything to strengthen or renovate Chinese society, Buddhism clings to it as ivy clings to a crumbling tower, deriving its nourishment from the rottenness of the structure.

While at the monastery we were shown a tank full of large fish which are in no danger of the treacherous hook : also a herd of porkers safe from the butcher's knife. The latter were reserved to die of old age—a fortune so rare for swine that I have never heard a statement of the age a pig may reasonably hope to attain. Compassion for brute animals is an amiable feature of Buddhism, as well as of Brahmanism, from which it is derived.

The Buddhist doctrine of metempsychosis indisputably tends to lower the sense of human dignity, and if it conduces in any way (which may be doubted) to the better treatment of lower animals; it does so at the expense of humanity to man. As generally held, this doctrine is largely responsible for the prevalence of suicide, leading those who are hopelessly wretched to try their luck on another throw of the dice.*

The influence of Buddhism is observable everywhere and among all classes of society, but most of the people can give no reason for their faith, or appearance of such, beyond that it is the custom, or that it was what their forefathers practised, and therefore must be observed. There is no doubt that abject fear of evil spirits is a powerful motive, even with those who profess to pay no attention to idolatry. An official once told us that those in authority of course did not believe in idols but, as the means of enforcing the law are feeble, the governing class supports the worship of them, as they terrorise the people and are a check against lawlessness. We suggested that the idols might be similar to "scarecrows," and the answer was "Exactly"! And yet that official, in spite of his words, was an abject slave to the popular beliefs during his life, and at his death a large number of priests were chanting and going through all kinds of mummeries, probably at his dying request.

The facility with which the "Three Religions" blend together, and the ease with which society swallows them all, without apparently caring to notice any distinctions, are very striking. It is not even necessary to be "everything by *turns* and nothing long," for in China one may belong to all the creeds at once! Dr. Arthur H. Smith says :—

It is not uncommon to meet with learned disquisitions upon the question as to the number of Buddhists and Taoists in China. In our view this question is exactly paralleled by an inquiry into the number

---

* "A Cycle of Cathay," p. 38.

of persons in the United Kingdom who use tenpenny nails as compared with the number of those who eat string-beans. Any one who wants to use a tenpenny nail will do so if he can obtain it, and those who like string-beans and can afford to buy them will presumptively consume them. The case is not different in China as

THE GREAT BUDDHA AT PEKING.
A full-length figure of Buddha, seventy-five feet high.

regards the two most prominent "doctrines." Any Chinese who wants the services of a Buddhist priest, and who can afford to pay for them, will hire the priest and thus be "a Buddhist." If he wants a Taoist priest, he will in like manner call him, and this makes him "a Taoist." It is of no consequence to the Chinese which of the two he employs, and he will not improbably call them both at once, and thus be at once "a Buddhist" and "a Taoist." Thus the same individual is at once a Confucianist, a Buddhist and a Taoist, and with no sense of incongruity. Buddhism swallowed Taoism, Taoism swallowed Confucianism, but at the last the latter swallowed both Buddhism and Taoism together, and thus "the three religions are one!"*

Besides these three religions there are at least twenty millions of Mohammedans in China.

---

* "Chinese Characteristics," p. 294.

CHAPTER X.

LANGUAGE AND LITERATURE.

ALMOST the first object of interest that occupies the mind of the missionary on his arrival in China is the wonderful language of the people with its strange hieroglyphics and peculiar sounds. So long as he remains in the country, it continues a problem which he is never able to master, and, while it is a never ending source of interest and pleasure to some, it causes much labour and effort of thought to others, for without a grasp of its variety of tone and complete construction one can never feel quite at ease in a Chinese city.

To those unfamiliar with China and her people, the language will not be a topic of such deep interest as to those who have learned to appreciate its beauties as well as its difficulties, but without being wearisome we may perhaps note one or two facts concerning it which are worth remembering. A language which is the mode of expressing the thoughts of one fifth of the human race, and which has become to them an object of profound respect, is surely worth the attention of all those who take an interest in the lives of their brother men.

The Chinese tell us that their written characters were invented by the Emperor Fu Hsi in B.C. 3200, or by Chang Chi who lived 500 years after Fu Hsi. However this may be, the Shu King mentions the art of writing as early as B.C. 2253, and in B.C. 1000 it was in common use amongst the official classes.

The language is frequently referred to under two divisions, the written and the spoken. The latter varies considerably in certain parts of the empire. This is especially so in several of the coast provinces from Shanghai to Canton, where many separate dialects exist ; yet throughout fourteen of the eighteen provinces the Mandarin or official language is used, and whether written or spoken is well understood.

But it may be better considered under divisions, or rather styles of composition, from which a good idea of its general usage may be obtained.

(1) *The Classical.* This is the style in which the Confucian and other classics are written. It is difficult to understand without explanation. It is seldom, if ever, used in speaking or writing, except in the form of quotation.

(2) *The Literary.* This, in its various grades, is the ordinary book language of the educated class. It is used in Examination essays, etc., and is much more intelligible than the classical, though only used in its written form. A simpler style of the same is used in business correspondence, official documents, etc.

(3) *The Mandarin.* This is the common language current throughout the larger part of the empire, and is capable of being both spoken and written. In this style is printed by far the largest proportion of the Bibles and Tracts issued by the various Societies, though the number of purely native books in mandarin is very small, compared with those in the literary style. There is a growing tendency to use this mode wherever the official language is known.

The literary style is comparable to that of a highly technical treatise on some scientific subject, while the Mandarin or spoken language corresponds to ordinary English, as used in newspapers and current literature.

The characters, or ideographs, which form the written language, are composed of two parts, the radical and the phonetic. There are two hundred and fourteen of the former. These form the ground work of the whole characters, and are hieroglyphics representing such common words as wood, water, fire, man, heart, head, etc., and these, combined with the phonetics, or primitives, form the various characters that go to make up the language, and determine to some extent their meaning. For instance, every character relative to grass or to vegetables would have the grass radical, or a word signifying anything made of metal would be, in part, composed of the metal or gold radical.

Each character also conveys a distinct idea, without reference to any part of speech, doing duty as noun, verb, or adjective as the circumstance may require. There is really no alphabet, unless the 40,000 characters which compose the language may be considered one, for each character has a distinct form of its own, and is not made up of a number of letters, as are our Western languages.

Those who may have felt the difficulty of acquiring the declensions, moods, and tenses of European languages, would find Chinese quite a relief, for there is no inflection of its words, an auxiliary character or a change of position of a word is the method used to express variation of meaning.

There are no less than 40,000 different ideographs defined in the Emperor K'ang Hsi's great dictionary, but only 6,000 or 8,000 of these are in ordinary use; at the same time the paucity of sounds is a very remarkable feature of the Chinese language.

In Western Mandarin there are only about 380 separate and distinct sounds for expressing the whole of the 40,000 characters, the result being that there are a large number of words of exactly the same sound and with a vast variety of meanings. In the ordinary Chinese dictionary under the sound "i" or "ee" no less than 230 separate characters are found with varying meanings, such as descendants, to trust, also, doctor, clothes, right, friendship, etc. To confine the expression of the thoughts of a whole nation to such a limited number of sounds seems impossible, and to lessen the difficulty, a remedy is found in the addition of what are known as Tones, of which there are five in Western China. Some idea of these may be obtained by pronouncing the word "pan" in five of the notes of an octave. These tones form one of the serious obstacles in the way of all who would attain to a good use of the spoken language. Through the great similarity of sound ludicrous mistakes are made, and grave ones also, as, for example, when a foreigner says that he wishes to buy a wife

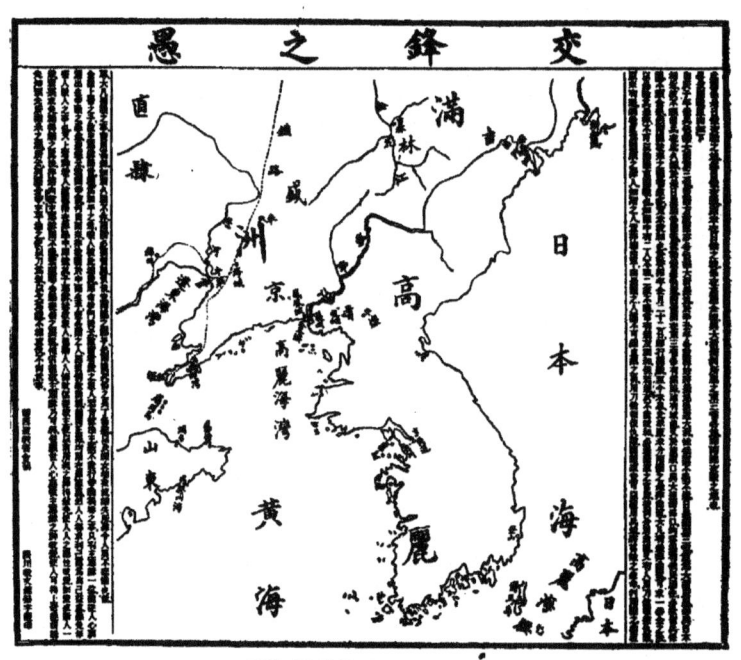

THE FOOLISHNESS OF WAR.[*]

Reproduction of a Chinese placard written and translated by Leonard Wigham, B A. The Original is printed on thin yellow paper, 19 inches by 17½ inches in size. The placard is read from right to left, beginning at top right-hand corner, and reading down each column.

when really he is only in need of a simple flag for his boat; or he may request a messenger to carry his heart away when really he is only intending to despatch a letter. Still worse

[*] The above illustration is inserted as showing Chinese characters, and also as an interesting Poster which was issued by the West China Religious Tract Society. The Map will be recognized to be the seat of the late Russo-Japanese War.

has been the revolting and blasphemous mockery of the "Jesus religion" in the anti-Christian placards, issued from Hunan Province, in which was substituted for the character "chu," meaning "Lord," another character of the same sound, but pronounced in a different tone meaning "pig."

The Chinese language is, like the people, in many respects a paradox. While it is one of the most difficult to acquire thoroughly, to obtain a knowledge of the ordinary talk of the people is by no means arduous, and from its monosyllabic character and the simple construction of the colloquial it is one of the least abstruse of languages. But the student who has only a knowledge of the spoken language has merely touched the fringe of the subject. An ability to write the complex characters with even a passable caligraphy, a power to read the ordinary works of scholars with ease, and to compose in a pure idiom in literary style, are attainments only reached by very few. It may indeed be said that the Chinese language is the most difficult in existence, largely owing to the style of composition recognised by scholars as classical.

LITERATURE.

The devotion of the time and powers of such a large proportion of the most intelligent of the people to literary pursuits has, not unnaturally, resulted in developing a vast amount of talent; and this, added to a knowledge of the art of printing, which the Chinese early acquired, has produced an enormous quantity of literature, on almost every conceivable subject. Works on Chinese history, philosophy, theology, fiction, politics, poetry, drama, art, topography, travel, etc., and cyclopædias—monuments of industry and learning—are to be obtained in every important city in the empire, the results of the labours of scholars of all ages from B.C. 1000 to the present day. Of these it is impossible to write fully, but mention may be made of a few of the leading writings of the Confucian school which have influenced the nation, and which are recognised as the standard literature of the people. The most important of these are known as the "Four Books" and the "Five Classics." The former consist of (1) a collection of the sayings of Confucius, or the Confucian Analects; (2) the Great Learning, a work by Tsen Sen, a disciple of the sage; (3) the Doctrine of the Mean ascribed to a grandson of Confucius, and (4) the Works of Mencius. The "Five Classics" (Ching), or Canonical works are :—(1) The Book of Changes; (2) the Book of History; (3) the Book of Poetry; (4) the Book of Rites; (5) the Spring and Autumn Annals. These nine books, with the commentaries of the noted scholar Chu Hsi upon them, form the foundation of the national literature.

The teaching of the Great Learning is the illustration of the virtuous nature which man receives from heaven, which from various causes has been perverted; the great aim of man's life being to restore that nature to its original purity. The method of attainment is taught by the example of the ancients, as follows :

> The ancients who wished to illustrate illustrious virtue throughout the empire first ordered well their own states. Wishing to order well their states, they first regulated their families. Wishing to regulate their families they first cultivated their persons. Wishing to cultivate their persons, they first rectified their hearts. Wishing to rectify their hearts, they first sought to be sincere in their thoughts. Wishing to be sincere in their thoughts, they first extended to the utmost their knowledge. Such extension of knowledge lay in the investigation of all things.
>
> The exercise of the utmost of his powers in the cultivation of the whole character is the supreme duty of man, and lies at the root of all besides.*

The result of all this will be States rightly governed, and peace reigning throughout the empire.

In the Analects we have a record of the mind of Confucius on a great variety of subjects; his views of the ancient literature of the nation, the current rules of propriety, his teaching regarding "letters, ethics, devotion of soul and truthfulness." Filial piety

* Legeg's "Translation of the Classics."

and parental submission he considered to be duties of the first importance, being the root of all benevolent actions, the former to be evidenced by careful attention to the funeral rites for parents, and sacrifices after death. His idea of the complete man was, "He who in view of gain thinks of righteousness; who in view of danger is prepared to give up his life; and who does not forget an old agreement, however far back it extends."

Perfect virtue "is to behave to everyone as if you were receiving a great guest; to employ the people as if you were assisting at a great sacrifice; and not to do to others as you would not wish done to yourself." Faithfulness and sincerity are to be held as first principles, and "when you have faults do not fear to abandon them."

Propriety in Confucian ethics ranks with benevolence, righteousness and sincerity, and the Sage impresses his disciples with the great importance of the possession of this virtue, for its restraints are a means of keeping a man in the right path, and through it is the character established. "Without the rules of propriety, respectfulness becomes laborious bustle, carefulness timidity, boldness insubordination, and straightforwardness becomes rudeness."

"The efficient government of the state" was a favourite topic with Confucius. The empire he considered the "Middle Kingdom," and his designation of its states is "all under Heaven," all else were barbarians. It was as one family; the emperor, the father of his people, for whom he should ever care with parental love, they rendering to him the filial respect due to a parent. The personal example of the ruler he considered to be one of the most powerful factors in the rectification of the character of the people, and the good ordering of the state.

Government is properly conducted "when the person in authority makes more beneficial to the people the things from which they naturally derive benefit; when he lays tasks on the people without their repining; when his desires are set on benevolent government; and he realises it when he maintains a dignified ease without being proud, when he adjusts his clothes and cap, and throws a dignity into his looks, so that, thus dignified, he is looked at with awe, and so is majestic without being fierce. He does not put his people to death without having instructed them, which is cruelty; he does not require from them suddenly the full tale of work, which is oppression; nor issue orders without urgency, and later insist on them with severity; nor does he pay wages and give rewards in a stingy way, which is mere officialism."

The Doctrine of the Mean, or "The Law of the Golden Medium" is a work the teaching of which is difficult to understand. It treats of the moral nature conferred on man by heaven, which is the law of his life, and he who accords with this nature walks in the paths of virtue, from which will result a state of equilibrium and harmony, issuing in a condition of happy order throughout heaven and earth.

The Philosopher Mencius (B.C. 372-289), whose works constitute about half of the four books, lived over 100 years after Confucius. Though a disciple of the sage, his teaching is in no way inferior to that of his master, and it was largely through the high honour paid by Mencius to the work of the older sage that Confucius has attained to his present lofty position in the regard of the people.

The natural goodness of human nature found an able exponent in the person of Mencius, and a considerable portion of his works are the record of his discussions with his contemporary, Kao, who taught that man's nature was neither good nor bad. It is mainly owing to his discussions on human nature that Mencius has acquired the rank of sage.

Confucius taught that " Man is born for uprightness. If a man be without uprightness and yet live, his escape from death is the effect of mere good fortune." Mencius, in answer to the statement of the philosopher, Kao, that nature was as indifferent to good and evil as water is indifferent to east and west, said, "Water indeed will flow indifferently to the east or west, but will it flow indifferently up or down ? The tendency of man's nature to good is like the tendency of water to flow downwards. There are none but have this tendency to good, just as all water flows downwards. By striking water and causing it to leap up, you may make it go over your forehead, and by damming and leading it, you may force it up a hill ; but are such movements according to the nature of water ? It is the force applied which causes them. When men are made to do what is not good, their nature is dealt with in this way."

Mencius recognised fully that, so far as the manifestation of human nature was concerned, appearances were against him; but to him the appearance was not the real nature of man, but the result of outside influences perverting the real goodness within, which did not receive sufficient nourishment to overcome the destructive forces at work. This he illustrated by the trees of the New mountain, which were once beautiful but were unable to retain their beauty owing to the work of the hatchet, even the buds and sprouts, which were the result of the activity of the vegetative life day and night, and of the nourishing of the rain, being destroyed by the browsing of cattle ; owing to which the mountain presented a bare and stripped appearance, as if it were never finely wooded. But this was not its real nature. And so man loses his proper goodness of mind, as the mountain is denuded by the hewing down of the trees day after day. But there is a development of its life day and night and, in the calm air of the morning, the mind feels in a degree those desires and aversions which are proper to humanity, but the feeling is not strong, and it is fettered and destroyed by what takes place during the day. The restorative influences of the night are not sufficient to preserve the proper goodness of the mind ; man's nature therefore becomes perverted, but this does not prove that man had not this goodness by nature, nor represent the feelings proper to humanity.

This doctrine handed down throughout the ages is the orthodox belief of every Chinese, and is the earliest lesson learnt by every child at school, where the first characters he is taught state " Man at birth is naturally good."

There is much to be said for the aspect of the doctrine as enunciated by Confucius that "man is born for righteousness," and there is nothing contrary to the Gospel of Christ in Mencius' view, that in man there are natural principles of benevolence, as well as of uprightness and propriety, which do not come from without, but are the inherent possession of every human being.

Those interested in political science and social economy may care to follow the views of the philosopher on the necessity of "a benevolent government." For the accomplishment of this he considered two things were necessary: "Education and Profitable Employment." The characters of the people were, according to Mencius, largely dependent on the richness of the harvest. He says: "In good years the youth of a country are most of them good, while in bad years they abandon themselves to evil." "If the people have no certain livelihood, it follows that they will not have a fixed heart, without which there is nothing which they will not do in way of self abandonment, of moral deflection, of depravity and of wild licence."

It is only the educated, the men of a superior order, who can stand the strain of an uncertain livelihood. Education and the good government of the people were therefore topics upon which Mencius laid great emphasis.

The important position which the "Four Books" hold in the life of the nation, is the excuse for devoting so much space to their contents. Many Chinese boys are able to repeat them all before they are ten years of age, and they constitute the principal class books of every Chinese school.

"The Five Classics" form the subject of study for more advanced students. "The Book of Changes" is amongst the oldest works in existence. It is said to have been written about B.C. 1100 by Wen Wang, who has left on record a system of philosophy, based on the mystic eight diagrams of the mythical Emperor Fu Hsi, and the doctrine of the production of all things from a male and female principle in nature.

The Book of History, a compilation of Confucius, consists of records as far back as the Flood up to the Chow dynasty (B.C. 1122-255).

Another book of history is the Spring and Autumn Annals, the only classic which was written by Confucius. It simply gives brief records of the doings of the ancient state of Lu of a most uninteresting character, yet supposed to be of the utmost importance as stating the proper relation of sovereign and princes.

The Book of Rites, a work of the twelfth century B.C., is a classic guide to the laws of ceremony, and some of its main principles are observed to-day by people of all ranks throughout the country, from the emperor to his meanest subject.

We do not naturally connect poetry with the prosaic people of the Celestial Empire, much less with its sedate and ceremonial-loving sage. Nevertheless poetry, in the view of Confucius, holds first rank in the educational influences for the training of the mind, and the Book of Poetry is generally considered to be his compilation. It consists of selected portions of the odes made in the early part of the Chow Dynasty. Confucius summed up the design of the three hundred odes in one sentence,—" Have no depraved thoughts."

The following translation of two Odes will give some idea of the poetry of ancient China.

OFFICER'S WISHES FOR HIS SOVEREIGN.

Heaven protects and establishes thee,
With the greatest security;
Makes thee entirely virtuous,
That thou mayst enjoy every happiness;
Grants thee much increase,
So that thou may have all in abundance.

Heaven protects and establishes thee;
It grants thee all excellence,
So that thine every matter is right,
And thou receivest every heavenly favour.
It sends down to thee long-during happiness,
Which the days are not sufficient to enjoy.

Heaven protects and establishes thee,
So that n everything thou doest prosper.
Like the high hills, and the mountain masses,
Like the topmost ridges, and the greatest bulks;
That, as the stream, ever coming on,
Such is thine increase.

DISMISS YOUR TROUBLES.

Do not push forward a waggon ;—
You will only raise the dust about yourself.
Do not think of all your anxieties ;—
You will only make yourself ill.

Do not push forward a waggon ;—
The dust will only blind you.
Do not think of all your anxieties ;—
You will only weigh yourself down.

One cannot pass from this subject without calling attention to the fact that the change now passing over the people of China is resulting in the production of a vast amount of literature, such as has never been seen in this empire before. This is mainly the translation of works of Western science and art, while books on travel, political economy, and many other subjects are not wanting. The catalogues of the various publishing houses, both under Chinese and foreign management, give evidence of the great reform movement now in progress. Works translated and printed at the coast, are recast, printed and issued in the interior, and the country is thus being permeated by a new leaven, by which the influences of the past are being necessarily affected.

CHAPTER XI.

EDUCATION.

THE first book of the "Selected Sayings" of Confucius, or the Confucian Analects, has for its title the word "Learn," and the sage at once, by his initial statement, impresses his disciples with the fascination and delight of acquiring knowledge.

"Is it not pleasant to learn with constant perseverance and application? for through learning are we enabled to comprehend goodness, and restore the original perfection of our nature." Ever since the days of the sage, learning has been held in the highest esteem by the people of China, and the educational system, which has in the course of centuries been developed, is to-day the pride and glory of the nation.

Knowledge of the Four Books and Five Classics is the gate by which riches, honour and official position are attained. Every parent endeavours to give his son at least some education, and it has become a proverb, "If the sons are not taught it is the father's fault."

The high regard which the Chinese pay to learning is seen in the position given to the instructor of youth. The teacher ranks foremost amongst the various classes of men. According to Mencius, the teacher comes before the government minister, and is the compeer of father and brother, and to-day "Teacher" is one of the persons worshipped in what is known as the Heaven and Earth Tablet, where Heaven, Earth, Sovereign, Parent, and Teacher form the family shrine in every household.

The great Viceroy Chang Chih Tung, in his work written a few years ago, "China's Only Hope," urges the necessity of solid learning for the salvation of the empire. Differentiating between what is, and what is not such learning according to the Confucian school, he says : " The superficial Chinese commentaries which pass current for truth, the unconnected, non-cohesive eight-legged essays, the effete philosophies, countless antiquarian works, false but high sounding poetry of China, are not Confucian learning." " Confucian learning consists in the acquisition of extensive literature ; and the strict observance of what is right ; in the profound and careful meditation of the old, in order to understand the new; in the making of one's self the peer of heaven by means of perfect sincerity, and thus influencing men and all things for good."

This view of education has influenced the whole empire for ages past. It is this education that has given the Chinese the same ideals, the same modes of thought, from Yunnan to Manchuria. Dynasties have come and gone, the people have been conquered, but they have overcome their conquerors by means of their education, and at the present time the thought most prominently before the minds of the people is education.

China has no Kindergartens, no School Board system, no National Schools, no Denominational Seminaries, no Colleges, no Universities, in the Western sense of these terms.* She has, nevertheless, her schools. Hardly a village throughout the whole eighteen provinces is without its group of lads intent on learning how the superior man bends his attention to that which is radical, filial piety and fraternal submission. In the lowest parts of the great cities, in some miserable hovel, the revered, long finger-nailed teacher will be found instructing the youths how the ancients governed their kingdoms and, at night, in many homes are boys struggling to learn by feeble rushlight the task for to-morrow's class. There being no Government elementary schools, the children

* Recent Educational reforms have, in some measure, altered this state of things.

are, for the most part, educated in private ones. These are sometimes schools opened by the teachers themselves, as a means of livelihood, and attended by the children of any who care to pay fees; family schools, where one, two, or more families will club together and engage a teacher to educate their sons; or

A TIBETAN FAMILY.
Tibetans may often be met with in West Sz-chwan. The Tibetan traders also come to the City of Chentu to do business.

"charity schools." The latter are common in some parts of the country, where a person, desirous for the welfare of the people of the district, or to accumulate merit for himself, employs a teacher to instruct the children of the poorer classes who cannot afford to pay fees. The education given in them is extremely deficient, the teachers often being very remiss in the performance of their duties. In each county town, prefectural capital and provincial capital there are colleges under official direction for a select number of students, where the professors are more registrars or examiners than teachers.

Many children begin their education at about five or six years of age. The third week in the Chinese New Year is a favourite time to introduce the child to the schoolmaster. He is taken by one of his parents to the selected school, and after making a deep bow or prostration to the teacher, he is initiated into the painful and laborious process of acquiring Chinese knowledge. He has no picture books, no play letter-blocks at home, to prepare for the future struggle. There is no attempt to make learning easy. He commences with a small book called " the Three Character Classic," written in rhyming sentences of three characters each, and in the first sentence he is plunged into the depths of moral philosophy, as to the goodness of human nature, and reasons for the depravity of man.

The teacher gives the sound of the first six characters, and the boy goes to the table appointed him, sits down, and there at the top of his voice repeats the six sounds until he has memorised them. No explanation is given him as to the meaning of the words or sentence, and the child has no more idea of what he is learning than an English lad would have if the first lesson given him were six Greek words from the Gospel according to John.

For four or five years this arduous and monotonous task is continued persistently, until the Four Books and Five Classics have been memorised. At sunrise the boy is found in his place in the schoolroom, and at dusk he returns home, and while two intervals are allowed for meals, there are none for play. Playgrounds are unheard of, propriety and sedateness leaving no room for amusement.

Each boy constitutes a class, children not being taught in groups. Of the twenty or more children in a school, no two are learning the same lesson. The teacher instructs the boys one by one, and as the portion allotted is memorised, each one " backs the book," *i.e.*, recites it with his back to the book, which lies on the table in front of the teacher.

The mystery of the formation of the Chinese hieroglyphics is learnt by tracing them with a brush and Chinese ink, upon thin paper, copies being placed beneath.

The first period of Chinese education is finished when the Classics have been memorised, and numbers of children never go beyond; many are, therefore, able to pronounce the characters in any ordinary book, without having the slightest idea of their meaning.

During the second period the teacher explains the meaning of the books which have been memorised, and the student is expected to remember the explanation. The books contain no vocabulary, and no dictionary is consulted by the student.

Then follow lessons in simple prose composition, and the writing of distichs or " Parallels," a form of composition highly esteemed by the Chinese, corresponding in some degree to the parallelism of Hebrew poetry. These couplets are in much demand by everyone at the New Year. They are pasted upon the door posts of a house, one on either side of the door. They are also presented at the time of marriages, birthdays, deaths, or at any special season. The following is the translation of the sentences on a pair of scrolls received by the writer a few days ago, which illustrate this form of composition. The words for " blessing" and " voice," which conclude each line, form in combination, in Chinese, the word for gospel.

> Desiring that everyone should long enjoy eternal life's blessings,
> It was as if all had heard an angel's voice.

But in all this, it may well be asked, where do those subjects come in which are considered the ground work in the education of our Western youth ? What time is given to arithmetic ? How much geography is taught ? Has science no place whatever in a Chinese curriculum ? Until the last few years, the answer to all these questions would have been in the negative. An ordinary Chinese teacher despises figures, they are for the shop-keeper or merchant ; and as to geography, he might know something of the names of the various kingdoms of China as they existed several hundred years before our era, but as to the whereabouts of the great nations of the earth, he is in complete ignorance.

It will be seen that Chinese education, pure and simple, is very different in scope from ours, being only a study of their own sacred books, history, philosophy, etc., and the composition of the Chinese language. Truly, that is a stupendous task, at which the students labour from youth to old age, and even then some fail to obtain the degrees they seek at the examinations, which are to a large extent the aim of those who devote themselves to learning.

EXAMINATIONS.

The various official examinations, which take place throughout the different provinces every year, are a very prominent feature in the life of the people, and an important factor in the development of the character of the literary and ruling classes. All consider them to be one of the greatest evidences of their high civilisation. The question is often asked with a certain amount of sarcasm :—Are there any examinations in your Western countries ? An answer in the affirmative often elicits great surprise—equivalent to a tacit acknowledgment that there may be some civilisation even in the West. The day for these questions is, however, fast passing away, as great numbers of the people are now better informed in regard to Western countries.

Until recently there have been no school or college examinations which would in any way be comparable to those in vogue in Europe. The Chinese examination system aims at providing the best men in the empire for the work of the state, and is, therefore, the door of entrance into the civil service. Success in examinations also secures much local prestige and influence.

In every province, examinations are held in three grades of cities: first in each "Hsien" or county town, second in "Fu" or prefectural capitals, third in the "Seng" or provincial capital.

In county towns the local magistrate holds periodical examinations for students in his jurisdiction preparatory to those held in the prefectural capital. On the near approach of these county examinations, students desirous of entering for them purchase at the magistrate's office the necessary papers for the examination. These consist of a certificate form and paper on which the questions are to be answered, which he takes to the local Temple of the God of Literature. Here his certificate is endorsed by the salaried licentiate, who acts as the student's guarantor. The licentiate enters the name in his register, and places his seal on the paper. The student hands these to the magistrate's clerk, who, in exchange, gives him a receipt which enables him, as a candidate, to enter the Examination Hall.

On the day of examination the students are introduced to the examiners by their licentiate guarantors. Generally about 2,000 competitors enter for these local tests, which consist of five separate test examinations, the last resulting in a selection of one or two hundred candidates. The first four of these are pretty sure of obtaining the desired first degree at the examination in the prefectural capital.

The composition of the famous eight-headed essays on topics in the Chinese classics, and the writing of poetry, constitute the main subjects on which students are examined.

Twice in every three years, examinations are held by the prefect (Fu) for the candidates of the various "hsiens" (or county towns) within his prefecture, at which a similar process is gone through to that already described.

But these two (Fu) examinations are only preliminary to that held by the literary Chancellor twice in three years in each prefectural city, the latter being open to all students who have entered in their own "hsiens." In this examination there are only three separate sittings, two of a day each, and the final one

128   *Education.*

of an hour for writing a paper in the presence of the Chancellor. Recently the papers set at these examinations have been considerably changed in character. Of late years questions have been asked at the first session on mathematics, geography, Chinese and Western history, politics, international law, etc. Only two subjects may be taken. Essays on the ethics and philosophy of the Chinese classics are

FIRST HOUSE FOR FRIENDS' MISSION, CHENTU.
The Chinese Viceroy visited this house and pronounced it to be "Very Good."

written on the second day. The fortunate competitors at this examination obtain the first degree (Hsiu Tsai, or Budding Genius), sometimes compared to the Western B.A., and often they number only one per cent. of those who have entered.

Once in every three years, in the eighth moon, the examinations for the second degree (Chü Ren, or Promoted Scholar), is held in the provincial capital, and is conducted by two special Commissioners of Education. Only those who have obtained the rank of " Budding Genius " are permitted to compete. Three sessions of three days each are occupied with this examination,

How the Competitive System Works.

at which advanced papers on the subjects already taken at the "hsien" and prefectural cities, are set, great accuracy and a high style of composition being required.

In the city of Chentu between fifteen and twenty thousand licentiates compete triennially for the honour of obtaining this degree. The examination halls, or rather cells, consist of narrow rows of tiny rooms, each one being about 5ft. 9in. by 3ft. 8in. in size, and only 5½ft. high. Each row of cells is designated by a selected character, which is conspicuous on the end cell of each row. The names of successful candidates at the first two sessions are not published, only the number of the cell each one occupied, and the character representing the particular row.*

The competitors come from all parts of the province, even from the extreme borders, and vary in age from twenty to over threescore years. They take provisions, bedding, candles, writing materials, and even servants with them into the examination halls.

Great excitement is manifested in every corner of the province when the results are published, for the whole neighbourhood, as well as the most distant relation of the successful candidate, shares in the distinction obtained. Relatives and neighbours are feasted, presents made, large sheets of coloured paper stating the candidate's name and his degree are sent to all friends, who place the document in a prominent place in the front of their houses, and the proud possessor of an M.A. degree has the words "Wen K'wei" hung over his own door.

Yet even this examination, successfully passed, does not guarantee any official post. Those who seek such must proceed to Peking to compete for the Doctor's degree, the possession of which entitles the holder to obtain an appointment.

A final examination is held within the imperial palace in the presence of the emperor, which, if successfully taken, entitles to admission into the Hanlin College. Upon the first in the list is bestowed the title of "Chwang Yuen," or Laureate.

* See illustration on p. 45.

It is important to bear in mind that in China not all who come to a certain standard are given degrees, it is only a fixed number of the best who get the degrees—sufficient for the government service.

Thus the competitive system works, and, at the top of the ladder, are found what are supposed to be the ablest and choicest men of the empire, chosen from every rank of life, providing the emperor with the best material from which to select his ministers.

The system, though it has many failings, has proved an admirable one for China, fostering the education of the people, giving the humblest in the land an opportunity of a share in the government of the nation, and providing a class of men capable of holding the reins of government. In the future, the same system, brought into line with the advance of modern civilisation, may prove more than ever to be one of the most powerful elements in the preservation and stability of the nation.

MISSION EDUCATION.

Perhaps nowhere, with the exception of Japan, have the educational agencies sustained by the various Missionary bodies exerted a greater influence in changing old standards, and creating new aspirations after more solid education, than in the Celestial Empire, and work along this line is now beginning to be fruitful.

In the first place, in connection with almost every Mission station, the free primary school was established, in which simple lessons in geography, arithmetic, and elementary science were taught, as well as the Chinese classics and Christian books.

These were followed by day and boarding schools of higher grades, and now in the chief cities of the empire educational establishments of considerable size and influence are being conducted by missionaries. While these institutions may not have produced the number of converts expected, the influence they have had upon all classes has been very great.

The missionary has been the pioneer in carrying this great civilising agency to the limits of the empire, and to-day in its remotest villages there is a demand for education according to the new standards. The method of memorising a large amount of literature without knowing its meaning is being changed to the more useful way of acquiring the meaning at the same time that the sound of the character is learned. Mathematics and the sciences, as well as foreign languages, are fast becoming primary subjects. An educational association has been formed by the missionaries, for the furtherance of Christian education. This association purposes to bring into China our western school systems and curricula, and has endeavoured to influence the educated and official classes towards a change in the subjects for public examinations; many of its members have also done most valuable service in translating text-books for school and college use. These are now in great demand throughout the eighteen provinces; indeed, they cannot be supplied fast enough to meet the need.

Several institutions, missionary, mercantile and governmental, in various parts of the country, have set apart men specially to translate text books in Western learning.

In nearly every one of the county, prefectural and capital cities, government schools and colleges are being established, which are to be teaching institutions, where Western as well as Chinese subjects will form part of the curriculum.

China appears at last to have really set her face towards reform; the spirit of inquiry is abroad, and the younger men of the literary class, as well as a few of the older prominent officials, are in favour of the new movement. Evidence of this is shown in the following extract from "China's Only Hope," already referred to, although, during the last year or so, its author appears to be actuated again by some reactionary tendencies. Speaking of what should be done in the way of reform in the educational system, Chang Chih Tung says:—

Let us plant schools in every province, circuit, prefecture, department and magistracy; universities in the provincial capitals and Peking; colleges in the prefectural cities, high schools in the Hsien, projected on the graded system. Let the curriculum of the high schools be the Four Books, native geography and history, arithmetic, geometry and the elements of science: that of the colleges, the higher branches of the four classes, history, government. foreign languages, and literature; and that of the Universities of a still higher grade." *

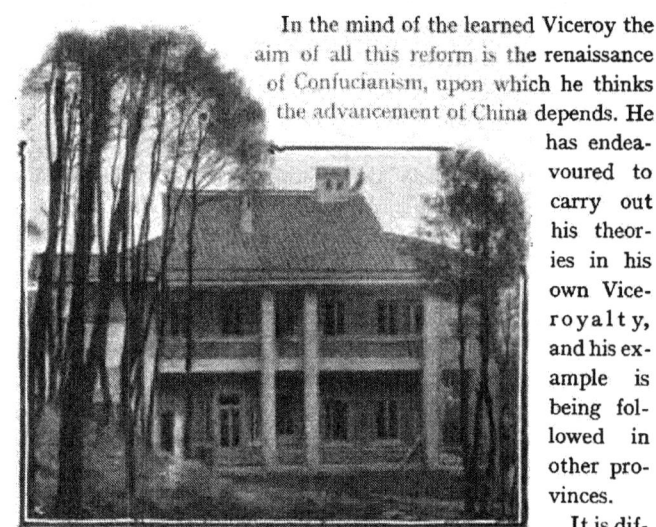

In the mind of the learned Viceroy the aim of all this reform is the renaissance of Confucianism, upon which he thinks the advancement of China depends. He has endeavoured to carry out his theories in his own Viceroyalty, and his example is being followed in other provinces. It is difficult to forecast what will be the effect of an adoption by China of Western education and civilisation, but it is of the utmost importance that the Christian Church should make her influence felt to the very greatest extent in this new movement.

MASTER'S RESIDENCE. BOYS' BOARDING SCHOOL, CHUNGKING.
See also the frontispiece.

* Events are moving fast in China and, since this chapter left the hands of the authors, a Decree has been issued at Peking, abolishing the old system of examinations, based on the Chinese classics, after the end of the present year. In future, the candidates for office are to be chosen from among the graduates of the modern universities, recently established in Peking and most of the provincial capitals, as advised by Chang Chih Tung.

CHAPTER XII.

CHRISTIAN MISSIONS.

ABBE HUC, in his "History of Christian Missions in China, Tartary, and Tibet," states "we are fully justified in giving credit to the tradition which dates the propagation of the Christian Faith in China to Apostolic times," and that "as early as A.D. 411 the Metropolitan See of China was founded by Actacus." He tells us that " as early as the third century the Chinese were counted amongst the nations who had received the Gospel."

THE NESTORIAN CHURCH.

From the sixth to the fourteenth century, the Eastern Syrian or Nestorian Church was a great and learned missionary Church, and in the year A.D. 635, under their leader, Olipin, they established themselves at Si Ngan, the capital of the province of Shen-si, which was then also the capital of the whole Empire.

Marco Polo, when travelling through China in the thirteenth century, found Nestorian Christians in many places. That Christianity—the glad tidings of the Gospel—was, at an early date, preached in certain parts of the Chinese Empire, and a Christian church established, is proved by the discovery of the now famous Nestorian Tablet, in the city of Si Ngan. Some workmen, while digging for the foundation of a house, in 1625, found this marble tablet, upon which is an inscription in Chinese and in some strange characters of another language. This celebrated monument is evidence to-day of the Missionary zeal of the Nestorian Church, and records the fact that in the seventh century " the great Law was promulgated in the ten provinces of China, and its Christian Temples were in a hundred cities." But, beyond this, little if any permanent trace can now be found of the results of Christian missionary effort before the thirteenth century, unless it be found imbedded in the native sects which have sprung up, and which survive to this day with higher truths than the common religions.

ROMAN CATHOLICS.

In the reign of the Emperor Kublai Khan, John de Monte Corvino, a Franciscan Missionary, who had passed the greater part of his life in Tartary, was appointed Archbishop of Peking. He was joined, in 1308, by three monks of his own order. For a time this movement was crowned with great success, the old missionary was cheered by the arrival of new comers and they helped one another. Conversions became so numerous that in 1312 further assistance was sent to the Archbishop. This wonderful movement, of which Abbé Huc gives such a thrilling account, disappeared so completely with the fall of the Mongol dynasty, and the confusion that ensued, that it was again forgotten that the Gospel of Jesus Christ had ever been promulgated in China. The Christian Churches, which had been established at the cost of enormous sacrifices, were never deeply rooted, and in time of persecution some centuries after, they were destroyed.

The next effort for the evangelisation of China was made, not from the North-West frontier through Tartary, but from the South-East, the Missionaries endeavouring to obtain an entrance in the province of Kwang-tung. The men connected with this attempt in the sixteenth century were Xavier, Michael Roger and Matthew Ricci.

St. Francis Xavier was impressed with a desire to visit the Chinese through hearing constant reference made to them, while in Japan. After several heroic attempts to reach Canton, he died on the Island of St. Johns in 1552, in sight of the vast empire in which he had hoped to preach the Gospel.

Father Michael Roger and Matthew Ricci were more successful, and in 1582, concealing their main purpose, they placated the Viceroy of Kwang-tung with presents, pleasing him with the working of a clock and such like, so that he permitted them to live in a Buddhist Temple in the neighbourhood of Canton.

Thus were commenced the great Roman Catholic Missions, which have since extended to the confines of the whole empire. They have succeeded in winning their converts to such a faith in Christ that, during the past two centuries, thousands of them have suffered torture and death rather than deny their Lord. While many of the methods of the Roman Catholic Church for the propagation of its faith, and some of its doctrines, are opposed to what we consider true Christianity, it must be admitted that in times of greatest persecution the converts have again and again proved their love to Christ, stood the test, and remained faithful.

A MANDARIN IN FULL DRESS.
By kind permission of the "FOREIGN FIELD."

It is at the same time to be regretted that, in too many cases, the Roman Catholic organisation has been and still is used for political purposes, both by missionaries and natives. One of the crying evils of to-day, throughout the length and breadth of the land, is the arrogance and official presumption of the Roman Catholic clergy, the undue exemption claimed by their converts from the jurisdiction of local officials, and their misuse of their connection with the Church to persecute and browbeat their neighbours. These things, in many places, have created great friction between the Roman Catholic Church and the Chinese people, resulting often in serious riots, and destruction of both life and property.

Mrs. Bird Bishop thus sums up the impressions formed on this subject during her extensive travels, as recorded in her book entitled, "The Yang Tse Valley and Beyond."

> Roman Catholic Missions in Sz-Chwan are unpopular owing to
> 1. Exorbitant indemnity demanded for riots in 1895.
> 2. The claim of the clergy to equality with officials of high rank.
> 3. The secrecy of the services and of the last rites of the Church, and the non-admission of the heathen to services.
> 4. The opposite methods adopted by Protestants (p. 102.)

PROTESTANT MISSIONS.

It may not be without passing interest, as consistent with the present aim of this record, to note that there next seems to have been a desire on the part of Friends to carry the Gospel to China, as early as 1661, when George Fox exclaimed, "Oh that some Friends might be raised up to publish the Truth in China!" Soon after that date, it is recorded that "John Stubb, Henry Fell, and Richard Castrop, were minded to go to China, but no masters of ships would take them." The two former did eventually get as far as Egypt (Richard Castrop having died at sea) intending,—probably in ignorance of the distance and the difficulty of the undertaking,—" to proceed thence by caravan, but they were stopped by the British Consul."

It was not until the year 1807, when Robert Morrison went to Canton, that Protestant effort made a successful commencement on behalf of the vast population of the Chinese Empire. The honour of having sent him to China, at a time when entrance into the country seemed hopelessly forbidden, belongs to the London Missionary Society. It has been well said that he was " A God-chosen man for a God-chosen work, at a God-given time, who proved that he possessed such a God-honouring faith as was bound to be honoured of God ! "

Protestant missionary work in the Chinese Empire may naturally be considered in four geographical divisions :—Southern, Central, Northern, and Western, each covering a large extent of territory, with populations varying in language and character.

SOUTH CHINA.

BRITISH PIONEERS.

The efforts of the first forty years were almost entirely confined to the Southern provinces, in particular to Kwang-tung and its capital Canton, Fu-kien and its capital Fu Chow, and Cheh-kiang the capital of which is Hang Chow.

At Newcastle-on-Tyne, in 1782, was born Robert Morrison, the man who became the pioneer missionary of the Protestant Church to the Great Closed Land of China. He was a last and boot maker by trade, and his prayer was that " God would station him in that part of the mission field where the difficulties were the greatest and most insurmountable."

It is important to the would-be missionary to note how unusually complete was his preparation. He had cultivated memory, and could repeat Psalm cxix. He practised mnemonic tests, which must have been invaluable in acquiring a language, such as Chinese, made up of tones and aspirates. The study of medicine and astronomy, and transcribing obscure manuscripts also united in training the man to deal with the educated people to whom he was sent. The *spirit* and *faith* which possessed him were well evinced before he started, when, to the almost contemptuous question,—" Young man, do *you* expect to move that great nation?" he promptly replied, "No, Sir, but I expect God to." That faith had to stand the test of seven and twenty years, most of which were spent outside the Empire, but he cheerfully plodded on, translating, compiling a Dictionary and seeking to extend the Redeemer's Kingdom. Though he had to wait seven long years for his first convert, and a whole lifetime without being allowed to preach publicly in China, foundations were well laid, and his followers in the great work know that his labour was not in vain.

Like Carey, Morrison had spent a large part of his youth in manual labour, but was filled with such an intense desire to fit himself for the ministry, that, notwithstanding twelve or fourteen hours' work each day, he yet found time for self-improvement and study. He first thought of Africa as his sphere of missionary labour, but God had another field of service for him. Neither his father nor his relations, for a time, were in sympathy with his desire to be a minister, much less a missionary, nevertheless, he prepared for the work to which he felt called, studying between seven at night and six in the morning. He also commenced the study of Chinese while in London, with a Chinaman who happened to be there. The East India Company, whose ships traded to China, would not grant a passage to the missionary, so Morrison was forced to proceed by way of America, sailing round Cape Horn and across the Pacific, and carrying with him letters of introduction from James Madison, Secretary of State (U.S.A.), to the American Consul at Canton, where he landed in September, 1807.

The question was,—how to reach the people? "First of all, Chinamen were forbidden by the Government to teach their language to any foreigner, under penalty of death; secondly, no one could remain in China except for purposes of trade; thirdly, the Roman Catholic missionaries were bitterly hostile."

The many helps which now abound for acquiring the language did not then exist. For a year Morrison lived in the house of some New York merchants, but he was unable to walk the streets.

A GROUP OF CHINESE WOMEN.

It seemed impossible to get near the people, yet he laboured on under most disheartening conditions. With the hope of better success he adopted Chinese dress; he even grew long finger nails, but then abandoned the plan as useless.

In 1809, he was engaged by the East India Company as translator, and thus having a more definite position, he was better able to prosecute his missionary work, to which he devoted every moment that was free from official duties. In 1812 he finished his Grammar of the Chinese language, and on the 31st

December in that year he writes: "I bless the Lord that this year the New Testament has been completed in Chinese, and is now nearly all printed. Oh! that it may be the means of great good! Lord! own it as Thine own Word; let it not return unto Thee void."

Considering the circumstances and the difficulties to be overcome, the achievement was great. Truly it may be well said of Morrison that "he had the patience that refused to be conquered, the diligence that never tires, the caution that always trembles, and the studious habit that spontaneously seeks retirement." It was thus that "Morrison laid the foundation of the Church of Christ in China."

In 1813 he was joined by William Milne and his wife. Milne was an Aberdeenshire man, an apt scholar, full of spiritual fervour, of good judgment, and admirably adapted to be Morrison's colleague. It was Milne who said "To acquire the Chinese language is a work for men with bodies of brass, lungs of steel, heads of oak, eyes of eagles, hands of spring steel, hearts of the Apostles, memories of angels, and lives of Methuselah." He might also have added "and the patience of Job."

In order to train Chinese, who might enter China without attracting the same suspicion as foreigners aroused, and as a base from which to carry on the work while the doors remained closed, Malacca was chosen as the site of the Anglo-Chinese College, and Milne was its first president. There he carried on his study of Chinese, helping also in the translation of the Bible and other works.

In 1819, Dr. W. H. Medhurst arrived in Malacca, as Milne's colleague, and laboured there for many years.

These three men,—Morrison, Milne and Medhurst were the pioneers of the great Protestant enterprise in China of the nineteenth century, and they will ever be remembered, like the three great India missionaries, Carey, Marshman and Ward, as men of indomitable patience and perseverance, indefatigable as translators, great students, able workers, chosen of God, and devoted to His service for the salvation of the heathen.

To the London Missionary Society also belongs the honour of being the pioneer of Medical Missions in China.

In 1838, Dr. William Lockhart, the first medical missionary, was sent to Canton by the London Missionary Society. Finding it impossible to establish himself there, he removed to Macao, where he opened a hospital, but after a brief stay was compelled by the Chinese authorities to leave. Returning again in 1840, Dr. Lockhart and Dr. Hobson carried on hospital work. In 1847, the latter succeeded in establishing a Medical Mission in Canton, where he was eminently successful. He also translated a number of well-known medical works. Then also the name of Dr. Peter Parker, who began work in Canton in 1835, will always be remembered as one of the pioneers of Medical Missions.

AMERICAN PIONEERS.

The first American Society to send Missionaries to China was the American Board, founded in 1810, and its pioneer labourers were E. C. Bridgman and David Abeel, who arrived in 1830. The former is well known for his work in connection with the Society for the Diffusion of Useful Knowledge in China (not the present Society of similar name), and as a member of the translation committee of what is now known as the Delegates' Version of the Bible. He was also for twenty years editor of the *Repository*, a valuable monthly periodical dealing with subjects relating to China.

S. Wells Williams, author of "The Middle Kingdom," one of the best and most trustworthy works in existence on China and the Chinese, went out as a printer, in connection with the American Board, in 1832. He published an English-Chinese Dictionary, which became a standard book for students of the Chinese language, though it has now been superseded by one by Prof. H. A. Giles.

CHANGED CONDITIONS.

It is not surprising that Missionary Societies, having thus begun to realise the responsibility of the Christian Church towards the millions of China, at once took advantage of the changed conditions which followed the signing of the Treaty at the close of the war in 1842. The London Missionary Society at once decided to remove their Anglo-Chinese College from Malacca to Hongkong, and all the Missionaries in the Straits Settlements met there to consult with reference to establishing missions in the treaty ports. Dr. Legge, with three assistants, took charge of the college. Later on it was decided that Dr. Medhurst and Dr. Lockhart should open a Mission in Shanghai. In 1844, A. and J. Stronach, of the same Society, established themselves in Amoy, where one of them soon became a well-known and popular figure in the streets and temples of the city; he learned by heart long quotations from the Chinese classics, so as to be better able to meet the arguments of those of the educated classes who attacked Christianity. He also largely helped to fix the style of the Chinese used in the translation of the "Delegates' Version" of the Bible.

The American Presbyterian Mission began work in Amoy, Ningpo and Canton, while the American Baptist Mission opened work in Hongkong, but in 1860 they removed to Swatow, a port 180 miles distant from Hongkong. Through the influence of Dr. Gutszlaff, two German missions, the Rhenish and the Basel, decided to begin work also; Genaehr and Koester were the pioneers of the former; Lechler and Hamberg of the latter. Mr. Lechler tried for many years to establish himself in the neighbourhood of Swatow, but without success. Mr. Hamberg devoted himself to work among the Hakkas, a race who were formerly emigrants from Central China. He was joined later by Mr. Lechler and Mr. Koester. Genaehr's work consisted principally in training native teachers and preachers. Both missions persevered amid much that was peculiarly disappointing and difficult. In 1866, Dr. Faber, whose literary attainments were of a high order, and whose translation work and original studies in Chinese are well known throughout the Empire, joined the Rhenish Mission.

The Protestant Episcopal Church of America sent out two missionaries to commence work in Canton in 1835, but these, finding it difficult to obtain intercourse with the natives, decided to go to Singapore, and later found a favourable field for their labours in Batavia. In 1842 they established a mission in Amoy, which was given up after three years, and then, one of them, Dr. Boone, was consecrated Bishop, and settled in Shanghai. This city is now one of their most important centres of missionary work in China. They have also extensive and influential evangelistic and educational agencies in Hankow and Wu Chang.

The work of the Church Missionary Society was commenced in 1844 by George Smith and Thomas McClatchie. Together they visited the five treaty ports in order to find a suitable home for the mission. Mr. Smith was much impressed with Fu-chau, but the Society was unable at that time to commence work there. Mr. McClatchie settled in Shanghai, visiting Ningpo, where the American Baptists had been labouring since 1843, and American Presbyterian Mission since 1844. He urged his Society also to start work there, which they did in 1848, and Ningpo and Shao Hsing, became the principal centres of the Church Missionary Society in the Cheh-kiang province. In 1875 the Ningpo College was founded, and became a valuable agency in the work; and, in the same town, in 1901, a Native Church Missionary Society was formed for further extension. In 1850 the Church Missionary Society occupied Fu-chau and laboured perseveringly, encountering great difficulties for eleven years before baptising their first convert. Medical work, commenced in 1860, opened the way for rapid progress. Severe persecution was met with, and in August, 1895, occurred the terrible Ku-cheng massacre. This was followed by a great advance.

In 1847 the American Board and the American Methodist Church had begun missions in Fu-chau. The labours of each of these societies have been greatly blessed, and the patient seed-sowing and prayerful waiting have resulted in a large harvest. Evangelistic effort, house-to-house visitation, education of boys and girls, theological training schools, and medical work have all had a prominent place in their efforts in the province of Fu-kien. The American Board also occupies a part of the province of Canton, at the earnest request and with the support of Christian Chinese in California; and their work there has proved successful.

CHAPTER XIII.

CHRISTIAN MISSIONS.
(Continued).

CENTRAL CHINA.

IN Central China we again find the London Missionary Society foremost as pioneers in the spread of the Redeemer's kingdom. On the opening of the new treaty ports to foreign residence, in 1858, they at once availed themselves of the splendid opportunity presented, and commissioned Griffith John and Robert Wilson to establish a station in one of the three cities clustering together at the mouth of the Han. In a native house in the heart of Hankow, therefore, the two missionary families took up their residence in 1861, converted a portion of the premises into a Chapel, and here the first Protestant Mission in Central China was inaugurated. From the beginning until the present day, preaching, first in the streets, and later in halls on main thoroughfares, has been a prominent feature of the work. For over forty years the daily preaching of Jesus Christ and His gospel has been maintained in this centre in the various halls of the Mission, with a zeal that has never flagged, and the tokens of God's blessing have been very encouraging.

Speaking at the opening of the Theological College, Hankow, in the spring of 1904, Dr. John said :—

It is now nearly fifty years since I settled in Hankow, and throughout all these years the one aim of my life has been to preach the Gospel of Christ to this people. The one thought that has been uppermost in my heart since my arrival in Hankow has been to saturate the people with the mind of Jesus, and fill this atmosphere with the music of the cross. To do that I have laid myself out to preach the Gospel, to lay a good foundation, to build a strong church, strong in character, strong in numbers, and to inspire others with the same aim.

Dr. John, and his colleagues of the London Missionary Society in Hankow, felt at first that it was their duty to devote themselves to this work of preaching, and to leave the matter of education to the few who were qualified to do it. But about ten years ago, with the beginning of the change that is now taking place in the Empire as regards education and reform, they considered the time had come for the London Missionary Society to provide education for Church members, and to attempt also to influence the children of the merchant class. They therefore prepared a scheme of education which they are now endeavouring to carry out, the present College and Theological Training Institute being part of this programme. Dr. John, notwithstanding his fifty years of evangelistic and literary work, has thrown his untiring energies into this new educational department, and also said, in the address above-mentioned :—

I am still an enthusiastic evangelist, as well as an enthusiastic educationalist. My heart is in this work of preaching Christ, my soul is in it ; do not think I have abated one jot or one tittle in my enthusiasm, or my interest in evangelistic work. No, far from it. I believe it is the grandest work a man can do. *There is no grander work under heaven, than preaching the gospel of Jesus Christ.* I am now more than seventy years of age, and I have greater confidence in the evangelisation of China than ever before. I was enthusiastic forty years ago, when I came to Hankow, but I am to-day more enthusiastic for God's cause in this land than when I arrived in this city.

These inspiring words from such a veteran enable us to learn something of the spirit that during the past half-century has animated the wonderful effort of the London Missionary Society in Central China, resulting in the well-established and energetic Church in Hankow, whose influence extends throughout the provinces of Hupeh and Hunan.

Since 1866 the London Missionary Society have also conducted one of the most successful Medical Missions in China, where Dr. Mackenzie, Dr. Gillison and others have preached the gospel of sympathy and love by relieving the sufferings of thousands of the vast population of Central China. A hospital was first erected in 1866; in 1873 a more commodious building was provided, and in 1888 a hospital was built for women and children.

The American Baptist Missionary Union sustains an encouraging work in the city of Hanyang and neighbouring villages, under the superintendence of J. S. Adams.

The Protestant Episcopal Mission opened stations in Wuchang and Hankow in 1868. Medical, educational and evangelistic work is now carried on by it at a large number of stations.

Thus throughout Central China the missionary efforts of these societies, and of others of which our space does not allow detailed notice, have been remarkably successful. Large and flourishing churches have been founded in Hankow, Wuchang and Hanyang; work has branched out in every direction, stations have been opened in many towns and villages, and the Gospel has been proclaimed throughout the whole of the province; men whose lives have been transformed have, in their turn, gone forth to seek and to save their own countrymen.

The work has extended not only to the limits of Hupeh, but even beyond, and in the neighbouring province of Hunan, which formerly was strongly anti-foreign in sentiment, there is a remarkable missionary movement in progress. Hundreds are being added to the church, and thousands are inquiring the Way of Truth. No less than six societies are at work in this province where but ten years ago not a single missionary was to be found.

THE CHINA INLAND MISSION.

With the exception of the labours of the London Missionary Society in Hankow, no missionary work to any extent had been begun in the interior of the Empire prior to 1865.

In 1862, Captain Blakiston wrote, "I believe I shall not be wrong when I say that there is not a single Protestant Missionary a hundred miles distant from an European settlement." J. Hudson Taylor, who had gone out to China in 1853 in connection with the Chinese Evangelisation Society, was so impressed with this fact and with the claims of the millions of China that, through his instrumentality, the China Inland Mission was organised in 1865. Its one aim and purpose was the evangelisation of the whole Empire in the shortest possible time, rather than obtaining the largest number of converts in a limited field. With this object in view, during the following two decades, long itinerating journeys were undertaken by various members of the Mission. Nearly the whole Empire was thus explored, and the Gospel carried, by word and by printed page, from one end of the country to the other. From Ta-li-fu in the South-West to Manchuria and Mongolia in the North-East, from Kan-suh in the North-West to Hainan in the South, mission stations were opened in the capitals of twelve provinces, as well as in subordinate places. The knowledge thus gained of China and its people, and of the spiritual work that was waiting to be done, led the Mission to see the importance of immediate and large reinforcements. Its pioneers were led to pray that during the years 1882-4 seventy new workers might be sent to the field, and an appeal, signed by seventy-seven members of the China Inland Mission, was issued to the Christian Church, in which the following words appear:—

> We plead then with the churches of God at home to unite with us in fervent, effectual prayer, that the Lord of the harvest may thrust forth more labourers into His harvest field, in connection with every Protestant Missionary Society on both sides of the Atlantic.

God answered that prayer, and during the three following years, seventy new workers joined the China Inland Mission.

Again in 1886 another appeal was issued by the Council of the Mission, for one hundred new workers in the following year. This request was also granted, and their faith honoured; the men and women were welcomed to China, the needed supplies were forthcoming; and a great impetus was given to the work of God in that land. The labours and influence of J. Hudson Taylor, in stirring up the Christian Church throughout the world to its duty in proclaiming the Gospel of Christ to the Chinese, cannot be over-estimated, and the blessing that has thus accrued to this Empire can never be told. The story of the growth of the China Inland Mission, the self-denying labours of its workers, the suffering of its martyrs, are among the marvels of missionary labours of the nineteenth century.*

NORTH CHINA.

The district which we may term Northern China included the provinces of Chi-li, Shan-si, Shan-tung, and Manchuria, as well as the North-West provinces of Shen-si and Kan-suh; forming one of the most interesting and important fields of missionary enterprise.

No Protestant missionary work had been possible in the North of China until the close of the war of 1860; but after the declaration of peace, several missionary societies directed their attention towards the capital of the empire.

The American Board of Foreign Missions was the first to enter the new field. Henry Blodget went to Tientsin in 1860, and commenced what has proved one of the most successful missions. The work grew and expanded, and stations have been also opened by this Society in Peking, in Kalgan, a centre of Mongolian and Russian trade, in Pao-ting fu, the capital of the province of Chi-li, and in Tungchow, an inportant city on the Pei Ho, a short distance from Peking. In Tungchow, the American Board has established the North China College, a large and important educational institution, with a theological seminary. The London Missionary Society now unite with them in carrying on the work of this college.

* Since above was written, J. Hudson Taylor, the Founder of the China Inland Mission, has passed away, aged 73 years. He died, as he would have wished, *in China*, at Chang-sha, the capital of Hunan on June 3rd, 1905.

Since 1861 the London Missionary Society has also conducted a flourishing work in Tientsin and Peking. The Hospital work of this mission in both cities has been particularly noteworthy. The names of Dr. J. K. Mackenzie, Dr. Roberts, and Dr. Dudgeon will ever be associated with the history of successful medical missions in North China.

The same district has been the principal centre of the American Presbyterian Mission. This was begun in 1863, by the Dr. W. A. P. Martin, who subsequently became President of the Tung Wen Kuan (Imperial College), and of the Imperial University, and has since filled an important post in connection with the educational institutions of Chang Chih Tung, the progressive Viceroy of Hupeh.

In eastern Shan-tung, Dr. Nevius, also of the American Presbyterian Mission, carried on extensive and systematic itinerating work for many years, the result of which was the establishment of a number of self-supporting Churches. The Teng Chow College, under the care of Dr. C. W. Mateer, is a leading feature of the Presbyterian work in North China.

Methodists were also among the pioneers of missionary effort in North China. Mr. Innocent, of the English Methodist New Connexion, arrived in Tientsin in 1860, where a church has been gathered, and a work developed in both Chi-li and Shan-tung. The American Methodist Episcopal Mission has made both Peking and Tientsin centres of much missionary labour. Its educational establishment, the Peking University, occupies an important position and exerts a great influence in the capital of the Empire. The Church building of this mission in Peking is one of the largest in China, and an audience of from 800 to 1,000 persons attends the morning services every Sunday.

The work of the Irish and Scotch Presbyterians in Manchuria, where they have the field all to themselves, has been greatly blessed. It suffered heavily during the Boxer outbreak, and again in the course of the recent war between Japan and Russia. The work of the Baptist Missionary Society in Shan-si and Shen-si and Kan-suh, can only be briefly mentioned, but here, as in other portions of the Empire, God has wonderfully blessed the labours of His servants. Established in 1877, its work has continued to flourish. One of its missionaries, Dr. Timothy Richard has rendered a very valuable service to Christian missions in China by his work in connection with the supply of Christian literature. As Secretary of the Christian Literature Society (Shanghai), he has had the opportunity of influencing the thought of thousands of the Chinese—an opportunity which he has used to very good purpose. Reference in passing must be made to the work successfully carried on by the China Inland Mission in the Northern provinces.

All the Churches of North China have passed through their baptism of fire and persecution, and the men and women who willingly suffered martyrdom during the Boxer troubles of 1900, rather than deny their Lord, have shown the genuineness of their faith in the Gospel of our Lord and Saviour Jesus Christ. Detailed accounts of the martyrdom have already been published separately, and widely circulated, so there is no need to attempt to repeat them here.

The progress of the various missions referred to, has proved that God honours the faith and perseverance of His servants; they asked and expected great things of God, and He did for them more abundantly than they asked or thought. He opened the door, and no man has been able to shut it. Every attempt to do so has resulted in a wider sphere of work, calling the Christian Church to come and help. China is open to the Gospel message to-day as never before. There is an unprecedented demand for Bibles, tracts and Christian literature, and so numerous are the calls from towns and villages throughout the Empire for a messenger of the Gospel to be sent to them, that the missionaries now in the field are too few to give an effective response.

MASTERS AND PUPIL-TEACHERS OF THE BOYS' SCHOOL, CHUNGKING.
Leonard Wigham is the central figure, dressed in Chinese costume.

CHAPTER XIV.

CHRISTIAN MISSIONS.
(Continued.)

WEST CHINA.

THE first Protestant missionaries to visit Sz-Chwan, the most westerly province in China, were Griffith John of the London Missionary Society and Mr. Wylie of the British and Foreign Bible Society. They made a long journey from Hankow, up the river Yang Tse to Chungking, and on to Chentu; thence overland by a part of the great and ancient main road which leads from the West to Peking, as far as Han-chung in Shen-si, and returned down the river Han to Hankow. They travelled 3,000 miles, taking five months to complete it, and Dr. John records that "from the day we left Hankow to the day we returned to it, we never saw a foreigner, with the exception of two or three Roman Catholic priests, and never came across a single Protestant convert."

No continuous effort was made to gain a footing in Sz-chwan until the China Inland Mission entered the province in 1877. In May of that year, Mr. John McCarthy succeeded in renting premises in Chungking, and widespread evangelistic tours were afterwards accomplished by various members of that mission, by a member of the American Presbyterian Mission, and by Mr. Mollman, an Agent of the British and Foreign Bible Society.

The first married couple to take up residence in Sz-Chwan were Mr. and Mrs. Nicoll, who settled in Chungking, where Mrs.

Nicoll did valuable work as a pioneer amongst the women. She received visits from them daily, and they used to come in crowds; she then paid return calls on them in their homes. Though we do not hear of one woman being added to the church in those days, Mrs. Nicoll did not labour in vain. To this day her name is lovingly remembered by women who ask, " Will she never come again ? " and when one is talking to them of the Gospel they will frequently say " Why, that is what Li Si Mu (Mrs. Nicoll) used to tell us ! "

After the planting of stations by the China Inland Mission in the two principal cities of Chungking and Chentu, long itinerating journeys were made from these centres into the neighbouring provinces of Yunnan and Kwei-chau. In the latter the China Inland Mission still remains the *only* Society at work, but the Bible Christians have joined them in Yunnan, with a band of earnest and capable workers.

In 1881 the Methodist Episcopal Mission commenced their West China Mission in Chungking, and this has now become one of the largest missions in the west. The Mission has large hospitals in Chungking and Chentu. In these cities also the mission is active in educational work; and many churches are growing up under its care in the towns and cities which lie along the main road between them.

In 1888 the London Missionary Society commenced work in Sz-Chwan, taking Chungking as its centre. Here, and in a large district to the south and south-east, evangelistic, church, school and medical work are as well balanced, and kept in such active development, as the limited number of its missionaries will allow.

The American Baptist Missionary Union followed two years later, taking up their quarters along the river Yang Tse, at Sui Fu and westward as far as Kia-ting, Ya Cheo, and Ta Chien Lu, right away to the borders of Tibet.

In March of the same year, 1890, the first premises of the Friends' Mission were opened in the city of Chungking, particulars of which will be found in the following pages.

In 1892 came the Canadian Methodists, a band of earnest men and women, with Dr. Virgil Hart as superintendent of the mission. They settled in Chentu and Kia-ting, where

MEN'S SIDE OF CHUNGKING MEETING HOUSE.
The Characters in the left-hand panel, above platform, are a translation of Matt. xi. 28, 29 ; those to the right John iii. 16.

extensive evangelistic and medical work is now established, with much out-station country work, which is well looked after. And last, but by no means least, their printing press is now a vigorous branch of the work. Large premises have been erected at a cost of many thousands of taels in Chentu, and the press, which was at first in Kia-ting, is now removed there.

The same year, 1892, also saw the commencement of another mission in Sz-Chwan. Under the guidance of J. Horsburgh, a self-denying and whole-hearted missionary, a band of men and women were sent out by the Church Missionary Society, who have taken as their district the north of the province, and away to the north-west. Their numbers have so increased that they have been enabled to open several stations.

Meanwhile the work of the three Bible Societies, the British and Foreign, the Scotch National, and the American, has been carried on in the whole of the western part of China, by their energetic and enthusiastic agents.

The China Inland Mission—first in the field—has developed and organised its work so that in the north-eastern part of Sz-Chwan Bishop Cassels has a well-settled diocese, with a number of workers under his direction, from Kwan Yuen in the north to Wan Hsien in the south with headquarters at Pao-ning. In and around Chungking, Sui Fu, Lu Cheo, Kia-ting, and Chentu the work has grown, until the China Inland Mission workers now number nearly two hundred.

The work has spread marvellously throughout these three western provinces, Sz-Chwan, Yunnan, Kwei-cheo, in the past fifteen or twenty years. From the many thousands of people who are now constantly coming in contact with Christian influence in the street chapels, dispensaries, hospitals and schools, an ever increasing number of converts may justly be expected.

In 1888, there were but three foreign women, one in each of the three provinces; to-day there are over a hundred scattered throughout them, whose work, amongst the women and children of the densely populated districts, forms a fair proportion of the whole missionary enterprise.

It must not be assumed, however, that missionary work has gone on steadily and without interruption. In no province probably, has there been more frequent interruption and unsettlement. Again and again there have been serious riots; but the threatenings of disturbance have been as great or greater hindrances, involving periods of protracted unrest.

In 1886 the work in Chungking was completely stopped by a riot, the missionaries having to take refuge in the Magistrates' Yamen, where they were detained a good while. Later they were expelled from the city, and were sent off at night by boat, at high-water season, when the river was in its most dangerous condition.

Two members of the China Inland Mission were very severely handled by the mob in a riot in 1892 at Sung P'an in the far west; while in 1895 all the missionaries were driven out of Chentu, no less than thirteen little children sharing—with their parents—in suffering for the sake of the Gospel; all again had to flee down-river, and their homes and the mission premises were destroyed.

A rebellion amongst the natives, headed by Yu Man Tsz, was the cause of much anxiety and uncertainty in 1898-9. Members of Friends' Mission, with others, lived for some time on house-boats at the river-side, ready to flee if necessary, but reluctant to leave unless compelled to do so.

In 1899, in spite of the difficulty and danger of travel, owing to the Yu Man Tsz trouble, a very successful Conference of Missionaries was held in Chungking, at which about seventy or eighty were present. Nearly a week was spent in healthy and friendly discussion on all the important branches of missionary work. Papers were prepared by workers in the three provinces, the one feature of all that was written being its practical bearing on the needs of the work.

The Conference was attended also by J. Hudson Taylor, and Charles Inwood, and their wives, and their counsel and help were greatly valued. Important missionary policy arose out of this conference. As a practical result there were three new departures, all of which give evidence of the healthy development of the missionary cause in the West as a whole.

1. An Advisory Board was formed, to consist of a representative from each Missionary Society in the field, for reference and advice as to division of territory, for the economy of the working force, and other matters of general interest.*

2. The West China Religious Tract Society was established. Hitherto the missionaries in the West had obtained their supplies from a Society in Hankow.

3. The *West China Missionary News* was commenced. This is a monthly periodical bearing upon and uniting in interest the various departments of work in all the scattered stations of the three provinces, edited at first by Mary J. Davidson.

Again, in 1900, came the terrible upheaval in the North, the massacre of hundreds of Christians, foreigners and natives, the siege of Peking, and the compulsory order from the British Consul for all British subjects to leave the West for the coast. Not one Protestant missionary remained in the whole of Sz-Chwan or Kwei-cheo, though three solitary ones did continue quietly and bravely at their station in distant Yunnan, and were unmolested by the Boxers. The strain of life in which the missionaries spent these hot summer days of 1900 is well depicted in the following words of one who lived through it with them, though not herself a missionary.

The Peking Syndicate men forced their way out of Shen-si heavily guarded, and themselves guarding a certain number of others, who escaped with them; yet they knew how much more critical their precipitate flight made the position for those who remained behind. Thus began the flight. From the Yang Tse valley, from far away Yunnan, round by Tonquin and Hongkong, from the Tibetan border, from Kan-suh, and from Shen-si and Sz-Chwan we all got in alive; for happily the West did not rise. The Viceroy of Sz-Chwan determined, after many vacillations, to throw in his lot with the Yang Tse Viceroys, who, realising that whatever Russia might do in the North, would only

* A map shewing the division of the Field recommended by this Advisory Board, in 1902, faces p. 160.

leave their region more defenceless before Great Britain, determined to treat her as an ally, and themselves to keep the peace. And they did it with a statecraft and firmness that cannot but move us to admiration. They were Chinese Viceroys, loyal to China; their fear, of course, being lest Great Britain should at once seize the Yang Tse as a set-off to Russia getting Manchuria, as per agreement.

To the same writer, Mrs. Archibald Little, her husband, and Mr. J. W. Nicholson, who shared with the rest of the foreigners all the perils and anxieties of these days, the missionaries of Sz-Chwan, who were the last to leave, owe a debt of gratitude for the generous hospitality and help given to the refugees when they passed through Chungking. There are those who gratefully remember the kindness and are glad thus publicly to acknowledge it.

Though the enforced absence of all the missionaries from the field in 1900 may appear, as it seemed at the time, a disappointing break, the workers returned six or eight months after to find that, not only had most of the converts remained faithful, but that the whole aspect of the people had undergone a radical change. The door was opened as never before and, to quote the words of one of the missionaries on his return, is only to give utterance to the prevailing experience of the many; he says:—

A mighty movement is going on. Instead of going about seeking an entrance, as in past years, received with indifference by the better classes, or with a bitter, though veiled opposition, now we find the people longing to drag us off in every direction, begging and imploring that we will open a station in almost every town and village.

In 1902, the work in the northern part of the F.F.M.A. district, as well as that of other missions in different parts of Sz-Chwan, suffered severely from a recrudescence of the Boxer movement. Property was destroyed, converts persecuted and several lives lost.

It is not possible by statistics to convey any adequate idea of the progress that Christian missions have made in the Chinese Empire, or of the great influence they have had in bringing about the stupendous change that is now taking place throughout the whole of the eighteen provinces, from the sea coast to the far western borders, but the following facts may give some impression of the work that is being done in this vast Empire.

The late Dr. Legge informed the writer a few years ago, that, shortly after his arrival in China, he entertained all the Protestant missionaries in the Empire, and all the Protestant converts, at a meeting *in his study !*

Dr. John says,—" When I arrived in Hankow in July, 1861, there was not a Protestant Christian in the whole of this region, and among the heathen it would have been hard to find one who knew anything about the truth as it is in Jesus." "In 1856 there were not five hundred native Christians in the whole Empire in connection with Protestant Missions. In 1866 they could not boast of 2,000 in all."

In 1877, there were twenty-nine Societies represented in the Empire, including three Bible Societies, and the number of converts had risen to 13,035, with ninety-two stations, and 318 organised Churches. In 1890 forty Societies were at work, with a total of 1,296 missionaries, 522 Churches, and 37,287 converts. In 1900, there were sixty-seven different organisations, 2,785 foreign missionaries, 6,388 native workers and 112,808 native Christians.

During the past four years the progress has been unprecedented in certain parts of the Empire; converts have been added to the Church by the hundred—where in the past they came in ones and twos—and the spirit of inquiry is met with in every province. The door is open wide. It is but for the Christian Church to embrace this opportunity to redeem the obligation resting upon her to preach the Gospel of Jesus Christ to the vast multitude who seek for something, they know not what, but who believe we have that for which they thirst.

In these pages it has been only possible to give an account of missionary work in the Celestial Empire, in barest outline. The reader is referred to the histories and reports of the various societies mentioned, for detailed information regarding them.*

* For a brief, but excellent, history of Christian Missions in China, see "Rex Christus," by Dr. A. H. Smith. (London: Macmillan & Co.)

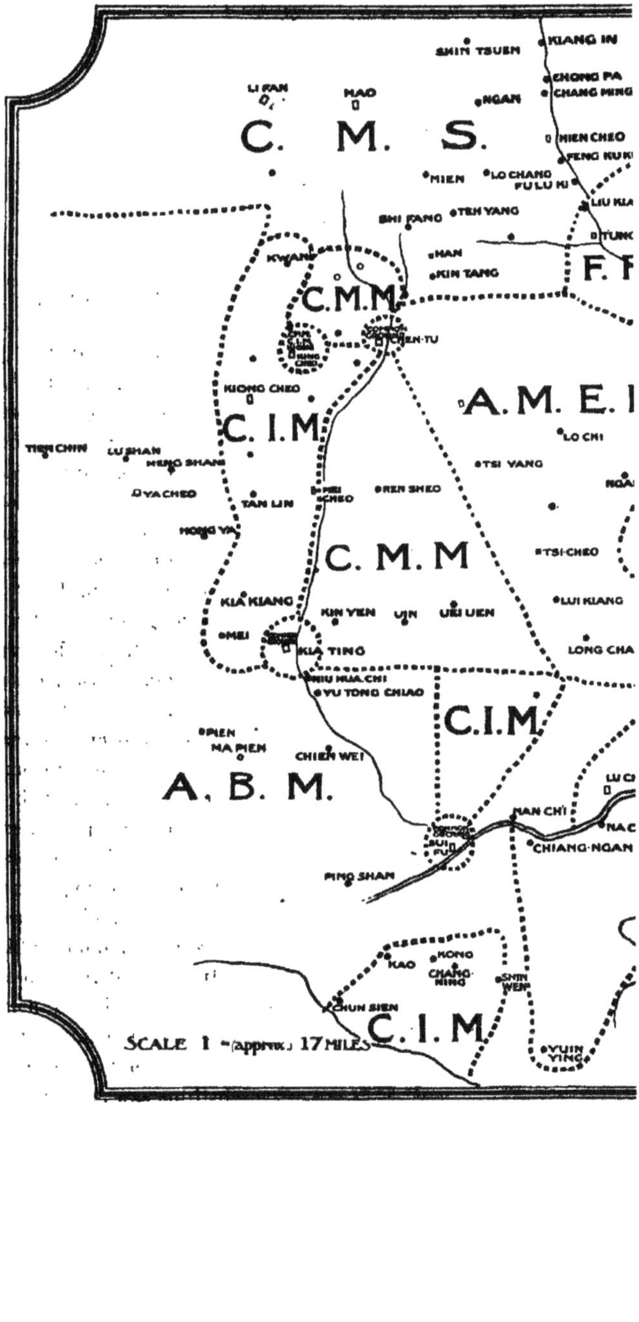
SHIN TSUEN
KIANG IN
CHONG PA
CHANG MING
LI FAN
HAO
NGAN
C. M. S.
HIEN CHEO
MIEN
LO CHANG
FU LU KI
TEH YANG
SHI FANG
HAN
KIN TANG
KWAN
C.M.M
CHEN-TU
A.M.E.
KIONG CHEO
C. I. M
LO CHI
TIEN CHIN
LU SHAN
MENG SHAN
TSI YANG
YA CHEO
TAN LIN
MEI CHEO
REN SHEO
HONG YA
C. M. M
TSI-CHEO
KIA KIANG
LUI KIANG
KIN YEN
UIN
UEI UEN
MEI
KIA TING
NIU HUA CHI
YU TONG CHIAO
C.I.M.
PIEN
MA PIEN
CHIEN WEI
A. B. M.
NAN CHI
SUI FU
CHIANG-NGAN
PING SHAN
KAO
HONG
CHANG NING
SHIN WEN
CHUN SIEN
C. I. M.
YUIN YING
SCALE 1" = (approx.) 17 MILES

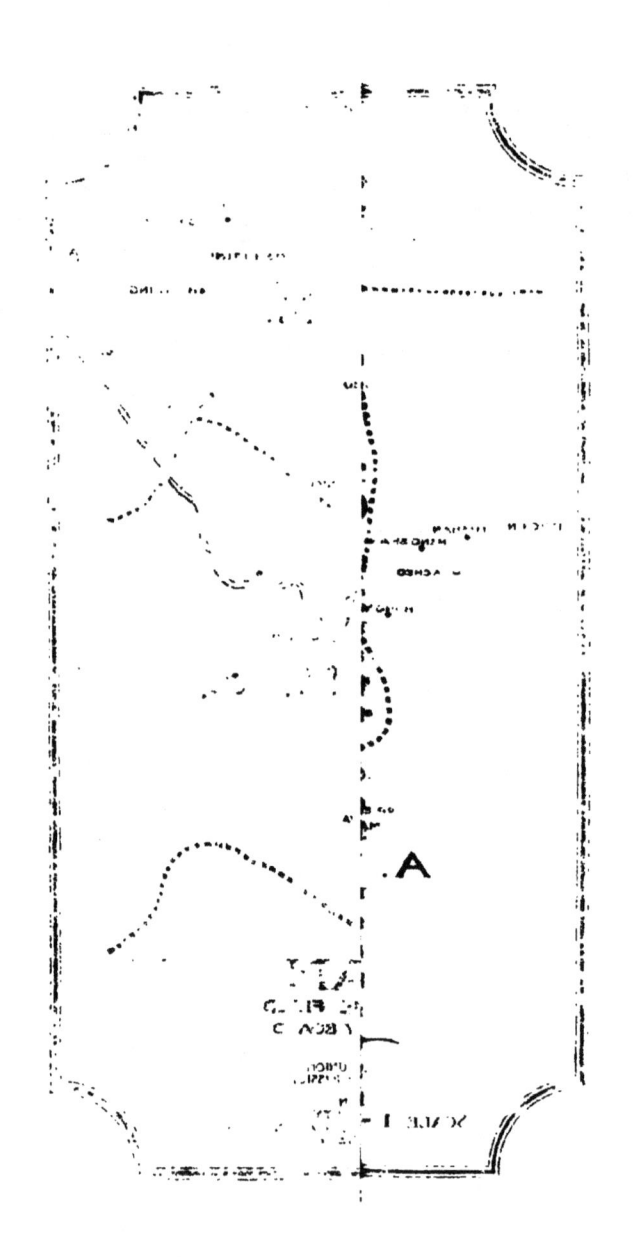

CHAPTER XV.

BEGINNING OF FRIENDS' MISSION IN CHINA.

IN February of the year 1875, the British Consular Agent, Margary, while travelling in the Province of Yunnan, was attacked by bandits and killed. The murder of this British Official having, it was believed, been committed at the instigation of the Governor of the Province, a series of negotiations took place in Peking, which ultimately resulted in the signing of the Treaty of Chefoo, by which liberty was obtained for all British subjects to travel throughout the length and breadth of the Empire, "without let or hindrance."

The granting of this privilege gave a great impetus to the work of the itinerating missionary, and the China Inland Mission, whose aim was to carry the gospel to the then unoccupied provinces, at once took advantage of the opportunity. They sent missionaries to explore the unknown land, and at the same time made known the great need for men and women to devote themselves to missionary work in the towns of the interior. J. Hudson Taylor by his work "*China's Spiritual Needs and Claims,*" and by personal advocacy of the claims of China upon the Home Churches, during the years 1876 to 1884, greatly stimulated interest in Missions in this country. The publication of accounts of the journeys of men who had traversed the interior, telling of the now opening door into the great land which had been so long sealed, and of the new opportunities for preaching the Gospel, also contributed to develop interest.

One of the articles published about this period, by Dr. George King, was entitled, "Shall the Gospel be preached to this generation of the Chinese ? " Several members of the Society of Friends reading it, were impressed with the fact that the Society had no representatives engaged in missionary effort in China, and felt that the time had come for them to have a share in the privilege of spreading the knowledge of Christ in the Far East.

About this time also Robert J. Davidson of Hillsborough, in the North of Ireland, was feeling himself called by God to devote his life to the spread of the Gospel in China. In the spring of 1883 he wrote to Thomas W. Fisher, who was local Secretary of the F.F.M.A. in Ireland, asking him whether the Association was prepared to commence work in that land, and to entertain offers for service there. Some delay occurred before any reply was forthcoming, and then it contained little hope of Friends entering upon so great an undertaking, but R. J. Davidson's letter was sent to the Honorary Secretary at Leominster. In reply, H. S. Newman wrote that there " did not appear any immediate prospect of Friends sending missionaries to China," but that in the issue of *The Friend* for the current month was a letter showing that others were also feeling the claims of that vast Empire, and were prepared to find the means to support a missionary, if any one was found who was believed to be called of God to the service.

The following is the letter referred to above.

SHALL THE GOSPEL BE PREACHED TO THIS GENERATION OF CHINESE?
(To the Editor of *The Friend*).

DEAR FRIEND,—No doubt many of your readers have seen an article entitled "Shall the Gospel be preached to this generation of Chinese?" It was recently read at a small Friends' Foreign Mission Association working meeting, in consequence of which £60 annually has been promised by Friends in ——— Meeting, for the support of a Missionary in connection with the China Inland Mission.

Any Friend willing to offer himself or herself to Christ for this service (subject to the approval of the China Inland Mission) is requested to communicate with "China," care of Editor.

Shall the Society of Friends remain any longer unrepresented in this wholly unsectarian Society for the spread of the Gospel in China, where it has no mission of its own, even though the population is nearly one-third that of the whole world? Surely some one will offer. If, however, no reply is received by the end of October, the money will be sent to the China Inland Mission, and the missionary whom they send we shall look upon and sympathise with as our representative.

Will your readers pray the Lord of the harvest to send forth the right labourer? I am, yours truly,

"CHINA."

July, 1883.

Replies to this offer were received from Henrietta Green, R. J. Davidson and two other friends. Some members of the Committee of the F.F.M.A. felt the whole circumstances to be a direct call of God to the Society to consider its duty to the Chinese, and that the time had come to commence direct work in connection with the Association rather than that Friends should join some other Mission; and accordingly these friends were asked to meet the Committee. Henrietta Green, who had conducted a successful mission work at Elsenham, in Essex, having recently recovered from a serious illness, felt that her restored life must be devoted to the work of God in China. Her desire was entered into most sympathetically by the committee of the Association in September 1883, and the important decision arrived at that the F.F.M.A. should widen its sphere of influence and that Friends should not be behind their brethren in endeavouring to carry the Gospel to the Chinese. The step thus taken in faith, in obedience to the guidance of the Spirit of God, was the beginning of the Friends' Mission in China, which has grown to be one of the most important branches of the F.F.M.A., having now twenty-four missionaries on the field.

Having thus decided to commence a Mission in China, the question naturally arose as to where in that vast Empire the Mission should be planted. J. Hudson Taylor was then in England, and he, with other members of the China Inland Mission, was consulted as to the most suitable place for Friends to begin work. In the previous year Chentu, the capital of the great Western Province of Sz-Chwan had been occupied by Protestant Missionaries for the first time. Missionaries at work in Shen-si had found immigrants from Sz-Chwan more devoted to religion than the people of other provinces. Their temples were kept in better repair, they spent large amounts on idolatry, and Roman Catholic missions had been very successful in gaining adherents in the province. It was therefore urged that they might be specially susceptible to the influences of the Gospel.

At that time only two cities in the whole province, Chungking and Chentu, were occupied by missionaries, and of these there were only six or seven all told, both men and wives. There was thus scope enough among the millions of the province, for many missionary societies to carry on work, without overlapping the labours of others.

The information thus gained favourably impressed those responsible for the selection of a locality for the Friends' mission, and the workers on the field to-day thank God for the guidance then given. The province of Sz-Chwan certainly has attractions and advantages for good missionary work not shared, in like measure, by any other of the eighteen provinces.

The committee of the F.F.M.A. accepted Henrietta Green's offer, and she went to London for special medical study, in preparation for her future work. Thus at the call of God, and in dependence upon Him, she went forth bravely as a pioneer of Friends' Missions in an untried field, ready at all costs to do what she believed was her duty, and the Church at home, as well as the people in China, have reaped the benefit of her faithfulness. She helped to create in the Society of Friends an interest for missionary work there, in days when the claims of the Chinese had little weight in the Church.

Henrietta Green sailed for China, with a company of the China Inland Mission workers in September, 1884, with the purpose of carrying out the plan already decided on, of commencing work in Chentu. This purpose she was never able to accomplish, for on reaching Hankow she found that the British Consul declined to grant passports to single ladies for travelling further west, owing to the war then going on between France and China. Thus her way inland closed, and she gladly accepted a home, for the time being, with Mr. and Mrs. Arnold Foster, of the London Missionary Society, in Hankow. Eventually she took up work in that neighbourhood, opening a dispensary for women and children in a village near by, where many gratefully received her patient self-denying ministrations. A little later on she severed her connection with the F.F.M.A., settling down to work in and around Hankow. In February, 1887, she returned to England on account of ill-health, but went out once more to China in January, 1888, in the hope of continuing the work that was so dear to her heart. Then followed a year of weakness and increased sickness and, in April, 1889, she had to leave that country. In May, 1890, closed the earthly life of our first Missionary to China.

To some this may seem a short record of missionary work ; to others it may be a cause of regret that the first object was not attained, and Sz-Chwan never reached. But with those who knew Henrietta Green intimately in China, there is no place for these thoughts. It was well said in the Memoirs, printed for private circulation, " Short as her time in the mission field was, her influence will last on, mighty on the right side—the side of undoubting faith in, and implicit obedience to, the guidance of the Holy Spirit." Even the heathen Chinaman who was engaged as a teacher to help her in acquiring the language said, "You are a good woman and God will bless you." A fellow-missionary who knew her well has expressed his belief in the "much, real solid fruit" that has resulted from her Christ-like ministry to the Chinese in Hankow, so that of her it may be truly said, "She was faithful to what she felt to be the will of God for her and was blessed in that faithfulness."

In 1885 Robert John and Mary Jane Davidson were accepted by the F.F.M.A. for work in China. R. J. Davidson was the eldest of a family born in Ireland, whose father had wished before his death that some of his sons might be missionaries in China.

Mary J. Davidson was already well-known in Mission work in London. They left England in September, 1886.

On the night of their farewell meeting, at Hart's Lane, (now called Barnet Grove), Bethnal Green, London, the scene of their previous missionary work, the placards of the evening newspapers announced a great riot in Chungking in West China. The missionaries had been driven from their homes, and their houses and churches burnt. This was not encouraging news for those about to start on a journey which would take them through that very place. It was felt at the time that this might seriously affect plans for proceeding to West China, as the war had done in H. Green's case, and so it proved.

On the 18th November Mr. and Mrs. Davidson reached Hankow, having called at Nanking on their way up-river, to consult J. Hudson Taylor as to the possibility of moving westward. It was found impossible to proceed to Chentu, *via* the Yang Tse and Chungking, and Mr. Taylor then suggested an alternative route, *via* the river Han, as far as the city of Hanchung and from there overland to Chentu. This appeared a round about way of reaching Sz-Chwan, but it was thought that as a very successful work was being carried on among the Sz-Chwan immigrants in the neighbourhood of Hanchung, it would be a good centre from which to approach the province. The missionaries, however, consulted the Committee, and awaited instructions from home before attempting that long journey. A house was rented in Hankow for a few months where much valuable experience of missionary work, and intercourse with missionaries of various societies, was obtained. Specially do our missionaries remember, with deep thankfulness, their intercourse with both Dr. Griffith John of the London Missionary Society, and the saintly David Hill of the Wesleyan Mission. They were as fathers to our mission in those early days, and the influence of their inspiring example and advice has never been lost.

In February, the missionaries received a cablegram, which had been delayed twelve days on the way, that read as follows :—" proceed Hanchung this Spring," and arrangements were made accordingly. The last night before starting on their long up-river journey was spent at the Wesleyan mission, and David Hill " accompanied them to the ship " and lifted his voice in prayer for a blessing on their untrodden way, and bid them "God-speed." For ten long and weary weeks they journeyed up the river Han, in a small, windowless house-boat. Mr. Botham, of the China Inland Mission went with them and was a congenial companion and interpreter. At last on a Sunday morning in May, 1887, the city of Hanchung was reached, and a hearty welcome was given to the travellers by Dr. William Wilson and his wife, of the China Inland Mission.

The first itinerating journey into Sz-Chwan was undertaken by R. J. Davidson in July, 1887, but only the range of hills dividing that province from Shen-si was crossed, and some books were sold in the villages on the other side. Robert J. Davidson, having had some medical training in England, was asked by Dr. Wilson to take charge of his dispensary work during his absence on furlough, so that until the spring of 1889, with the help of an able native assistant, that work was steadily pursued, as also the study of the language.

Yet the objective of Sz-Chwan was kept well in view, information being gained from missionaries, and from natives of the province who had become residents in Hanchung, which all helped to a better understanding of the method of procedure in opening up work in an unoccupied city. Hanchung was then the only city in the province of Shen-si open to missionary effort. Attempts had been made by several men to obtain a footing in Si-ngan, the capital, but without success, and the knowledge gained by these various experiences was helpful and instructive.

The view was held by Friends at home that our Mission should endeavour to occupy a portion of the province of Sz-Chwan in which the work might be carried on without overlapping that of other missions. This was the plan already adopted in India and Madagascar, where a certain portion of the country is set apart, by mutual agreement [between the various Societies, as the F.F.M.A. district. In accordance with this view, an effort was made to accomplish this purpose.

Just about this time the city of Pao-ning, in the North-East of Sz-Chwan, was opened to missionary work, and considerable difficulty was experienced in obtaining a residence there. Only in three other places in the whole province was resident missionary work being carried on. There was therefore a wide field quite untouched by Christian workers, where there was ample room for Friends, without entrenching upon the spheres of others. Dr. Wilson's medical assistant, Sie, came from the prefectural city of T'ung Ch'wan, and, when he heard that we were looking to go into the province of Sz-Chwan, he suggested our aiming to settle in the large prefecture of that name, as a most suitable sphere for our efforts, and affording the opportunity we desired of a district in which other Societies were not labouring. The political division of the province into prefectures (Fu), each of which governs a number of counties (Hsien), made what seemed a suitable division.

Our aim was to find such a district near Chentu, and, when we learnt that T'ung Ch'wan was only three days from the capital, it seemed as if it might be the place in which the Lord would have us labour. Mr. Sie offered to render what assistance he could in renting a house in T'ung Ch'wan, and expressed his willingness to return to his old home, and, through his friends and neighbours, help to obtain a footing in the district. These were days of difficulty, little understood by present arrivals on the mission field. It was difficult to find anyone willing to rent to the foreigner, and when one was found, after much trouble, another difficulty arose—the officials were much opposed to the residence of missionaries in their cities. Foreigners had then only Treaty rights to *travel* in the interior of China. No provision was made for their residence beyond the Treaty Ports and, where houses were rented in other cities, the missionaries remained only on sufferance, both of the people and of the officials. If opposition were shown in any form, there was little hope of doing much permanent work. Eighteen years have brought immense changes and, though there is still no definite treaty right, a certain prescriptive right now prevails, and houses can be rented and property bought in nearly every city in the vast Empire.

In those days, it was generally necessary to pay a number of preliminary visits to a city, trying to make friends with the people, and getting them accustomed to the sight of the foreigner, before making any attempt at securing premises.

In the end of 1887, the first visit of this kind was paid to T'ung Ch'wan. The city is situated on the river Fu, a tributary of the Chia-ling which joins the Yang Tse at Chungking, and is on the main road between Pao-ning and Chentu. There is good river and postal communication between the city and Chungking, and it is the principal market for the extensive silk trade of central Sz-Chwan. It lies in a small, well-cultivated plain, with the river Fu forming its eastern boundary. A small stream flows through the plain from the west, skirting the southern wall, while immediately outside the western gate is a rocky eminence surmounted by a temple which overlooks the whole city.

There are a good number of trees throughout the city, so that viewed from a distance, it gives the impression of being well-wooded. The people are generally well dressed and clean, though the prefecture as a whole is poor. The soil is not suited for the growth of rice, and the population has to depend mainly on the adjoining prefecture of Mien-cheo to supply this. Yet T'ung Ch'wan was in many respects well suited as a locality for a first attempt at settlement. In the following year, therefore, when another visit was made, a small house was rented, with the hope that it might be occupied by our missionaries, on the return of Dr. Wilson to Hanchung. Meanwhile a knowledge of the language and customs of the people was being acquired, besides some practical work being done in the Hanchung Dispensary, and the experience thus gained proved invaluable in the following years.

At the same time, the spirit of opposition to the foreigner

was also quietly at work. The county official, the Hsien magistrate of T'ung Ch'wan, informed the Viceroy of the province that foreigners had rented premises in his city, and asked for instructions which were only too readily forthcoming. The foreigner had no right to rent a house outside any treaty port; and he must not be permitted to take up residence there. As soon as he arrived with any intention of staying, he must be asked to "move on" or take all risks, for his passport only stated that he was permitted

THE FIRST PREMISES RENTED IN T'UNG CH'WAN.

to travel, and travel he must if he passed that way. Still it was hoped that a personal representation on the spot might improve the feeling, and as long as we held possession of the house, a tiny unpretentious one at a modest rental of only about fifty shillings a year, this hope was entertained. More than a year thus passed, but even time brought no more friendly feeling.

When Dr. Wilson returned to Hanchung, in May, 1889, he was accompanied by Caroline N. Southall, who had been accepted by the F.F.M.A. for our China Mission, and who was warmly welcomed as a fellow-worker.

CHAPTER XVI.

IN THE PROVINCE OF SZ-CHWAN.

IN July, 1889, R. J. and M. J. Davidson, with their little child, just seven weeks old, left Hanchung for their settlement in Sz-Chwan; Caroline N. Southall remaining behind for a time, busy with the language. A ten days' journey across the mountains and over the great main road to Chentu was lengthened into a tedious one of seventeen days, owing to heavy thunderstorms and intense heat, and the little baby arrived " more dead than alive," early a sufferer for the sake of the Gospel! They halted at Pao-ning, where Bishop Cassels of the China Inland Mission had kindly offered hospitality, and there the mother and baby were welcomed into the ladies' house, where the kindness of Miss Elizabeth Hanbury (now the wife of Dr. Wilson, formerly of Hanchung) was a further link in the chain of providences which marked those early days of the mission in so many ways.

R. J. Davidson at once proceeded to T'ung Ch'wan to make the final arrangements for the settlement of the mission, but no sooner had the District Magistrate realised that the foreigner had come to *stay*, than he began to coerce the landlord of the little house that had been rented, threatening to punish him if he did not see that the foreigner gave it up. Both the Prefect and District officials refused to be interviewed by R. J. Davidson, but sent him messages through the landlord saying he had no "right" to be there. Letters were written, but all without effect. The magistrate knew that he was backed by the Viceroy, so the screw was tightened on the aged landlord, as the most effectual way of dealing with the missionary. The landlord was a Mohammedan, and had behaved with no common courtesy and kindness from the beginning, taking R. J. Davidson and his native companion into his own house, and liberally providing for their needs. He felt, as he said, a bond of union between them, in the use of the name "Lord," when speaking of God whom he also worshipped, such as was not realised with the heathen. At last the old man appeared one day with a criminal's chain round his neck, accompanied by a number of lictors, and prostrating himself before the foreigner said, " I have never been so disgraced in public before. Can you do nothing to have me freed ? I do not wish to turn you out, but neither I nor my family can bear this disgrace, and the shame of public punishment by the magistrate." Then his sons and brothers besought that the house might be given up, or representation made to the British official. What could the missionary do but leave the city for a time ? "When they persecute you (through your landlord) in this city, flee ye into another." There was no other course but to go; the door was still closed and the time had not yet come to open it. Yet what was a sore disappointment at the time was no real hindrance to the work, for God had other purposes and plans in store for the China mission.

R. J. Davidson went out of T'ung Ch'wan with a heavy heart, for had he not walked round and round the walls of that city, and up and down its streets, and longed to preach to its people the everlasting Gospel, which he knew they needed so sorely, believing God wanted them to hear. Such as these are dark days of testing in the life of any missionary, when it becomes a very real thing to walk by faith and not by sight.

He turned to the only place which seemed open to him, the busy commercial city of Chungking, and the future developments of the mission proved how much cause he had to be encouraged by the first message he received on reaching there. In a letter from England came a little card on which was the promise, which has been so abundantly fulfilled—" He shall choose our inheritance." It was taken not only as a promise, but as the sincere desire of the missionary that there should be no self-choosing of any place, but that God Himself should plant the mission where He would, should Himself open the door; and in the full confidence that *when He opens no man can shut*.

T'ung Ch'wan being closed, another home for the Mission was sought and a brief visit was paid to Chungking. Missionaries, already there, pointed out the great need and importance of that city. The London Mission had only commenced their work a few months; the China Inland Mission had but that spring been reinforced since the riot of 1886,* and the few Missionaries of the American Methodist Episcopal Mission were busy reconstructing their work, after the havoc wrought. The city, in many respects of first importance in the province, has a dense and industrious population, and as the rendezvous of traders from all the country round, it offered a wide sphere for the best efforts of a large number of missionaries.

A temporary home, offered to our missionaries by Dr. and Mrs. Cameron of the China Inland Mission, was gratefully accepted, and it was arranged that the three members of our mission should take up residence in Chungking for a time, until further plans could be developed. Caroline N. Southall went overland to Pao-ning, and Robert J. Davidson returned there to take her with his family to Chungking, where a small house was rented until the following spring, when the large premisès in the White Dragon Fountain Street became the first real home of the Mission. The native house in the third court was adapted for a residence for the missionaries, and buildings in the first and second courts provided accommodation for a preaching hall, dispensary, girls' school, and a small preaching room near the street entrance.

* See reference to this on p. 157.

In March, 1890, the opening services were held, members of other missions being present and taking acceptable part. Then followed the struggle usual in those days. Crowds of sightseers attended the services, curious about the foreigner, and specially anxious to catch sight of the ladies. There was no idea of an orderly meeting, or attentive listening to the preacher; men stood in clusters round the door, or hustled in and out according to their own sweet will, occasionally leaving *en masse* in the midst of the sermon, on hearing the noise of theatrical performances commencing in the God of Thunder temple close by.

During the week the dispensary was opened, and an effort was made, with marked success as time went on, to win the confidence of the people, by kindly attention to their bodily ailments. Those who thus came were enlightened as to the object for which the missionary was amongst them, and many heard the Gospel message for the first time.

In the autumn of 1890 the missionaries felt so short-handed that they cabled to England asking if help could not be sent, and received the encouraging reply that Frederic S. Deane was just starting to join them. After giving some time to the language, he removed to the Nine Wells house on the Ta Liang Tsz (Great Ridge Street), and commenced there in 1892, the Boys' School, which has ever since had a prominent place in the work of the mission. That winter three more workers were added to the little band. Leonard Wigham joined F. S. Deane at the young men's house, while Alice M. Beck and Margaret Southall went to the other mission house. On these premises Caroline N. Southall had already started the Girls' School, which has also remained ever since an important branch of the work.

Thus the mission was planted, and the first years were marked by much toil and little apparent result. It was in fact a time of ploughing the ground, which was hard and full of stones, and only in looking back from the changed aspect of the present can the signs of progress be marked. Gradually the meetings became more settled. Men were recognised as repeating their visits and giving more attention to the preaching. The women were encouraged to keep their pipes in their hands, and to wait until the meeting was over for their smoke ; and the little school girls were taught to avoid spitting on the floor or talking to one another during service. At last there came a happy day for the missionary, who had long been striving to prepare the way of the Lord, when two men walked into his study with their arms full of idols which they desired to renounce, confessing their belief in the one True God, and Jesus Christ whom He has sent to be the Saviour of the world. One of these men still remains in more or less bondage to his opium pipe, from which he has made many attempts to be freed. An intelligent man, he understands the Gospel story but not its power and is still only classed as an inquirer. The other after long probation was received as a Church member, eventually becoming an evangelist, until his death in 1900, during the enforced absence of the missionaries.

Two other men of those early days deserve mention, both of whom accompanied the missionaries from Hanchung when they settled in Sz-Chwan. Chang first heard the gospel from Miss Elizabeth Hanbury, who spent much time and patience in instructing him. He still remains a member of the Church in Chungking, and has proved a faithful servant for many years. The other, Li, had been a butcher, but became a servant in the missionary's house. He learnt dispensing, and worked well, keeping his dispensary clean and tidy, and working in the house between whiles. He also did some able preaching in the street chapel, and seemed likely to be a valuable helper, but was suddenly cut off with fever, and is buried in the little Christian cemetery outside the city. These two men were the first native members added to our number.

Beside the anti-foreign feeling then prevalent throughout the province other influences proved marked hindrances to the work. Riots and rumours of expected riots often kept the missionaries on the *qui vive*, ready to leave should occasion arise. Clothing, when taken off at night, was put in an easy position for hurried dressing, and little pieces of silver were carried on the person, in case there was need to pay chair-bearers to carry the missionary to a place of safety. One little girl, the daughter of a fellow-missionary in the city, was found one day with her pocket stuffed full of handkerchiefs. When asked why she had taken so many, the child replied, "I thought they would be handy if we had to run again to the Yamen for safety." This gives a little idea of one side of missionary life in the interior in those early days, which it may not be out of place to recall when we consider the vast changes sweeping over the country at the present time.

In those days the missionary could not go from one city to another without official escort, and the daily official enquiry, as to when he would "move on," if he seemed inclined to make some tarriance. No wonder that one of them, on a long itinerating journey, weary of such constant attention from the officials, wrote home saying, "I feel like the little London shoe-black who replied to the policeman's 'move on' with the question, 'But, please Sir, where am I to move to?'" Children were taught to flee from the foreigner, when he passed by, as if he were a dangerous kidnapper. This was an accusation often brought against him, and men would carefully draw their queue before the nose to avoid the unpleasant odour of the poor foreigner, who was made in any and every way to realise that he was indeed, not only a pilgrim and a stranger in the land, but a very unwelcome one into the bargain.

As the year 1893 drew on, and the work, in spite of many discouragements and hindrances, was becoming more established, the number of our mission band was increased to ten by the arrival of Mira L. Cumber and Isaac Mason. It was felt that the time had come to procure permanent premises in Chungking. Accordingly two compounds were purchased, within a few minutes' walk of each other. One was in the Ts'ang P'ing Kai (Street of the Celestial Plain). This was the central one and a good dwelling house, a meeting-house to seat some three hundred persons, class rooms, and a dispensary, were erected on it. In the Ch'ao Yang Kai (Street turned towards the Sun), another house was built, and, adjoining it, a girls' school room and preaching hall. Many were the prejudices of the people which had to be respected. One site selected was considered too near the top of the hill, where a sacred temple forbade the foreigner's presence; and a less desirable one had to be bought instead.

THE SANATORIUM, OR "COUNTRY-HOUSE," JUST OUTSIDE CHUNGKING.

The garden-wall had to be built irregularly round the above, as shown on the left of the picture, to avoid the graves of the Chinese, of which there are a large number on every side.

In March 1894, these houses were occupied, and the new meeting-house opened.* The attendance at the regular services increased, while the behaviour of the audiences much improved, showing that the more settled meetings were appreciated.

Church meetings and membership were established, the latter being granted in response to the written application of the candidate, which was dealt with according to Friends' mode of procedure at home. In addition, a public confession of faith in the Lord Jesus, and of a desire to follow Him had to be made.

Thus the work took root, and in those years when life in the interior was often disturbed, there were many tokens of the

* See illustration of interior of Meeting-house, on p. 155.

wisdom of having a good centre in this busy city. Soon after our first missionaries settled there, it had become an open port, and the right to reside there was, therefore, settled by treaty.

The stifling atmosphere of the crowded city was a strain on the health of the missionaries, especially during the great heat of summer when the thermometer registers 90° or 100° Fahrenheit in the shade. The first property actually purchased in China was a small plot of ground about two miles outside Chungking, situated in the midst of thousands of graves. There a small sanatorium was erected, and this "country house" proved of immense value to our missionaries, and those of other missions, during the next few years, when the prejudice of the people made the beautiful hills on the South side of the river forbidden ground for the foreigner. We were indebted for this resort, largely, to the liberality and sympathy of the late William L. and Ellen Barclay, who followed the development of the Mission with keen interest.

And yet one other note of grateful remembrance must be given, or this record of the past will be incomplete. In the winter of 1892, Isaac Sharp accomplished the long and dangerous journey up the river Yang Tse to pay a visit in gospel love to our little band of workers. Many looked on his journey doubtfully, but, not only was the visit a refreshment and help to our own workers, it was the means of blessing to many in other missions also. The natives, with their reverence for old age, were greatly impressed by the fact of one, over eighty years of age, venturing to travel so far on such an errand, and it has had a lasting influence on not a few of them.

CHAPTER XVII.

FRIENDS' MISSION, CHUNGKING, 1894-1904.

WITH the erection in 1893-4, of the commodious houses, and the mission premises adjoining them, a second stage of the work may be said to have been entered upon.

The Girls' School, which was commenced and carried on for two years by C. N. Southall in the rented native premises, had given much encouragement, and the new quarters in the Ch'ao Yang Kai (Street turned towards the Sun) increased its usefulness and attendance. Here for several years Alice M. Beck (now Deane) laboured assiduously among the girls, making many a young life brighter and more hopeful through her own cheerfulness and helpful influence. Though few of the girls are with us now, most of them having married heathen husbands, not a few families and homes are brighter to-day in consequence of her teaching in our Girls' School. One of the very earliest scholars became a pupil teacher, and has been for years an assistant in the School; she has also become a Church member.

On the same compound as the Girls' School is a small street-preaching hall. This opens on to the busy thoroughfare known as the "Great Ridge," which practically divides the city into two parts, the upper and lower city. Here, as well as in the Meeting-house, a short distance off, in the Ts'ang P'ing Kai (Street of the Celestial Plain), large audiences attended the preaching of the Gospel. Many who came to these services were only passing through the city, and carried news of what they heard to towns and villages in distant parts of the country.

The seed thus sown is now bearing rich fruit in an unexpected way, in the expressed desire of hundreds and thousands, throughout the length and breadth of the province, to learn more of what the missionary has come to teach. F. S. Deane took a keen interest in this part of the work, not only in the preaching in the two halls, but also in the open air, in various spaces—here and there—in the city. He also frequently visited the military camp near by, making friends with the soldiers stationed there, and bringing them to some of the meetings. After only a comparatively short time in the country, I. Mason took an active part in this evangelistic work, accompanying F. S. Deane also on itinerating tours.

The work amongst women was not at first of an encouraging character. During the early years, C. N. Southall (now Wigham) was indefatigable in the attention she gave to the crowds of women who came to the meetings, and also to two or three whom she taught more regularly. The latter all afterwards became Church members. This work was also greatly furthered by her sister (now Margaret Vardon), as well as by A. M. Deane, each doing a large amount of house-to-house visitation, at a time when it was not as easy for a lady to walk about the streets of Chungking as it now is. Women have always come readily to the various meetings and classes, though the number who have become Church members is not large; but we believe that the good work accomplished during this period, 1893-6, has had its part in the wonderful leavening process which has been going on during the past two decades in the people of China. This leavening effect cannot be shown in statistics, nor tabulated as so much work done; but, in the long run, it is in this direction that the results of missionary labour must be looked for and the real progress of missions seen. The missionary does not perhaps see direct fruit from much of his toil and prayer, but with great joy he witnesses, as some of us have done, the change that is coming over the Chinese peoples, largely through the influences of Christian Missions.

The Boys' School, which we have already said was commenced in 1892, was situated on the "Great Ridge," in native premises, a short distance from the Girls' School. It continued to grow in numbers and usefulness under the care of F. S. Deane and, since 1893, under Leonard Wigham, who has had charge of it continuously, except when on furlough in 1897, and again in 1904.

In 1895, it was felt necessary to provide more suitable and

A VIEW FROM CHUNGKING.

commodious accommodation for the large number of boys who attended, and a good compound was purchased in the Tu Yu Kai (Street of the posting station on the road to the Capital), only four or five minutes' walk from the meeting-house. Here a residence and school were erected. This school, like the one for girls, was, at first, what is called in China a "I Hsio" or Charity School, the scholars being of the poorer class, and receiving their education free. The School has developed, provision has been made for Boarders, and fees are now charged.

In these schools a considerable portion of time is necessarily given by the children to acquiring a knowledge of their own language, and so Chinese teachers are engaged to teach the Chinese classics ; they also teach the children the characters of the Christian books, portions of the Scriptures, Bible history, etc., used in the School. The missionary gives the Christian instruction, having Scripture reading and prayer with the children daily, and also lessons in western subjects, arithmetic, geography, physiology, etc. Until recently, the latter did not form any part of an ordinary Chinaman's education. Here again we are seeing the result of the missionary's work in the great change which has taken place throughout the Empire in regard to education. He first taught these branches of learning in his school; the Chinese have appreciated their usefulness, and now call for reform in the education of the children. This was brought very prominently before us in Chungking, by the Reform Edicts of the Emperor in 1898, when hundreds of students of all ages from twelve to fifty came to us to be taught arithmetic and geography, with the English language added as an extra. We endeavoured to meet this desire as best we could until the *coup d'etat*, when the Empress Dowager took over again the reins of government.

In 1896, Edward B. Vardon, formerly of the C.M.S., was married to Margaret Southall, and joined the staff of F.F.M.A. workers in Chungking, taking charge of the Boys' School on L. Wigham's return to England on furlough, in the beginning of 1897.

In the same year, Isaac and Esther L. Mason, the latter having joined the mission in 1894, were able to take up residence in the T'ung Ch'wan prefecture, thus obtaining a footing in the district in which we had for many years been looking to work. The story of their labours, and the progress of the mission in that district, is told in the next chapter.

The mission staff, in Chungking, was reduced in numbers by the return to England, in 1897, of F. S. and A. M. Deane; owing to the serious illness of the latter. The work in the Girls' School was then taken up by Mira L. Cumber, whose time, for two years, had been occupied with classes for women, and dispensary work.

THE SCHOOL FOR MISSIONARIES' CHILDREN.
Erected on the Hills, on the South of river Yang Tse, opposite Chungking.
Opened in March, 1898.

During the hard uphill work of 1895, when riots in the capital and rumours of trouble throughout the province made the people afraid to have anything to do with the foreigner, it had been considered unwise to have open air preaching for long periods at a time, and dispensary patients, men and women, decreased by half the numbers. The missionaries lived for weeks together in constant fear of an outbreak. The people were unreceptive, scholars who had passed through the schools ceased to have anything to do with us, but the workers persevered, amid much discouragement, filled with the assurance that the time would come when there would be a mighty turning to God. They still looked hopefully forward to brighter days when the patient seed-sowing should bring forth an abundant harvest.

In 1896-7 there was a period of steadier and less interrupted work, but in 1898 the whole of the province again suffered, owing to serious troubles between the Roman Catholics and the Chinese in the neighbourhood of Ta Choo Hsien. There a petty rebellion occurred, raised by a coal miner named Yu Man Tsz, who with his followers held a Roman Catholic priest in captivity for months, persecuting and killing numbers of the Christians. The unsettlement went so far as to threaten that all the missionaries might have to flee,—many had boats ready at the river-side, and lived on them for some weeks, until things quieted down again. In this year A. Warburton Davidson joined the mission staff.

In the beginning of 1897 an estate was purchased by the mission, on the hills south of Chungking, for the erection of a school for foreign children; for the cost of which over seven hundred pounds had been raised by special subscription in England. A large and substantial house was built, which was publicly opened by the British Consul, in March, 1898, and the school established there has been greatly valued by the missionaries of the different societies working in the Province. Elsie M. Hunt, who came out to China in 1897, became the teacher, and has devoted herself to the interests of the school ever since.

But interruptions were not yet at an end, and in 1900 came the worst one, in the terrible crisis in the North, which led the British Government, through its Consul at Chungking, to insist on all British subjects leaving the West. This took almost the nature of a "flight." Very reluctantly they had to leave the work and the natives, when it seemed to them that their presence was specially needed. They were followed by the ss. *Pioneer*, with the British Consul on board, which stopped to take on some who had started in native boats, thus increasing the number of refugees on the little steamer to something like ninety, and down the rapids they rushed, at high-water too, arriving at Ichang in safety the next day.

THE HILL SCHOOL CHILDREN AT DRILL.
Five children of Friend Missionaries have been at School here: R. Huntley Davidson, Wilfred S. and Mabel Wigham, M. Irene Mason, and B. Ellwood Jackson.

It was fully eight months before any of our own missionaries were back again in Chungking. An attempt was made by two of them to return two or three months earlier, taking passage on the ss. *Sui Hsiang*, on her maiden voyage. Thus they hoped to reach the West without the tedious journey by native junk, and were on the vessel, in company with some twenty foreigners, when she struck a fatal rock at the first rapid of any importance.*
The steamer sank entirely out of sight in a very short time. The missionaries' lives were saved by some native lifeboats, which, stationed at dangerous places on the river, hastened to

* See illustration on p. 23.

their rescue; but all their goods went down with the vessel. They had to replace clothing, books, etc., lost in the wreck, and begin the long, tedious journey in the old way; and so spring was well on before they again entered Chungking.

On their return they found that, not only had the natives continued to hold the meetings, and to assemble regularly for prayer and exhortation, but a change, vast and unexpected, had come over the whole of the province. First in one direction, then in another, and in due time in our own district between Chungking and T'ung Ch'wan, inquirers and listeners were appearing in hundreds, asking for preaching halls to be opened, or even themselves offering to provide the halls if only preachers could be sent! The missionaries were almost staggered at what they saw and heard, yet could only accept the fact,—the door was open wide, in a manner and to an extent they had never known before. So, though very suspicious of ulterior motives, they could but step forward and grasp the opportunities to the best of their ability.

A CHINESE LIFEBOAT.
Provided by the Chinese to accompany house-boats up-river beyond the more dangerous rapids.

One Sunday evening about this time three well-dressed men attended service in Chungking, and, after sitting through the sermon, apparently listening with earnest attention, they appealed to the missionary to go to their city and open a

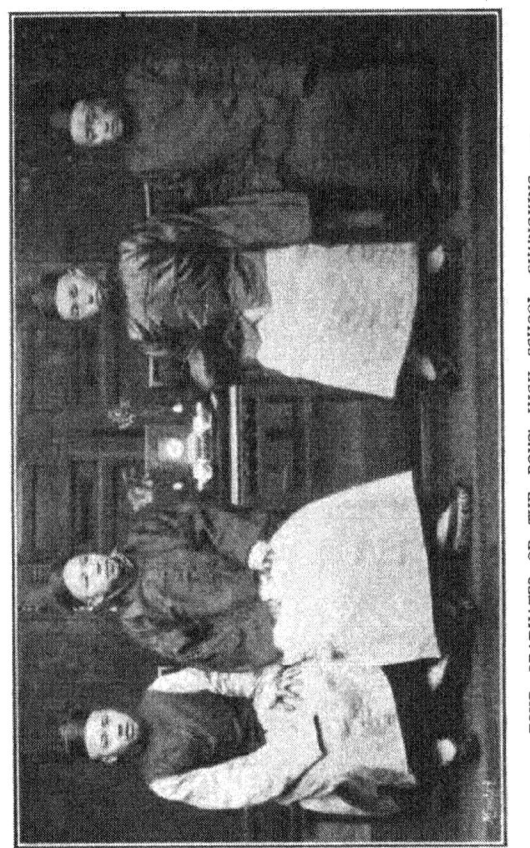

FOUR GRADUATES OF THE BOYS' HIGH SCHOOL, CHUNGKING, 1904.
All are Christians and two of them are Members of our Society.

preaching hall. They offered liberal terms (*too* liberal he feared to be genuine) but they came from T'ung Liang, a city he and others in the mission had already visited. It was a two days' journey (about 60 miles) distant from Chungking, with a population of about 20,000. T'ung Liang, and its near neighbour Ta Choo, were cities that had been the stronghold of the rebel Yu Man Tsz, and had therefore been considered difficult ground. Two of our missionaries, who were about to visit other parts of our district, determined to go round by T'ung Liang and accepted the invitation thrust upon them. With this step the work in all that district practically commenced, and T'ung Liang now forms the centre for important outstation work. In 1904 Benjamin H. and Florence E. Jackson took up their residence there so as to be on the spot for the care of this work.

It was soon found that these men had the " ulterior " motives feared. The inn keeper, who received the missionaries with such effusive welcome, turned out to be the very man who had caused the native Roman Catholic priest to be killed in the Yu Man Tsz riots; and at least one of the men, who pleaded to have the Gospel preached in their city, was found to be a thief and a liar! One of the others died soon after, but the third still remains a listener at the meetings. Yet they opened the door in the providence of God and, if they have not themselves been willing to come in, they have not hindered others from hearing and receiving the Gospel invitation. Our last message from the city of T'ung Liang is one of hope and encouragement.

During the past four years, the work, in every department, has continued to grow, and the number of missionaries has also increased. There are now in all twenty-four workers in the Friends' mission, of whom ten are men and fourteen women.

The Boys' School in the Tu Yu Kai became too small for our requirements and, after renting additional premises for a time, better accommodation had to be found. A fine New School Building and Master's Residence have been erected on the hills opposite Chungking, on the south side of the river Yang Tse. It is hoped that, under these new conditions, the Boarding School will be even more effective than in the past.*

Another preaching hall has recently been opened in a busy thoroughfare in Chungking, called the White Elephant Street, making the third one regularly in use; while in two villages outside the city a deeply interesting work has sprung up amongst people largely employed in the match factories.

INTERIOR OF MATCH FACTORY AT T'A CHI KEO.
In this factory, near Chungking, numbers of little boys and girls are employed. It was recently burnt to the ground, the consequent want of employment causing much distress.

The number of Church members has grown slowly, but steadily, for it was felt from the first that great care should be exercised in receiving persons into Church fellowship. There are several hundred adherents who have manifested a sincere interest in the Truth, and we look to them to form in days to come a strong healthy Church. Several of those who have joined us in membership have proved themselves earnest workers, and are now doing good service in the cause of Christ.

* The School Buildings were formally opened on June 10th, 1905. For illustrations, see frontispiece, and also p. 132.

CHAPTER XVIII.

WORK OF THE LAST DECADE.

NORTHERN DISTRICT.

IN May, 1894, in consequence of an urgent call to the relief of an aged wealthy man, who had met with an accident, R. J. Davidson and I. Mason travelled to Yang Tao Ch'i in the T'ung Ch'wan prefecture. This town is six days' journey from Chungking, and on their arrival it was found that the patient was dead and buried. Great curiosity and interest had been raised in the town, however, and a large number of people came to R. J. Davidson for medicine. A wish being expressed that a dispensary might be opened there, part of an inn was rented for that purpose. An introduction was gained to the district magistrate, who gratefully accepted treatment for paralysis, and from that time forward became a true friend of our missionaries.

The visit above referred to was a very brief one, but it had far-reaching effects in that it turned the thoughts of our mission once again to T'ung Ch'wan, and was the beginning of a work which has continued to increase.

Isaac Mason tells the story of subsequent growth as follows:

"In the autumn of 1894 I returned alone to Yang Tao Ch'i, and spent several weeks there, living at an inn, dispensing medicines, and preaching daily. Many subsequent visits were paid from Chungking, and these extended to the cities of T'ai Ho Chen and Se Hung Hsien. At the former place we found a man who had learned something of the Gospel at a China Inland Mission station. He had gathered a few people, and with these I held many meetings in dirty little rooms at the inns where I stayed. The man referred to proved untrustworthy, and has since run a chequered career which has left him in prison, and all of the original band at T'ai Ho have disappeared. Yet the work in that city has been continued for nine years, and is to-day

NEW SCHOOLROOM OF THE GIRLS' BOARDING SCHOOL, T'UNG CH'WAN.

an important branch of the T'ung Ch'wan work. First we rented a small place outside the city, and it was from this point that my wife and I really entered upon the work in what is now called the Northern District, first by visits, and afterwards by residence at Se Hung. In 1896 we felt justified in attempting residence at T'ai Ho, a busy, walled city, with much river traffic, six days' journey from Chungking (about 187 miles) on a main road to Chentu. It has the disadvantage of having no responsible official in residence, and the people are somewhat turbulent at times.

"In spite of continued efforts we could not find a house, so at last we went to Se Hung, fourteen miles distant, and there found accommodation. Now note God's goodness in guiding us in ways which were contrary to our wishes. Since we attempted to find a house at T'ai Ho Chen, the Roman Catholic premises have *twice* been torn down by rioters, and floods have *twice* invaded the city. Had we resided there, it is almost certain our house would have suffered the fate of the Romanist premises, even though we might have escaped damage by the floods. I am often reminded of Isaac Sharp's remark that 'Those who mark the hand of Providence, will never lack a Providence to mark.'

"After repairs to our rented premises at Se Hung, we went to live there early in 1897. For thirteen days our boat rode bravely up the river from Chungking but, on the fourteenth, when nearing our new home, we were wrecked in a rapid and, after an exciting experience, we spent the night on the cobbles with our damaged goods strewn around us. The morning brought but little comfort, as with it came rain, so we left our goods with our faithful servants, and pushed on to our destination, where we arrived hungry and tired, and in a 'grubby' condition generally. We had not a single friend to meet us, and nothing but bare rooms and native fare until our goods turned up.

"Yet this dispiriting entry was the commencement of three happy and not altogether unsuccessful years at Se Hung. By the time we were ready to commence work, we were better known, and were even treated to a band of music (!) along with scrolls and crackers, and had about 200 guests, from the district magistrate down to our poor neighbours.

"The first year we pegged away, preaching and dispensing daily, and also conducting religious services, and, while thousands heard, at the end of the year we had not a single professed 'inquirer'. In our second year we added a school, and so completed the trio of the usual branches of our work, viz.: evangelistic, educational and medical. The school, besides bringing under our influence the jolly little lads, also helped us to win a way to the adults. In no country is the teacher and the scholar held in greater respect than in China. As an attempt to reach scholars of more mature years, we once spent a whole night at the doors of the county examination hall, distributing Gospels and tracts to the hundreds of students as they came away from their essays. During that year we were often threatened by the Yu Man Tsz rebels, who were pledged to kill or drive out of the country all foreigners, and when at last the magistrate told us he could not guarantee further protection, and begged us to withdraw for a time, we reluctantly did so. It transpired afterwards that our boat was followed for some distance by those who thought to do us mischief, but our Father's protecting arms were round about us, and we escaped in safety. At that time the rebels had a French priest in captivity, held at ransom. They afterwards rioted at T'ai Ho Chen, but did not visit Se Hung.

"It was during that year of trial that we enrolled several inquirers, some of whom are members to-day. The school had a good attendance and our meetings were fairly well attended also. A mothers' meeting, conducted by my wife, was quite a feature of the work. Fifty or sixty women would come together weekly, and sit for hours talking with my wife who had no Christian woman helper at that time; then they would listen attentively while I gave an address, for which they invariably expressed their thanks. Then a cool-off in the shade of the garden, with sips of tea, or the musical box and picture books would fill up till dusk. It is not easy to measure the results of such work, but there can be no doubt that the seeds sown have borne, and will yet bear fruit.

"It was about this time also that I first visited Chin Fu Wan, twenty miles distant from Se Hung, at the request of people residing there. In those days it was hard to gain an entrance in country towns. We were mostly regarded with a kind of superstitious awe, and the general opinion seemed to be that it was best to leave us severely alone. To meet therefore with a dozen

THE MEETING HOUSE AT T'UNG CH'WAN.

men, ignorant of what the Gospel is, and to whom the name of Christ conveyed no meaning, but who evidently desired to learn was very encouraging; and, when their pipes were reverently laid aside, and attempts were made to follow the hymn or prayer, or the simple yet searching questions of a Christian catechism, one felt it was good to be there, and well worth the day's journey to meet with them. For two years we visited, and held meetings at an inn, and then we secured premises, and this outstation has steadily held its place, though not long ago most of the houses of our adherents were destroyed by 'Boxers.'

"In our third year we began work at Kwan Yin Koa, and also opened a day school in the city of T'ung Ch'wan. It was a cause for rejoicing to have actually gained a footing in the city, after R. J. Davidson's experiences long before. An attempt was made to annoy us, and the magistrate acted rudely, for which he afterwards apologised, and became a friend who insisted on my accepting hospitality as his guest during a later visit. He also gave a donation of about £13 to the mission.

"In 1899, A. W. Davidson came to reside at Se Hung and, after a few months' study, he attempted a visit to neighbouring markets, at one of which, named Yu Lung Chen, he was attacked and severely beaten. He was selling books in a temple yard when the horse-play began, and on retiring to his inn a crowd followed. He then made haste out of the town, but was pursued, and not knowing the way, was overtaken; so excited was the mob that but for God's restraining hand he might have been killed there. In consequence of his injuries we took him to Chungking, and later on he returned home for rest.

"We were now appointed to live at T'ung Ch'wan, and took up residence there early in 1900, not without regrets at leaving the pretty little city of Se Hung, and the friends there. That station has since been in charge of a native helper.

"There was not much difficulty in entering upon work at T'ung Ch'wan. The officials visited us freely, and the people came around as we opened a dispensary and held meetings for worship in a very dilapidated chapel made out of unused small rooms. Our friends rallied from a distance to give us a good start-off, some of them travelling fifty miles each way, and bringing with them a silken banner, to express their good wishes. One old woman hobbled on her little feet over thirty miles in her anxiety to be present. Admirable determination and perseverance crop up at times in the Chinese character, especially in those converted.

"Just as the work appeared to be taking root, the 'Boxer' outbreak occurred in the North, and an urgent message from Chungking advised us to leave at once. Things seemed so quiet locally that at first we decided to stay on, but a recall from our Consul following, we had reluctantly to hasten away. Notwithstanding the surface quietness, the terrible edict had already gone forth that all foreigners were to be exterminated. Hundreds of us in the interior were saved as by a miracle, by the action of a few brave Chinese ministers who dared to ignore the wicked command, and two of whom were reported to have deliberately altered the message into one of protection, and suffered death for their noble action.

"It was in this hour of peril and trying separation that we realised how much we loved the people and were beloved by them. We parted amidst honest tears of sorrow, and with feelings too sacred for words, and we blessed God as we felt that the work of the past had been worth while, and He had undoubtedly been working in our midst.

"It may be mentioned here that, though the province of Sz-Chwan was evacuated by missionaries, the 'Boxer' outbreak did not extend so far, and the natives left in charge were generally found faithful in keeping the work together until the missionaries were able to return. Including a visit to England, we were absent from T'ung Ch'wan about eighteen months.

"For part of that time R. J. Davidson had given some oversight by visits from Chungking, and at one period there seemed to be a considerable movement towards Christianity, but it was only a passing wave, and was too largely mixed up with selfish interest to produce much lasting result. One good result, however, was the opening of work in Yen T'ing Hsien, by a native, without any help or influence directly from a missionary.

"When R. J. Davidson paid a visit to that city he found regular meetings for preaching and worship being conducted, and evidence of real conversion, at least in the owner of the house, K'ang Sao Fu, a man who is now one of our trusty helpers.

"In the spring of 1902, we were reinforced by the arrival of Mira L. Cumber and Dr. Lucy E. Harris, the latter being our first qualified medical missionary in China. They took up residence near our house, and the dispensary was transferred to their premises. A Girls' School was commenced, and work amongst women was extended. Both departments of work grew and prospered, especially the Girls' School. Better premises became needful, and a Ladies' Residence, a Women's Hospital and Girls' Boarding School have been erected.*

"Unfortunately we were much hindered during 1902 by the local 'Boxer' rising, which for several months was a grave danger to our lives. Five of our out-stations were attacked, and two of them completely destroyed; one of our adherents was killed, and many lost their homes and possessions. We were brought into the fellowship of their sufferings, as stragglers—men and women—found their way to us, footsore and weary, having been hounded about for days and weeks, turned out and reviled by their nearest relatives and friends on account of their faith.

"Our city became so surrounded that we could not have left it if we had wished, and at last a night attack was made, when we heard the unearthly yells of the 'Boxers' threatening destruction to us, and we saw the cannon belching out fire as the attack was repulsed by the soldiers and citizens. For months these latter kept guard every night on the walls.

"Our work came almost to a standstill, as people feared to

* The Girls' Boarding School was opened in February, and the Women's Hospital in July, 1905.

be identified with us; but the refugees from the country stations kept us busy, and we had some inspiring meetings during those times of persecution. There was much bloodshed and wanton destruction all around, yet we were kept in safety, and were conscious of the protecting arm of our Heavenly Father around us. In the midst of it all, while loud were the threats of destruction, we kept steadily at work building larger premises, and when the rebellion was crushed, and the leaders were being executed or cast into prison, we exchanged our cramped little chapel for one four times as large, which we sometimes had quite full of people.* In the country too we made extensions after the persecution, and while we had regretfully to close up Kwan Yin Koa, and lost a few loosely-attached adherents, we took larger premises at no less than five of our out-stations.

"Before the outbreak a visit had been paid to P'ung Ch'i Hsien, and a work opened there, so that we had glimmerings of light in all the walled cities of our district. From P'ung Ch'i we extended to Hsiao T'ung Ch'ang and Yü Ch'i K'ou,—two market towns in the neighbourhood, where the work seems promising at present. Our great need is for faithful native helpers to take charge of the country work, and build up the Church with oversight from the missionary. Only in this way can we ever expect to reach and influence the masses around us.

"With the object of trying to meet this need, we have at times taken a few young men into residence, instructed them more fully, and given them practical training as helpers. This is a branch which is likely to be more developed amongst us.

"No account of the work in and around T'ung Ch'wan would be complete without a hearty word of appreciation respecting the native helpers who have shared the toil with us, and enabled us to undertake much more than we should ever have done without them. While not men of marked ability, some of them have shown a devotion and faithfulness which has been very gratifying. Foremost stands Mei Chi Hsiu, who has been with me from the

* See illustration on p. 195.

THE VISIT OF THE DEPUTATION TO TUNG CH'WAN, 1904.

In view of the above visit the Native Christians gathered at Tung Ch'wan from all the nearest out-stations for special meetings on two days (January 31st and February 1st). The company was photographed outside the Meeting House, before leaving. The three Members of the Deputation, together with Isaac Mason and Edward B. Vardon, may be seen on the extreme right; Dr. Lucy Harris on the extreme left; and, nearer the centre, Esther L. Mason and Mira L. Cumber.

beginning, first as language teacher, and then as general helper. He applied for membership during our first journey together, and has for years been a worthy member of the Society of Friends. When riots have driven us away, he has held the fort, and has won a respected name in the locality. Being the son of a magistrate, he gains ready acceptance with all classes, and is withal a humble man. His son Mei Ch'wan San came with us as a boy of twelve, and has developed into a useful young man who can give a very thoughtful address, and can be relied upon for honest and good work in visiting the out-stations. Four or five more who have been gleaned from this station are now helping in various branches, and their stories may be told at some future time. May the number of such greatly increase!

"Such is the general survey of the work during the last decade, until the time of the visit of the Deputation from the F.F.M.A., consisting of the Secretary, (Dr. William Wilson,) Albert J. Crosfield, and Marshall N. Fox, who visited China in 1903-4 with the object, in a time of unparalleled opportunity, of extending Friends' Mission there. The work might now be classed under heads, as follows :—

"*Evangelistic.*—From entering upon virgin soil, we have seen spring up a small yet promising

DEPUTATION TRAVELLING FROM CHUNGKING TO CHENTU.
The above is typical of this and other main roads in China.

Monthly Meeting of sixteen members and over 300 adherents in various stages of advancement. Religious meetings have been established in five cities and as many towns, and at most of these there is frequent preaching of the Gospel to passers-by. In T'ung Ch'wan city, besides regular preaching at the street chapel, a bookstall has been opened for the sale of Scriptures and tracts and wholesome literature generally. A colporteur has regularly worked our district, and by various agencies at least 2,000 Testaments have been circulated, besides many thousands of Gospel portions and tracts.

"Regular classes for instruction are held for both men and women, and visits are paid to homes, especially in the suburbs of T'ung Ch'wan, by Mira L. Cumber. A Society of Christian Endeavour has been established for some months. A few young men have been in training for evangelistic work, and Esther L. Mason and Mira L. Cumber have each had one or two women under special instruction as prospective helpers.

"Statistics do not fully represent the extent of Christian influence. God, who has opened the doors before us, and who has supplied our every need, and again manifested His power through imperfect instrumentalities, is doubtless working still in ways and places that we know not of.

"*Educational.*—A beginning was made in 1898 at Se Hung with about forty boys ; many of them were bright little fellows who will possibly retain all through life pleasant impressions of those days,—especially the times out of school, when we had our games in the garden and got very near to one another. Perhaps deeper lessons will 'stick' better because of those romps ! At any rate the missionary is not feared as a child-eater by those lads.

"At T'ung Ch'wan the Boys' School was the first branch of our work, as it was begun before we went to reside there, and one pleasant recollection of our entry into that city is of a string of merry lads coming to meet us with crackers, and then taking up procession with us through the streets. During the evacuation of 1900 the local teacher left from fear, and numbers dropped, but Mr. Mei kept the school open, and it is now in good premises and consists of nearly fifty scholars. Some of these are sons of country Christians whom we have taken as boarders. Besides more or less of the Chinese classics, our scholars always study the Scriptures, and memorise many portions. Worship is conducted every day, and Sunday attendance at meetings is

BOYS' SCHOOL BUILDING. TUNG CH'WAN.

expected. Text books on the lines of Western education are used, and geography and arithmetic, physiology and drilling have all been taught. A few of the older boys have learnt a little English from Esther L. Mason, and some of the girls from Mira L. Cumber.

"The Girls' School was commenced in 1902 by Mira L. Cumber. It had only about eight scholars the first year, but the following year there were thirty, and now nearly double that number, including boarders. There has recently been a movement among them in the direction of unbinding feet. They study much the same subjects as the boys, and many of them are bright and intelligent.

"The Se Hung Boys' School was discontinued for some time, but is now in full swing again with thirty scholars, and so also is the one at T'ai Ho Chen with about the same number.

"Thus about 170 scholars are under Christian instruction and influence and, as they take home their books and no doubt

GIRLS AT DRILL.
Pupils in the Boarding School at T'ung Ch'wan.

talk of what they hear and see, there is surely a leavening influence carried into many families unknown to us.

"*Medical.*—The medical work gained our first entry into the district, and it has always been a valuable adjunct to the other branches. With our travelling medicine boxes and rough and ready means, large numbers of patients were attended to in the early days, and when we left Yang Tao Ch'i and settled at Se Hung, the Dispensary was part of our daily work.

"I would add my testimony to the many already given as to the value of such work judiciously carried on. Prejudices have been broken down and confidence won, while the relief of suffering has often called forth real gratitude. Surely such efforts are ever a 'preparation of the Gospel of peace.' 'There is no speech nor language' where the voice of kind actions is not understood and appreciated.

"At T'ung Ch'wan we opened a dispensary and, before the evacuation and our furlough, we had many patients daily—as many women as men coming without any apparent hesitation. One does not hear of Chinese women doctors, so female sufferers perforce go to men for treatment, and, this being the natural order, I have never found difficulty in general dispensary practice. But better things were in store, and in 1902 Dr. Lucy E. Harris took charge of the medical work, and I was glad to let my 'quackery' give place to trained skill. Dr. Harris has seen a large number of patients, chiefly women, but including many men and boys. She has a small hospital for in-patients, with the prospect of a useful future."

The latest developments in Friends' Northern District are resultant on the visit of the F.F.M.A. Deputation, involving the opening of two new centres, as well as the erection of enlarged premises at T'ung Ch'wan. Dr. W. Henry and Laura A. Davidson have settled in this last-named city, and it is expected that the further development of the medical branch will prove a great help to the building up of the general work.

One of the new centres is Chentu, the capital of the province. Mission work has been carried on there for over twenty years by other societies, but it is such a large city that there is ample room for the F.F.M.A. to share in the labour. Robert J. and Mary J. Davidson have opened the work for Friends there and are to be joined by Dr. Henry T. and Elizabeth J. Hodgkin. Dr. Hodgkin is already well known through his work in connection with the S.V.M.U.

The other new centre, Sui-ling Hsien, is situated between T'ung Ch'wan and Chungking. The Methodist Episcopal Mission has been established there for a few years and has done good work, amid many difficulties. Isaac and Esther L. Mason now reside there, buildings have been erected, a street-chapel opened, and a day school with thirty boys and girls established. Edward B. and Margaret Vardon have taken up work at T'ung Ch'wan. The first work of the former was the building of the new Girls' School and Women's Hospital. This Hospital for Women has since been completed and, in July, 1905, was

THE WOMEN'S HOSPITAL AT T'UNG CH'WAN.
To the left of the picture a portion of the Wall of the City may be seen.

formally opened in the presence of the officials and gentry of the City. The School was finished and occupied in February, 1905.

Ten years ago the T'ung Ch'wan area was barren, stony ground, with no missionary. Now, including Chentu, the Friends' Foreign Mission Association has twelve missionaries in this Northern District. For this we thank God; but we cannot forget the large area and the population of the field committed to us, which calls for still more labourers, and for the continued prayer and support of the Church at home.

CHAPTER XIX.

R. J. DAVIDSON'S NOTES OF VISITS TO YEN T'ING, 1901.

SATURDAY, 26th *Oct.* 1901.—I left T'ung Ch'wan this morning about 5.30, with Yuen Ta Ch'en and Li Sao San. We had a most beautiful morning to start, one of the finest I have seen for a long time, with a beautifully fresh, almost cold, breeze. The air was clear and crisp, and as we reached the hills on the farther side of the river the prospect was magnificent, the high hills far away on the other side of T'ung Ch'wan being just visible in the distance.

The first twenty "li" (a li is about one-third of a mile) is up and down hill, but afterwards the road leads through a gully between the hills and is fairly level, though not so good as the one from Chungking. As I crossed the river at T'ung Ch'wan, and wended my way towards Yen T'ing, my thoughts travelled back to thirteen or fourteen years ago, when I first entered T'ung Ch'wan by that route. I have not been along the road since, and most of it is forgotten, but here and there glimpses of landscape, a house, an inn or a turn of the road would flash back familiarly.

At forty-five "li" from Yen T'ing we were met by two inquirers from there, who had come to meet us, or rather I suppose were on their way to the Fu to ask about us, as I had not arrived at the time they had first expected. We found the people had been waiting and were somewhat disappointed at my failure to arrive at the earlier date. This had been impossible owing to my having to attend to the renting of a house, which took longer than I had hoped for. The men turned back with us, and one of them went ahead to give the news of our approach.

We had a good journey and reached the river, three " li " from Yen T'ing, about five p.m., well before dark. After crossing the river we came to a " Filial Arch," one " li " from the city, where we found thirty or forty people waiting to receive us. I bowed to them, and they said a few words of welcome, let off some crackers, and escorted me into the city. I dislike these numbers to meet one with this ceremony, but there seemed no way to avoid it. They wished me to go at once to what they called the " Li pai t'ang " (the chapel) saying that everything was prepared. I felt in some doubt as to the advisability of accepting their invitation as I did not know what my going might involve. We do not yet know the people; they have started this " Worship " on their own account to a large extent, and who the man is that takes the lead I have yet to learn. His motives and aims are as yet a mystery to me, and until I know better where I am with him, and the whole business, it seems better not to go and reside in his house, so we came to the inn where I now write these notes.

Some of the inquirers from Yu Lung Chen and the man in charge there, Fu Ch'ang Ming, came to the inn to see me. I think they did not like my being there, but they took it very well. Shortly after our arrival someone appeared with red cushions and red cloth for the chairs and inn couch. I tried to find out a little about things, and learnt that the leading spirit is a man called K'ang Sao Fu, who is a well-to-do man in the city. He appears to have a good deal of influence in the place, looks about thirty-five or forty years old, tall and rather slightly built, and gives one the idea of manliness. I understand he was in Yu Lung Chen attending the meetings, and gathered that the doctrine was good. It was too far for him to attend there, so he decided to give part of his own house, the "tao wu" (guest hall) for the holding of meetings, which I understand he conducts himself.

Through his influence large numbers have attached themselves to the cause, or " Church " as they call it. The people call themselves " chiao hwei ti hsiung " (Church brothers), but they do not seem to know much of the customs of the Christian church. After the others had gone, I inquired of Mr. Fu, the caretaker at the neighbouring out-station of Yu Lung Chen, as to Mr. K'ang's antecedents. It occurred to me to inquire if he had had

I. MASON, AND SOME CHINESE NATIVE HELPERS.
Mr. K'ang is at the extreme left of bottom row; Isaac Mason on the right.

anything to do with the great gambling trouble, when the Yen T'ing Hsien made a raid upon it last spring, as I mentioned in the notes of my last visit. Mr. Fu replied that he had, and that the magistrate had settled the business without a trial some time since; the magistrate, I am told, says that K'ang has had a severe warning. After a while I went round to the " Li pai t'ang," escorted by several inquirers who had come for me, with two men carrying lanterns going before us! I was led up a main street and round the first to the right, also a main street, and a few doors up was guided to the entrance of a large house situated between two shops. As I entered I noticed a written paper on the door with " Fu Yin Tao T'ang," *i.e.*, Gospel Hall, on it, and some writing below, which I had not time to read then. At the door I was met by several people, also two boys stood, one on each side, holding hand lamps; these led the way into the interior, where a large company was assembled as if for meeting, all in most orderly fashion. The room, a large one, was lighted with foreign lamps, and native candles in stands, and on the walls were various papers covered with writings. On one of the pillars hung a large board with a long list of names of those who profess to believe the doctrine. At the top of the room stood the altar to ancestors, which had not been taken down, but it was covered with a red satin cloth on which was the Lord's Prayer in large characters. The large room with its number of lights and crowd of quiet orderly people was a sight not to be easily forgotten. As I went in I was received by the whole company, and took my seat at the top of the room. After a little while I spoke, telling them something of our customs and of the necessity of sincerity in their search for truth.

The man Ch'en Kwan San, whose sister-in-law came to us in T'ung Ch'wan to complain of his treatment, was one of those who now received me. I spoke very plainly, and I think we had a fairly good time, they assenting with apparent sincerity to all that I said. The whole movement is a strange one, and whether for good or otherwise I cannot yet say. I am moved with various feelings, and am praying earnestly for right guidance. If this man K'ang is repentant and desires to reform, and takes this way of doing it, it may be God's way of working in this neighbourhood. If he is a rascal and is using the Christian Church and cause as a cloak to screen him from trouble, while carrying on his evil practices, then he is a great scoundrel indeed, and is leading away large numbers. He professes to be changed, and conducts worship. Large numbers come to hear him, so I am told, but I have had very little conversation with him yet.

The people here have practically formed a church of their own, but have been waiting for us to give it formal sanction.

Early this morning Li Sao San got up and went off to read what is on the paper at the door, and found a number of very good facts and instructions. A notice had also been put up to say that I was expected on the 15th, and would preach on the 16th; inquirers were to come early, and idlers and children would not be admitted.

I understand that one inquirer had been severely reprimanded for going back to his own village and using the name of the Church to the injury of his neighbours. They say that this is a thing they will not permit, and if it is done they will have nothing to do with the persons who act in such a way.

Monday, 28th October. Just after breakfast yesterday Mr. K'ang sent round a present of a duck, a fowl, some eggs, and a basin of flour. Shortly afterwards he and several other inquirers, some of the principal people here, and some from Yu Lung Chen, came to call. At first we had some general conversation, then our talk turned to the character of those who are professing an interest in the truth, and as Ch'en Kwan San was present I spoke very plainly to him and the others, and I think he had a lesson; I also told Mr. Fu to go and see about him. This led to our talking of the people in Yen T'ing, and somehow Mr. K'ang himself told of what he had been, of the gambling business, etc., and said that he had thoroughly given it up. He told us that his parents had died when he was young, and he had no one to control him, and being possessed of some little money he was led astray; but he had now seen the error of his ways. He said that he had not joined the Christians until after the gambling business was settled. His idea was simply to give over his sins, to trust in Christ, and to devote himself to preaching the Gospel. This we subsequently learned he had done pretty thoroughly during the past few months. He made a very straightforward statement of his idea of taking up with Christianity; that some year or so ago he was in Chungking where he frequently attended the Methodist Episcopal Mission street-preaching hall, near the Tao T'ai yamen. I spoke to him of the ancestral tablet in the "tao wu" where the meeting is held, and he replied that he had not worshipped it for several months, and was prepared to take it down; but that his wife and some other members of his family advised him to leave it for the present, and not to worship it, but wait until he had learned more of the truth before removing it. He said that the next time we came we should find it removed. I did not press him to take it down, feeling most strongly that any such action must be of his own free will. He seems quite prepared to take the necessary steps. I was extremely pleased to have had this statement before the morning meeting, as it throws a good deal of light on what I wrote yesterday. Yuen and Li were also much relieved by what we heard, for it gave us all the impression of evident sincerity. If all we have seen and heard is arrant hypocrisy, then it is of the most extraordinary kind.

We went to Mr. K'ang's house for meeting, and found a good company assembled, which increased after we arrived. Everything was clean and tidy, the forms properly arranged in the centre of the room, chairs and small tables at the sides and two chairs at the top for the speakers. Mr. K'ang made all arrangements, and we had a very orderly, and I think useful meeting. Those present were very attentive, and gave the impression of earnestness; not coming simply for curiosity as one so often finds is the case, but meeting to worship God and hear His truth.

After meeting I asked the inquirers to stay awhile, so that I might examine them. I commenced with Mr. K'ang, and found that he knows a good deal of the truth; and he told me of his relations and his trying to influence them. I found that he had commenced the work in the fifth moon, and had continued the meetings regularly, conducting and teaching in them himself. He has a rough register of attendance, also a clean one kept beautifully, so that one sees at a glance how often people have attended. He has also a separate list of inquirers, besides the one on the board hung up; and a book in which he enters the names of those who show most interest. His register is a copy of Mr. Fu's at Yu Lung Chen, only better kept. I was quite surprised with the order in which I found everything. He seems modest and speaks fair, as well as being polite and respectful.

The next man I saw was his cousin, a man a good deal older, who has a Chinese degree of B.A. He tells me he is of one mind with his cousin in this matter, and desires to be true and faithful. This man has been at Chentu, and knows Dr. Parry, and has heard the doctrine from him, as well as having read some for himself.

Several others, more distant relatives of Mr. K'ang, were also introduced. I interviewed between twenty and thirty, and Yuen examined between ten and twenty. Several knew very little, but two or three gave wonderfully clear answers. I was particularly pleased with three, who gave very clear statements of the truth, as well as definitely expressing their decision to be right out for Christ.

One man Cho gave one of the best testimonies I have ever heard in China from an inquirer. In any inquiry meeting at home this man would have been classed as one of the most hopeful converts, without hesitation. He stated most distinctly, as well as humbly, his own sense of sin, and that this had been brought to him most vividly by the Gospel; that he had found pardon and forgiveness through Christ's atoning death, and now his sincere desire was to follow in His footsteps. I could hardly believe my ears as this young man told me these things, with such apparent reverence, humility and contrition as I have rarely seen. What could I do but believe that God had been here working His own blessed will in a way we had not thought of. One's mind may be full of doubt and suspicion of the sincerity of such confession, owing to past experience, but I must acknowledge I was bowed in thankfulness to God for such evidence of His grace. My discernment may have been at fault, but somehow two or three of these testimonies seemed to carry conviction with them.

R. J. Davidson's Notes of Visits to Yen T'ing

I was simply filled with thankfulness, and could only pray God to carry on the work which He Himself had begun in this quiet, dead-alive, and almost lonely city among the hills in central Sz-Chwan.

Another testimony was extremely interesting; that of a man who lives one li from the city. He has devoted a large amount of time to learning the truth, knows his catechism by heart, is very much in earnest, has learned to pray morning and night and to thank God for his meals. He says he must pray before he sleeps.

It was simply extraordinary to hear these things from people who had never seen a foreigner before—at any rate had never spoken to one—and had little if any teaching but what they had obtained from Mr. K'ang and their catechisms and Testaments. Here is a nucleus of a church all ready to our hands. God give us grace and wisdom to know how to deal with this people. They have made mistakes no doubt, but on the whole I think they have done wonderfully well with the little knowledge they have. I cannot but feel deeply thankful that I have been permitted to see such work in this land.

Several came to call on me in the afternoon, and at 4.30 the local magistrate sent me word that he would like to see me in response to my request for an interview. So I went to call on him. I was anxious that there should be no misunderstanding about the relation to the work here, and, if any of these people were using the name of the Church to screen themselves from the law, I would endeavour to make things right. I found the magistrate a comparatively young man, who could speak English pretty well, a very rare accomplishment for officials in West China ! We were able to talk matters over in English and so avoid being overheard by the attendants, which in this particular case was a great advantage. He at once asked me what we meant in the Church by the term " T'ing Yu " or listener, and I explained how we used the title for those who come to hear, expressing themselves willing to learn, but whom we are not prepared to class as inquirers until we have further knowledge of them.

We then talked freely of the opening of the work here, and he told me of Mr. K'ang and his antecedents, that he was a small expectant official, and that not only had he been gambling but he had used his influence to terrorise people, and that he had not been a good man. The magistrate was quite aware of his present attitude and the Church, and said he knew we would not screen him if he ought to be punished, but he told me very distinctly that Mr. K'ang was quite changed. Since he had joined the Christians he had nothing against him whatever, and he gave every evidence of repentance. I was extremely pleased to hear this. The magistrate also expressed his pleasure at the change, and said that while we could not prove it real, we could accept what there was and wait to see how he continued. He added that for such a good work he would be the last to stand in the way, and when his people were helped to do right he was well pleased. He was extremely friendly, and invited me to a meal to-day when he said we could talk over things better. He tells me that nothing is reported in his Yamen against those who profess to be Christians, and he believes we do not wish to have lawsuits. He said the caretaker Mr. Fu at Yu Lung Chen was an honest man, but he had no talent!

In the evening I went again to the " Li pai t'ang " (the chapel) where several were already gathered; the numbers increased and we had a good meeting. I spoke for only a short time, then Li and Yuen gave testimony, the latter's text being about Paul and " not being ashamed of the Gospel of Christ." Both spoke nicely, and after singing I asked if any of the local people wished to say anything. Then Mr. K'ang got up and spoke exceedingly well. He seems to have quite the gift of a preacher, and judging from what he said I imagine the people get fairly good teaching. He spoke of the necessity of taking down the family gods and ancestral tablets, and of his wish to serve the Lord, and trusted they would all be of one mind with him.

Three or four others also spoke very nicely indeed, for the first time I should think, but really with point and earnestness.

We arranged for another meeting to-night, and conversations to-day. The day was not over then, for, after I returned to the inn, several of the inquirers called again, and the magistrate returned my call, and renewed his invitation to dinner. There was an eclipse of the moon, and tom-tomming went on for hours. After the magistrate left, some of the inquirers stayed and talked till quite late.

These people deal very strictly with any attempt to use the name of the church to injure others, and have struck off the names of one or two because they have tried to do this. The notice put up at the door of the meeting-house states, amongst other things, that the teaching of Jesus has spread to every country. "He came to save the world, and to persuade men to turn from evil and follow that which is good. All those who would be His followers must have a sincere heart, throw away the false, and follow the truth; they must not cherish covetousness, each performing his own duties in his sphere of life, so that the people and the Church may be on friendly terms. If there are those who use the name of the Church and do outside that which is evil, trusting in their power to impose on the people, it will be difficult to distinguish who is who. Now all you who are Christians and those who are outsiders, let not those who are of the people cheat the Church, and the Church is not to cheat the people, etc., etc."

YU LUNG CHEN, 30*th October*, 1901. All Monday, I was kept closely at it with callers in the inn, who came to inquire further about religious things. Two young men were very anxious to know how to use a reference Testament, one of them being the man who gave such a good testimony on Sunday. In the afternoon I went to dinner with the magistrate, and had a long talk with him about Church affairs, and about some of the people who now profess an interest in Christianity. I told him of some of the things I had heard about Mr. K'ang and he said there was no foundation for them. I have done my best to try and find out if Mr. K'ang and these people have really any very wrong motive in joining us, and I can find none. Some of them appear very satisfactory. In the evening we had a good meeting; several engaged in public prayer for the first time, and it was a great encouragement to see them. Mr. Hwang and Mr. Fu from Yu Lung were very interested. We left Yen T'ing yesterday morning, three of the inquirers accompanying us to this place. Mr. K'ang and a cousin were of the party; they said they wanted to hear more, and would return in time for Sunday's meetings. I was met, on arrival here, by quite a number of people some way from town, and crackers were let off for some distance along the road; on reaching the door people lined the way, and three great crackers or salutes were fired off. I found that I had also been expected here for some days, and people from the villages round had been waiting, but had been forced to return to their homes; some because their money was spent, others on account of their crops. Still, last night there was a good houseful at meeting and I think a most helpful gathering. I find that 267 names are on the register here but that includes the 83 at Yen T'ing. Mr. Fu tells me that these people attend three or four times before he enters their names, and those who cease to attend he crosses off. Some of these are not sincere, and have used the name of the Church to injure others, and the true inquirers are very anxious that this be put a stop to as soon as possible, and press me to make some rules and arrangements whereby it can be checked. They say that Mr. Fu is an honest man, but has no power whatever to control things, and if something is not done serious trouble may arise. They tell me many others would join if there were more control, and more hope of arrangements being made to look after the people, but while things are as at present they will keep aloof. I told them of our prospect of having more workers next year in T'ung Ch'wan, but they said T'ai Ho Chen would suit them better, if we could have some one there. This was said quite independently of any suggestion of mine.

YU LUNG CHEN, 31st *October*, 1901. Have had an extremely busy time here, quite a number of people came yesterday, and

I was not able to see them all; some came late, others had gone away, but in the evening the place was packed with most attentive listeners. No doubt a wonderful work is going on here, and I find much progress in knowledge since my last visit, and many express a desire to be truly penitent. Last night in the meeting, after Li and Yuen had spoken, Mr. K'ang gave a fine testimony, told of how he came here without much, if any, idea of what he wanted, except that he thought his being a member of the Church might add to his prestige, but having bought a catechism and other books, he awoke to the truth; he told them that they knew of his past, and now he was anxious to serve Christ. The people seemed greatly impressed. Li Sao San heard them whispering to one another, "That is K'ang Sao Fu" in great astonishment. Last time I wrote of the need of some one here, now I say it is simply indispensable. When the Lord gives us a good work, shall we not enter in and undertake it? For many years I have prayed to see a genuine interest in the Truth, and longed to see men give evidence of real conversion as I have seen at home. Now I think I have seen it; anyhow it was so good I could only humbly thank God for the work He is doing. I may be mistaken, and influenced by sentiment to some extent, but somehow these things which I have seen and heard are different from those I have experienced elsewhere. I can only pray and ask your prayers that this good work, which I believe has been begun of God, may be carried on.

Passing through T'ai Ho Chen, and spending one day there, in which I did not hold any regular meeting, but only interviewed some of the people, I went on to Kwan Yin Koa, arriving there on 2nd November. My last visit to this place was in company with Isaac Mason in June of last year, when we came at the request of a few people who professed to be interested in the Truth, and were anxious to have help from us. They began holding meetings among themselves in a house belonging to one of the leaders of those interested. Isaac Mason and I were on that occasion received with great *éclat*, firing of crackers, show of tawdry decorations in dirty rooms, with red silk curtains, etc., and with a great appearance of zeal for the Truth. There were between twenty and thirty inquirers.

Immediately after our visit rumours of the troubles in the North reached this district. The people got frightened, no one was really in charge, or had capacity or knowledge enough to teach or lead them, and the result was the withdrawal of many inquirers.

On our arrival yesterday we were warmly welcomed by a few, but with nothing of the enthusiasm of last year. I examined several who say they attend meetings on Sundays, but only one or two know anything at all of the Truth. The way that these people attach themselves to the Christians, without the slightest knowledge of what they are doing, is almost incomprehensible to a foreigner. Some of them told me they believed the doctrine, but when asked what the doctrine was, they pleaded entire ignorance, some not even knowing the name of the God whom we worship, and yet they said they had been joined to the Christians and attended meetings for a year! There seem three or four who are slightly more intelligent than the rest, and who know something of the Truth. They all—I think with some justice—excuse themselves by saying that they " have no one to teach them, and how can they hear or understand without a teacher ? " One of their number would like to do more. At present he leads the meetings when possible, but his farm and other claims prevent him from doing all that he desires. He certainly requires training and teaching himself, if he is to teach others. There are now two probationers and about fifteen inquirers. I spoke to them very plainly about showing more earnestness in trying to find out the Truth from the Testaments and books they possess, and I hope by our next visit some progress may have been made. The work here is a great contrast to that around Yu Lung Chen, and yet a year ago this seemed much more promising.

CHIN FU WAN, *4th November*. Since my last visit to this place, in June, 1900, a small shop has been rented on the street of this busy market, and a native placed in charge. The village is situated on the main road between Wan Hsien on the river Yang Tse and the capital, Chentu. On market days over 10,000 people crowd its one long street. This occurs once in every three days, and on the intervening days little, if any, business is done.

On our arrival on Saturday, shortly after noon, the street was almost impassable with the crowd of people who had come to market. Yesterday, Sunday, hardly anyone was to be seen; here and there at a tea shop, a little crowd gathered round a table to watch the card players. Cardplaying and gambling seem to be the occupation of many, on the off market days. They read no books, no papers come their way; if they have something to eat and nothing to do they seem to be quite satisfied! Dirt, horrid smells, filthy homes, do not seem to affect them in the slightest; they know of no desire for anything cleaner or better, at least so it seems. "Dead in trespasses and sins," and one might add "in sloth and dirt," is a fitting description of many of the people we meet. What can be done? Would that the Spirit may come and breathe upon the dry bones, for they are very dry, that they might live. Life, spiritual life, is the one great need of this people.

Twenty or thirty gathered with us in the morning for worship, and in the evening rather more; most of them listened attentively, and recognised truth as truth when they heard it, showing that in the hearts of this people God is at work. Seventeen persons have entered their names as inquirers. I examined several and found some of them had a fair knowledge of the Gospel, and one or two appeared really desirous of doing right.

November 4th. Reached T'ung Ch'wan to spend a few days more here, before proceeding south again; thankful for what I have been permitted to see, and glad to have had these two young men with me. Yuen's message at Yu Lung, the last night we were there, was very good. His text, short and to the point, was "Be real as well as nominal."

CHAPTER XX.

OUR AIMS AND FUTURE PROSPECTS.

FOR the proper prosecution and development of missionary work in this land it is of the utmost importance to have a definite purpose in view, and to make all our efforts contribute to the attainment of that object. Our great aim is to bring as many of these people as possible under the influence of Christian truth, and to lead them to a knowledge of God as revealed in our Lord Jesus Christ. Therefore, whatever department of mission effort we engage in, whether as physicians, preachers, educationists, or workers among women, all our energies are bent toward the accomplishment of this one supreme end, the salvation of men and women. This aim is a great and glorious one, and demands the consecration of our highest powers.

Those who have laboured longest, and with the greatest success, are at one in their belief as to the power of the Gospel in the hearts of the Chinese, and as to the latent possibilities for good in the character and life of those who come under its influence. Who can, even in a small measure, estimate the forces that shall result from the planting of the truth of God in the hearts of the people of China ? We believe, with all our souls, in Jesus Christ, and that He alone can satisfy our needs, and the needs of the Chinese, and woe is unto us if we do not present Him in such a way that they may learn to love and obey Him. Our aim is, by word and deed, to proclaim in all our districts the Lord Jesus Christ as the way back to the Father of us all, and that in Him all the cravings of man's better nature may be satisfied.

This we take to be the general purpose of the Friends' Mission in China, as elsewhere; but it is necessary to have some definite plans in order best to carry out this purpose in detail. We have already given some account of what has been, and is being done, in the various centres where we have missionaries, but a forward view may add a spirit of strong hope and expectation to that of thankfulness and rejoicing, already obtained through looking back over the way that the Lord has led us.

A FAMILIAR ROAD.
On the way to the Hill School for Missionaries' Children, seen on the hill-side above.

We may best formulate our desires for the future consolidation and progress of the mission, by considering the agencies now at work in our various centres:

SOUTHERN DISTRICT.

Stations: Chungking and T'ung L'iang.

1. CHUNGKING, the oldest station, is at the present moment strengthening the stakes, and the various branches of the mission there are looking forward expectantly to a lengthening of the cords. The work in the street-preaching halls in this city has always been a prominent feature and, with the addition of more

MIEN CHEO
C.M.S.

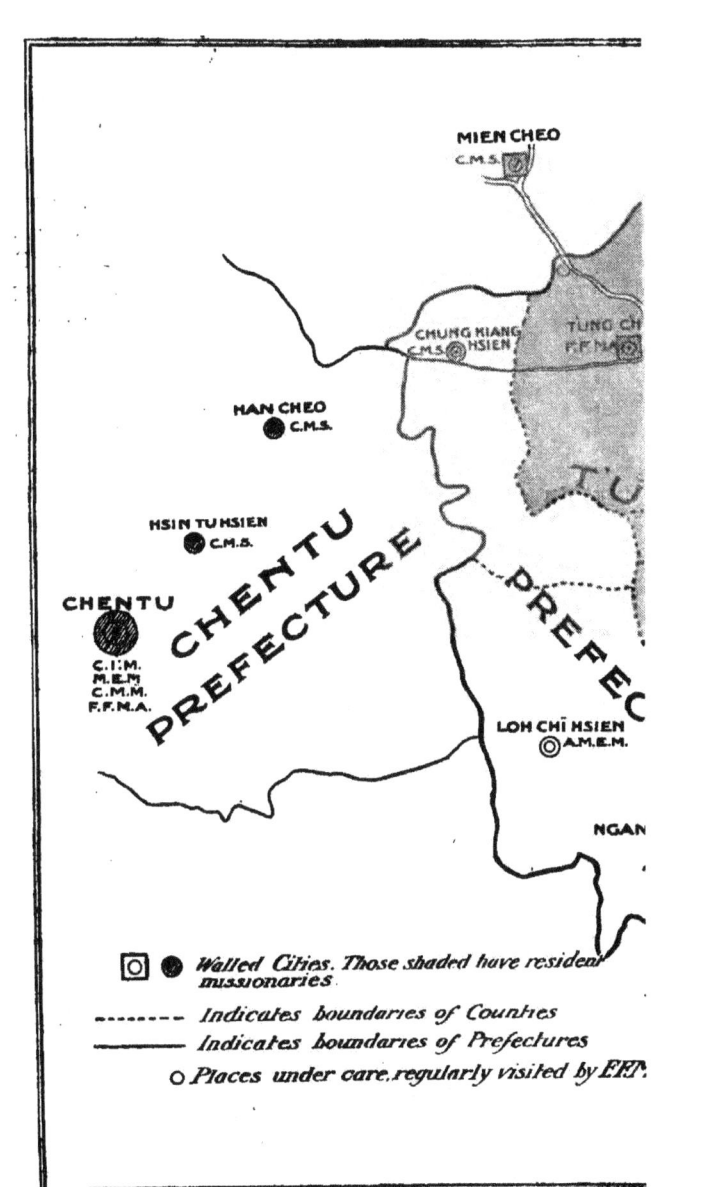

CHUNG KIANG
C.M.S. HSIEN

TUNG CH
F.F.M

HAN CHEO
C.M.S.

HSIN TU HSIEN
C.M.S.

CHENTU
C.I.M.
M.E.M
C.M.M.
F.F.M.A.

CHENTU PREFECTURE

T'U

PREFEC

LOH CHI HSIEN
A.M.E.M.

NGAN

▣ ● *Walled Cities. Those shaded have resident missionaries*
-------- *Indicates boundaries of Counties*
———— *Indicates boundaries of Prefectures*
○ *Places under care, regularly visited by F.F.*

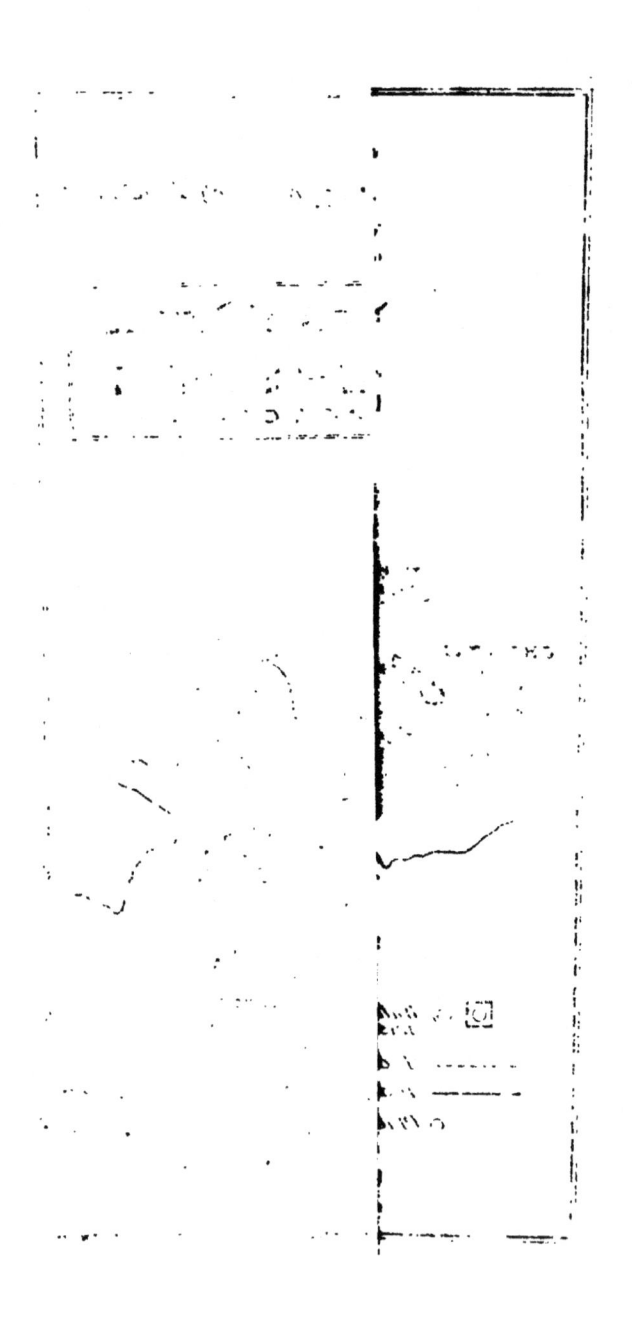

helpers we look for a greater scattering of the seed than ever before, by this means. It may not seem to result in an immediate harvest, but we are assured of a rich ingathering. The Bishop of Hongkong, speaking lately of this class of work, says :—" The pioneers of Protestant missionary work in China, the men who founded the Churches, were wonderfully successful, in spite of enormous difficulties, and in spite of having to wait many a long year before they saw results. These results were achieved by the ' foolishness of preaching,' by the steady, unwearying proclamation of an acceptable message, without hospitals or colleges, without complex machinery, but by the patient, persistent proclamation of Jesus Christ and Him crucified, in the town and in the country." The need for this regular, patient preaching of the Gospel is very great, and we have now several halls, besides the large meeting-house, in Chungking city and suburbs, where we look to maintain this evangelistic effort. In several other villages near the city we are anxious to have someone to proclaim the Truth. By this means we expect to spread widely the knowledge of the Christian religion, so that all may have the opportunity of learning of Jesus.

As mentioned in an earlier chapter, educational work among boys in Chungking has out-grown the building in which it has been carried on for some years. In the new building, which has been erected on the south side of the river, we shall be able to accommodate at least forty boarders, to whom we hope to give a thorough Christian education. We trust that from them may come our future School Teachers and Mission Helpers. We want so to work this institution that it shall make its influence felt, not only in Chungking, but throughout the province. As men at home to-day are thankful for the teaching and training they received at Ackworth, Sidcot, Saffron Walden, or others of our Friends' Schools, so may many a Chinaman in days to come praise God for our Friends' School at Chungking. Alfred Davidson has the care of this department during Leonard Wigham's furlough.

2. The new station opened at T'UNG LIANG has now a missionary living there. He has oversight of the work in the two counties of T'ung Liang and Ta Choo, which are considerably larger than any two English counties, and he and his family are the only foreigners resident in all that neighbourhood.

ONE OF CHINA'S BRIDGES.
The Chinese make very good stone bridges. This one is crossed on the way from Chungking to T'ung Liang.

There are scores of market towns and villages where men and women profess an interest in the Gospel, besides those in which we have native helpers at work. These places have to be visited periodically, the inquirers seen and taught, the helpers advised and strengthened, and the work already begun in the two county towns needs constant supervision.

Besides the carrying on of the regular meetings, there is also need for Elementary Schools. Classes for teaching local inquirers, as well as those from the country round, are of pressing importance, as well as simple Bible Schools for the helpers, which must have a share of the missionary's time. This work is comparatively new, but we aim at making it permanent, to carry the Gospel news to every village and market in the two counties, and we are hoping ere long to see Christians in every hamlet round.

Work amongst the women and girls, in both the city of Chungking, and the rest of the "Southern District," also calls for more labourers, and it was never in a more hopeful condition to reward the effort expended upon it.

NORTHERN DISTRICT.

Stations : T'ung Ch'wan, Sui-ling, and Chentu.

Turning to the "Northern District," where the local conditions are somewhat different from those in Chungking and its neighbourhood, we greatly rejoice in the opportunity afforded now of reaching the great population with the Gospel. We are looking forward to a still more extended effort than the mission has been able to make in the past. The number of foreign missionaries, as well as native helpers, has been considerably increased during the past year or so, but even yet not in proportion to the great needs.

3. In T'UNG CH'WAN the mission has prospered, and a broad foundation for future work is being laid, upon which we hope to build strongly and well. Medical work, the education of girls and young women, and the supervision of an increasingly large number of out-stations will be made the prominent features of our work in this city. Owing to various causes, particularly the prejudice of the people against entering a foreign hospital, the medical effort has not been so successful as we could wish; but with the new hospital erected in 1905, we anticipate much better results in days to come, not only in T'ung Ch'wan, but in the surrounding district.

One of the crying needs of to-day in China is the education of women. In this great province of Sz-Chwan we have never heard of a dozen schools for girls exclusive of those carried on by missionaries. Notwithstanding the great love of learning among the Chinese, they have kept their women ignorant, and the result is that, as a rule, they are much inferior to the men in intelligence and ability, and decidedly more superstitious. The wretched custom of footbinding has doubtless had part in restricting the development of womanhood, both

THE GIRLS' BOARDING SCHOOL PREMISES AT T'UNG CH'WAN.

intellectually and physically, but good progress is being made in Sz-Chwan in the crusade against this cruel and useless practice. The anti-footbinding movement is actively pushed by our missionaries as well as others, and is becoming popular amongst the intelligent natives. Viewing the general situation all round, we thankfully see much willingness on the part of parents for their daughters to be educated, and therefore feel we should make this branch of our work a prominent feature at least in one station.

T'ung Ch'wan presents advantages for such a work. It is healthy, property is comparatively cheap, and the cost of living not expensive; these facts confirm the wisdom of devoting our energies to helping the girls here. Girls who have been in the day schools in other cities can, if they so desire, go to T'ung Ch'wan Boarding School for further instruction. Some have already done so from Chungking. The girls educated in this school may make good wives for our native Christians, and some of them may help in the teaching of their sisters in other centres, for the demand for the education of women is fast increasing.

It will already have been observed that out-station work in this district has occupied a prominent place, and with the increasing number of towns and villages where men are desirous of Christian teaching, this department in the future must claim still more of our attention. The teaching of these inquirers, the training of necessary helpers, the constant itineration required to visit these stations regularly, present a prospect of missionary effort that at times almost overwhelms the workers. But we have been taught to expect great things from God, and we are not dismayed when He gives us great opportunities for usefulness. Fields lying untilled, or white unto the harvest, renew in our hearts the prayer, " Lord, send forth more labourers into Thy harvest field."

4. SUI-LING. The extending of our missionary effort to the cities of Sui-ling and Chentu is a great cause for rejoicing, and calls for increased prayer both in the field and at home. We rejoice in the command to go forward, and especially so when the great mountain of opposition which appeared to block our path so long has largely disappeared. We need to pray for wisdom and spiritual discernment to know how best to utilise the present opportunities, to recognise what work should be undertaken, and what left undone.

The city of Sui-ling, though only of " County " or " Hsien " rank, is one of the most important in the province, being favourably situated on a branch of the Chia-ling river, affording easy communication with Chungking, which makes it a great distributing centre for a large area. We are hoping to make this station an active centre of missionary work. A good street-preaching hall, which we have obtained on a busy thoroughfare, a large compound on which a school and residence have been erected, and the existence of an interesting work in the neighbouring city of P'ung Ch'i and surrounding villages, all go to prove that the

NEW FRIENDS' BUILDINGS AT SUI-LING.
The above are situated just outside the walls of the City of Sui-ling.

prospect of future growth and development of the Friends' Mission work in this district is by no means small. May the faith and loving gifts of the Church at home, which have made this advance possible, be richly rewarded in a large ingathering of men and women to the Kingdom of our Lord and Saviour.

5. CHENTU. Only in 1904 did the original purpose of the Friends' Foreign Mission Association to commence work in the capital of the province become an accomplished fact, and our aims now, in opening a mission station in Chentu,

MEALTIME; DURING THE BUILDING OF THE TWO NEW HOUSES AT CHENTU.
The nearer of the houses has been erected as a future home for Dr. Henry T. Hodgkin.

are of a somewhat different character from what they were twenty years ago. Then we simply looked to work, as the way might open, amongst the general population, whereas now we believe the call is to make a special effort to reach the literary classes, amongst whom comparatively little work has been done. Indeed some pioneer missionaries have rather avoided than sought intercourse with the educated people ; the labour amongst them has been specially difficult and unpromising. It has often been said that the simple country folk were the most receptive, and, as of old, the saying that " the common people heard Him gladly" has been true in China. Therefore the wealthy and educated, as well as the official class, have been largely left untouched by the teaching of the Gospel. Yet these are the men who influence the course of the nation, and who often have been our bitterest enemies. Is their opposition the result of ignorance which we might have dispelled had we endeavoured to do so ? It may be so, in part, and the time seems come to aim at reaching them. God has laid it on the hearts of Friends to do their share in bringing a knowledge of the Lord Jesus Christ to the literary classes, who stand as much in need of His salvation as others who have less learning.

THE LITERARY CLASSES.

How are these classes to be reached ? This question is of the greatest importance and one to which we must find a satisfactory answer if the work is to be done successfully. The usual methods of street-preaching, medical work or even educational efforts, do not bring this class about us to any large extent. It is therefore necessary to find some means by which we can get so into contact with this portion of the population as to be able to bring to them a knowledge of the Gospel. The distribution of books to students, at the various examination seasons, has been very useful, but this is not equal to the living voice. In one or two places in China, lectures have been given on scientific subjects, and museums have been furnished with collections illustrative of various branches of Western science and manufacture, natural history, and the progress of Christianity. To these the *literati* have been invited, and, in connection with them, there have been special lecture halls, reception rooms, library and reading rooms, in which visitors have an opportunity of hearing the Gospel. In the present stage of progress in China such institutions are proving most successful in reaching the more educated classes. The great desire for Western learning, including English, offers a means of reaching educated young men; and not them alone, for the daughters of the officials and gentry are almost equally anxious to acquire knowledge.

In the great western capital of Chentu, where numerous families of this class reside, we look to work along these lines, which have proved successful in other centres, such as Chincheo Fu, in Shan-tung, under the English Baptist Mission. The property already secured for the Mission gives scope for work on these lines, and the quarter of the city in which we are located is suitable for the purpose.

Thus, in detail, we bring forward the aims and prospects of the Mission in China, trusting that the Church at home may be encouraged in the work God has given it to do, and that with increased hope and prayer the Mission may be enabled to go forward in the discharge of the great trust committed to it, in bringing in the Kingdom of our God and His Christ.

CHAPTER XXI.

APPEAL.

WHILST thus defining in some measure our future prospects and aims, we would impress upon our readers the fact that they have developed before us, in a manner and to a degree, of which we had no anticipation a few years ago. China has been such a "closed door," and has opened so reluctantly to receive the messengers of the Gospel, that many of them have hardly expected ever to be other than " despised and rejected," as their Master was before them.

When, however, the marvellous Providence of God overrules the cruel enmity of the Boxer rising of 1900, and converts a nation of 400,000,000 people into an attitude of polite recognition of the influence of the missionary, so that his teaching is sought after and listened to by overwhelming numbers, it becomes a necessity that the facts be laid before the Home Churches. It can hardly be too strongly emphasised that the present is a unique opportunity for the enlargement of all missionary effort in China, whether we refer to purely evangelistic effort, educational, medical or literary work. As these lines were being penned we had a fair example of the press of work abounding on every hand. The doors being opened half an hour before the time, the meeting-house in the city of Chentu was quickly filled to overflowing with a quiet, orderly crowd of men and women, ready to sit a couple of hours to listen to the preaching of the Gospel. Seven days a week this could be repeated, if only the men were there to preach. In the towns and villages throughout the whole of Friends' District—which, by the way, is equal to the six northern counties of England—preaching, teaching and school work are waiting to be done. All the work—the foundations of which have been laid in past years in the steady toil which needed long patience—is now increasing so rapidly that the present band of workers cannot possibly compete with the demands upon their time and strength. In addition, the altered attitude of the people demands Western teaching, and the question has to be faced, Shall China get it *with* or *without* the Gospel? This is a question of world-wide importance, for Western training she will have. If she takes it with its excessive military influence, as in Japan, which seems quite possible, the world's peace may be endangered by the rise of a military Empire on the vast scale which her resources permit. The coming of Christ's Kingdom may be hindered unless the present opportunity be quickly and thoroughly grasped. The Christian Church will have cause to regret any neglect to respond to the call which has been sent to all the Home Churches, from the three thousand missionaries already in the field, who are bearing the burden, and what does appear to be the very " heat of the day." They appeal for more helpers, more support, more prayer. Shall they appeal in vain? The men who are best acquainted with the facts of the present conditions are most emphatic in their call for help.

In all truly healthy work there must be growth and expansion. We rejoice that we can say that this is the fact in our own branch of the mission field in China. But the little band of twenty-four workers,—only ten of whom are men,—is quite inadequate to meet the growing work, and the expansion which the present crisis demands. We therefore appeal to our readers prayerfully to consider whether we, as a Society—and many of our members individually—have not at the present time a special call of God to respond adequately with our best offerings.

Especially would we appeal to the educated young men, who are about to take up their life work, to consider the cry from the land of Sinim, in the light of the Saviour's marching orders,—" Go ye into all the world, and preach the Gospel to every creature." That command is given to the disciples universally, as much as the Gospel invitation, "Come ye," and there should surely be a time in the experience of every Christian, for considering to what part of "all the world" it is God's will that he should go. Undoubtedly to some the right place is at home, and to such the Saviour's words apply,—" Go, tell thine own house how great things the Lord hath done." Yet before settling-in to home life, should not each follower of Christ consider the call to " tell it out among the heathen that the Lord is King "? Should any one question how one may be sure there is no mistake in the decision, we would answer, the call is threefold, and can be discerned step by step. First, there is the call of God in His written word already quoted, no one can gainsay that ; then there is the call in the individual heart and the *desire* to respond to the first call ; and third, the call in the outward providence of circumstances. May not the present special circumstances in China be the final call for some who have been seeking to know their life work ?

> His lamps are we to shine
>   And go where He may say ;
> And lamps are not for sunny rooms
>   Nor for the light of day,
> But for dark places of the earth,
> Where sin and want and pain have birth.

Let no one hesitate in the fear that the needs of the home lands are too pressing. On this point it may not be out of place to quote the recent words of a Scotch missionary in China (Dr. J. C. Gibson), who says :—" If anyone feels so impressed by the needs of home that he hesitates to consider other fields, let me suggest a simple method which will help to determine personal duty. Resolve that you will not offer yourself for any post for which there are other candidates as competent as yourself. In Great Britain there are about 38,000,000 souls, and among these there are about 44,000 ministers and over 700,000 Sabbath School Teachers. In China there are in all little over two thousand missionaries. The ratio of these workers to the population is as if you had in Edinburgh one minister and one Sabbath school teacher to do all the evangelistic and pastoral work in the city."

Again, in view of home and family claims, which might *seem* sufficient to deter some, this is his actual experience, and it is worth notice, " As an only son, when I went to the foreign field, I left at home my mother and three sisters, who might fairly have made a strong claim for my remaining at home, but from no one of them did I ever hear a single word of opposition. When I returned from my first term of service, only one of those four remained in life, and yet I never had a moment's reason for regret for the decision which I had made. I had ample testimony that the tie formed with the foreign field became to those who remained at home a signal means of grace, and the source of a large amount of happiness, which, if weighed in the right balance, fully compensated them, I believe, for any loss they might have incurred."

Dr. Griffith John, who has been for over fifty years a missionary in China, voices the heartfelt experience of many of his fellow-workers, when he says,—" I thank God most devoutly that I am a missionary. I have never regretted the step I took, and if there is a sincere desire in my breast it is that I may live and die in labouring for Christ among the heathen. I am prepared to offer a joy in this work such as will enable you to understand what the Master meant when He said 'My peace I give unto you.' The romance of missions is a home dream, *the blessedness of missionary life is a reality.*"

APPENDIX.

BOOKS FOR FURTHER READING.

BEACH, HARLAN P. "Dawn on the Hills of T'ang; or Missions in China." Student Volunteer Missionary Union. 2s. 6d. Pp. 175. An excellent handbook.

BISHOP, Mrs. BIRD. "The Yang Tse Valley and Beyond." John Murray. 21s. net.

BROWN, ARTHUR JUDSON. "New Forces in Old China." Fleming H. Revell Co. 5s. net. This is a valuable book on the present conditions in China and their significance.

BRYSON, Mrs. M. I. "Child Life in China." R.T.S. 2s. 6d. Illustrated, pp. 312. Well adapted for children.

DOOLITTLE, J. "Social Life of the Chinese." Illustrated, pp. 633. Good on Chinese customs.

DOUGLAS, ROBERT K. "China." ("The Story of the Nations" Series.) T. Fisher Unwin. Price 5s. net. A standard history of China, helping to a clear knowledge of the external history of the country from earliest times to the present.

GIBSON, J. CAMPBELL. "Mission Problems and Mission Methods in South China." Oliphant, Anderson and Ferrier. 6s.

MARTIN, W. A. P. "A Cycle of Cathay." Oliphant, Anderson and Ferrier. 7s. 6d. An account of a missionary's life in China, with interesting sidelights on the people.

MOULE, A. E. "New China and Old." J. Seeley and Co. 5s.

ROSS, JOHN. "Mission Methods in Manchuria." Oliphant, Anderson and Ferrier. 3s. 6d.

ROWNTREE, JOSHUA. "The Imperial Drug Trade, a re-statement of the Opium Question, in the light of recent evidence and new developments in the East." Methuen and Co. 5s. net.

SMITH, ARTHUR H. "Chinese Characteristics" Illustrated. Oliphant, Anderson and Ferrier. 7s. 6d. Excellent on Chinese character.

SMITH, ARTHUR H. "Rex Christus: An Outline Study of China." Macmillan and Co. 2s. 6d. net. Pp. 256. Another good handbook.

SMITH, ARTHUR H. "Village Life in China." Oliphant, Anderson and Ferrier. 7s. 6d. Good on country life.

STOCK, EUGENE. "For Christ in Fuh-Kien." C.M.S. 2s. 6d.

TAYLOR, Mrs. HOWARD. "One of China's Scholars." Morgan and Scott. 2s. 6d. net.

TAYLOR, Mrs. HOWARD. "Pastor Hsi: One of China's Christians." Morgan and Scott. 3s. 6d. net and 1s. 6d. net.

TUNG, CHANG CHIH. "China's Only Hope." Oliphant, Anderson and Ferrier. 3s. 6d.

WILLIAMS, S. WELLS. "The Middle Kingdom." 2 vols. Simpkin Marshall and Co. 42s. The most thoroughly informing book on China.

WALLACE, E. W. "The Heart of Sz-Chwan." Text Book of the Young People's Forward Movement. Toronto: Methodist Mission Rooms. 2s. 6d. net.

PRESENT F.F.M.A. MISSIONARIES TO CHINA, WITH DATE OF ARRIVAL IN FIELD.

CUMBER, MIRA L.	1892
DAVIDSON, ADAM WARBURTON	1897
DAVIDSON, HENRIETTA (*née* Simmonds)	1899
DAVIDSON, ALFRED	1901
DAVIDSON, CAROLINE E. (*née* Child)	1904
DAVIDSON, ROBERT J.	1886
DAVIDSON, MARY J. (*née* Catlin)	1886
DAVIDSON, W. HENRY, M.R.C.S., L.R.C.P.	1901
DAVIDSON, LAURA A. (*née* Morris)	1901
HARRIS, LUCY E., M.B.	1899
HODGKIN, HENRY T., M.A., M.B.	1905
HODGKIN, ELIZABETH J. (*née* Montgomery)	1905
HUNT, ELSIE M.	1896
JACKSON, BENJAMIN H.	1901
JACKSON, FLORENCE E. (*née* Ellwood)	1901
JONES, MARGARET B. M.	1903
MASON, ISAAC	1892
MASON, ESTHER L. (*née* Beckwith)	1894
MAW, WILFRED A.	1903
MAW, EDITH (*née* Benson)	1903
VARDON, EDWARD B.	1896
VARDON, MARGARET (*née* Southall)	1891
WIGHAM, LEONARD, B.A.	1891
WIGHAM, CAROLINE N. (*née* Southall)	1888

MARRIAGES IN CHINA OF F.F.M.A. MISSIONARIES.

Leonard Wigham, B.A., to Caroline N. Southall	Mar. 23, 1893
Frederic S. Deane to Alice M. Beck	Mar. 20, 1894
(F. S. and A. M. Deane returned to England in 1897).	
Isaac Mason to Esther L. Beckwith	Sept. 9, 1895
Edward B. Vardon to Margaret Southall	Nov. 17, 1896
Adam Warburton Davidson to Henrietta Simmonds	Jan. 25, 1901
W. Henry Davidson, M.R.C.S., L.R.C.P., to Laura Morris	Jan. 3, 1903
Alfred Davidson to Caroline E. Child	June 4, 1904

DEATHS OF F.F.M.A. CHINA MISSIONARIES.

Henrietta Green, ... May 24, 1890
[In China 1884-9, at first in connection with F.F.M.A., afterwards as an independent Missionary.]

Hannah Rosher ... Mar. 21, 1899
[In China 1897-99.]

F.F.M.A. STATISTICS FOR CHINA, 1904.

	Northern District.*	Southern District.*	Total.
NATIVE WORKERS (voluntary or otherwise):			
Evangelists	8	3	11
Teachers (Men)	5	8	13
,, (Women)	1	2	3
Bible-Women	3	4	7
Colporteurs and other Native Workers	8	8	16
Total Native Workers	25	25	50
CHURCH STATISTICS:—			
Out-stations (Places of Regular Meeting)	9	8	17
Organised Churches	2	1	3
†Members	22	34	56
Adherents	561	192	753
Sunday Schools	3	2	5
Sunday School Membership	150	113	263
Meeting Houses (or buildings used as such)	12	13	25
EDUCATIONAL STATISTICS:—			
Boarding Schools	1	1	2
Pupils (Boys)	—	17	17
,, (Girls)	13	—	13
Primary Schools	5	8	13
Pupils (Boys)	84	121	205
,, (Girls)	36	68	104
Total Number under Instruction	133	206	339
MEDICAL STATISTICS:—			
Dispensaries	1	—	1
Patients Treated (out)	1,423	—	1,423
,, ,, (in)	16	—	16
Total Attendance	4,439	—	4,439

THE WORK OF AMERICAN FRIENDS IN CHINA.

The Foreign Mission Board of Ohio Yearly Meeting, dates the founding of its China Mission from 1890, though its pioneer missionary, Esther H. Butler had been in the country for three years, learning the language and preparing for the work in the mission of another denomination. Their first station was established at Nanking. In 1892 a church was organised; in 1896 a girls' boarding school and a hospital were opened. In 1898 a second station was opened at Lu-ho-hsien, twenty-five miles north of Nanking, where evangelistic, educational and medical work is being pressed forward. The missionaries number nine—seven women and two men.

* The Northern District includes Chentu, T'ung Ch'wan, and Sui-ling; the Southern District, Chungking and T'ung Liang.
† Membership is only granted after eighteen months satisfactory connection with the Mission. After six months a man may become an Inquirer, six months later a Probationer, and then six months afterwards, a Member. Most of the other Societies admit to full membership far more speedily and the yearly accession to their numbers is, therefore, much larger in comparison.

RECENT STATISTICS OF CHRISTIAN MISSIONS IN CHINA.

(Extracted from article by HARLAN P. BEACH, F.R.G.S., *in* MISSIONARY REVIEW OF THE WORLD, *October, 1905.)*

According to statistics gathered by the writer for January 1st, 1900, the fullest that have hitherto been published, there were at that time 2,785 Protestant missionaries in the empire, of whom 1,188 were men and 1,597 were women. In 1904 the number had increased thirteen per cent. to an aggregate of 3,107 with 1,374 men and 1,733 women—one missonary, man or woman, to about 131,000 people.

TABLE OF COMPARISON.

	1900.	1904.	Increase. Per cent.
Protestant Missionaries in China	2,785	3,107	13
Chinese Helpers	6,388	8,313	30
*Communicants	112,808	131,404	17
Mission Stations	653	765	17
Mission Out-stations	2,476	3,666	48
Hospital Patients	691,732	880,304	27
Day Schools	1,819	2,100	15
Scholars in these Schools	35,412	43,275	22
Higher Educational Institutions	170	275	62
Students in these Institutions	5,150	7,283	41

PROVINCE.	Missionaries, 1900.	Missionaries, 1904.	Number of Different Stations, 1904.	Number of Communicants, 1904.*
Gan-hwuy	71	96	20	1,532
Cheh-kiang	209	217	32	12,367
Kiang-si	97	134	34	1,708
Kiang-su	299	375	15	4,727
Chih-li	254	221	20	8,468
Fuh-kien	255	269	35	29,924
Ho-nan	59	90	20	1,019
Hu-nan	136 (?)	102	11	663
Hu-peh	118	208	21	9,801
Kan-suh	80	52	12	89
Kuang-si	...	41	2	736
Kuang-tong and Hongkong	300	416	46	29,047
Kwei-chow	24	20	6	123
Manchuria	92	87	16	9,914
Shan-si	142	137	28	1,551
Shan tong	204	271	23	14,226
Shen-si	88	80	23	954
Sz-chwan	189	243	30	3,467
Yün-nan	22	36	6	77

* As Friends our classification is necessarily different. Approximately a Church member, in connection with the F.F.M.A., is our equivalent of a Communicant in the other Societies.

INDEX.

Abacus, 88.
Abeel David, 141.
Actacus, 133.
A Cycle of Cathay, 3, 4, 5, 8, 106.
Adams, J. S., 147.
Advisory Board, 158.
Agriculture, 78, 84.
Almshouses, 72.
American Baptists, 142, 143, 147, 154.
  ,,   Bible Society, 156.
  ,,   Board, 141, 144, 149.
  ,,   Friends, 241.
  ,,   Methodist Episcopal Mission, 150, 154, 173, 207, 214.
  ,,   Presbyterians, 142, 143, 150, 153.
  ,,   Protestant Episcopal Mission, 143, 147.
  ,,   Treaties, 8.
Amoy, 7, 142, 143.
Ancestral Worship, 76, 80, 82, 96, 214, 217.
Anglo-Chinese College, 140, 142.
Anti-Foot Binding, 49, 206, 228.
Arrivals, F.F.M.A. Missionaries, 240.
Arrow War, 8.
Arsenal, 48.

Bank, 52.
Baptist Missionary Society, 150, 234.
Barclay, Ellen, 178.
Barclay, W. L., 178.
Basel Mission, 142.
Beach, Harlan P., 12.
Beck, Alice M., 174, 179.
Beggars, 61.
Bible Christians, 154.
  ,,   Colportage, 204.
  ,,   Schools, 227.
  ,,   Translation, 140.
Bishop, Mrs. Bird, 21, 30, 136.
Blackburn Commission, 44.
Blakiston, Captain, 22, 148.
Blodget, Henry, 149.
Book of Changes, 114, 118.
  ,,   History, 114, 119.
  ,,   Poetry, 114, 119.

Book of Rites, 114, 119.
Boone, Dr., 143.
Botham, Mr., 167.
Bourne, Consul, 18.
Boxers, 7, 150, 151, 158, 184, 197, 198, 199, 235.
Boys' School, Chungking, 174, 177, 181, 182, 189, 225.
  ,,   ,,   Se Hung, 204, 206.
  ,,   ,,   T'ai Ho Chen, 206.
  ,,   ,,   T'ung Ch'wan, 204.
Bridgman, E. C., 141.
Bristles, 37.
British East India Company, 51, 138, 139.
British and Foreign Bible Society, 64, 153, 156.
British Treaties, 8.
Buddhism, 3, 58, 93, 102.

Cameron, Dr., 173.
Canadian Methodists, 155.
Canton, 7, 104, 135, 137, 138, 141, 142, 143.
Cash, 49, 54, 57, 58, 61, 62.
Cassels, Bishop, 156, 171.
Castrop, Richard, 136.
Chang, 101.
Chang Chi, 109.
Chang Chih Tung, 14, 122, 131, 132, 150.
Chang Hsien Cheng, 37.
Chefoo, 161.
Cheh-kiang, 137, 143.
Chentu, 32, 33, 34, 36, 43-50, 128, 153, 154, 155, 157, 163, 164, 166, 169, 171, 192, 207, 208, 215, 227, 230, 234, 235.
Chia Ling, 34, 37, 169, 229.
Chien-cheo, 34.
Childhood, 82.
Chi-li, 149, 150.
China, Area, 1.
  ,,   Climate, 1.
  ,,   Foreign Trade, 51.
  ,,   Geography, 2.
  ,,   Government, 11.
  ,,   History, 2.

Index.

China, Lexicon, 6.
  ,, Literature, 6, 113.
  ,, Manufactures, 15.
  ,, Minerals, 1.
  ,, Mountains, 2.
  ,, Name, 1.
  ,, National Characteristics, 36.
  ,, Physical Features, 2.
  ,, Political Relations, 7.
  ,, Popular Customs, 66, 71, 77, 81.
  ,, Population, 1.
  ,, Position, 1.
  ,, Productions, 32, 37.
  ,, Rivers, 2.
  ,, Trade, 38, 47, 51.
China Inland Mission, 147-151, 154, 156, 157, 161, 163, 164, 167, 171, 173, 194.
China Mission Handbook, 94.
China's Only Hope, 122, 131.
China's Spiritual Needs and Claims, 161.
Chinese Characteristics, 65, 108.
Chinese Evangelisation Society, 148.
Chinese Grammar, 139.
Chinese in California, 144.
Chinese New Testament, 140.
Chin-cheo Fu, 234.
Chin Fu Wan, 194, 221.
Ching Cheng, 37.
Ch'ing Dynasty, 5.
Chinkiang, 16.
Chin Ling, 32.
Ch'in Shih Huang, 2, 57.
Ch'in T'an, 25, 26, 27.
Chin Wang, 57.
Chow, 3.
Christian Endeavour, 204.
Chronicles of Cash, 57.
Chu Fu Tsz, 4.
Chu Hsi, 6, 114.
Chungking, 13, 36-42, 44, 50, 62, 153-159, 164, 166, 172-193, 197, 198, 207, 209, 224-227.
Church Missionary Society, 143, 156.
City Walls, 37, 42, 43, 44.
Civil Academies, 45.
Civil Service Examinations, 4.
Coal, 32.
Coffins, 72, 90, 91, 92.
Coinage, 49, 51-64.
Colleges, 98, 124, 131.
  ,, Missionary, 140, 142, 143, 145, 146.
  ,, Colleges, Provincial, 45, 124.
Conference, 155.
Confucius, 3, 75, 93, 97.

Confucianism, 81, 93-98, 132.
Confucian Analects, 114, 121.
Consuls, 50, 184.
Converts, 175.
Corvino, John de Monte, 134.
Cotton, 86.
Crackers, 92, 210, 219, 220.
Craftsmen, 78.
Crosfield, A. J., 23, 203.
Cumber, M. L., 176, 183, 199, 204, 205.
Customs, 18, 51.
Davidson, R. J., 162, 163, 165, 166, 171-173, 191, 197-199, 209-222.
  ,, M. J., 165, 166, 171-173, 207.
  ,, A. W., 184, 197.
  ,, Dr. W. H., 207.
  ,, Laura, 207.
Dawn on the Hills of T'ang, 1, 12.
Deane, F. S., 174, 180, 181, 182.
  ,, A. M., 174, 179, 182.
Deaths, F.F.M.A. Missionaries, 240.
Degrees Hsiu Tsai (B.A.), 45, 128.
  ,, Chü Ren (M.A.), 45, 128.
  ,, Doctor, 129.
Delegates' Version of the Bible, 141, 142.
Demon Possession, 90.
Deputation, F.F.M.A., 203, 207.
Devotees, 105.
Dictionaries, 6, 111, 141.
Dispensaries, 167, 173, 174, 184, 191, 197, 206.
Doctrine of the Mean, 114, 116.
Doolittle, J., 53, 77.
Dress, 78.
Dudgeon, Dr., 150.
Dutch, 51.
Dynasty of Chow, 3, 119.
  ,, Ch'ing, 5.
  ,, Han, 3.
  ,, Hsia, 3.
  ,, Ming, 4, 37.
  ,, Shu, 46.
  ,, Sung, 4, 57.
  ,, T'ang, 4.
  ,, Yuen, 4.
Education, 49, 121, 130, 182, 189.
Electric Light, 14.
Embroidery, 47.
Empress-Dowager, 11, 49.
Encyclopædia, 6.
Endicott, J., 16.
English Methodist New Connexion, 150.
Examinations, 4, 11, 45, 49, 110, 126.

Index.

Faber, Dr. E., 94, 143.
Face, 66.
Fans, 48, 51.
Farmers, 78.
Feasts, 88, 90.
Fell, Henry, 136.
Filial Piety, 72, 74, 76.
Filigree Work, 47.
Fisher, T. W., 162.
Five Classics, 114, 121, 124.
Food, 68, 79.
Foot Binding, 4, 5, 78, 82, 228.
Formosa, 10.
Fortune Telling, 90.
Foster, Arnold, 165.
Four Books, 114, 121, 124, 132.
Fox, George, 136.
Fox, M. N., 203.
France, 10.
Friends' Foreign Mission Association, 154, 162-165, 168, 170.
Fu (Prefecture), 127, 168.
Fu (River), 34, 169.
Fu Ch'ang Ming, 210, 211, 213, 215, 217, 219.
Fu-chau, 7, 137, 143, 144.
Fu Hsi, 109, 119.
Fu-kien, 137, 144.
Funeral Rites, 48, 68, 79, 92, 115.

Gambling, 69, 222.
Gas, 14.
Gate of Tsu, 24.
Genaehr, 142.
Geomancy, 90, 96.
Germany, 10.
Gibson, Dr. J. C., 237.
Giles, Professor, 5, 11, 141.
Gill, Captain, 44.
Gillison, Dr., 147.
Girls' School, Chungking, 174, 177, 179, 183.
Girls' School, T'ung Ch'wan, 199, 205, 229.
God of Literature, 127.
Goddess of Mercy, 105.
Golden Days, 3.
Gordon, General, 6.
Gorges, 22, 23, 24, 25.
Grand Canal, 2.
Great Learning, 114.
Great Wall, 2.
Green, Henrietta, 163-166.
Gutszlaff, Dr., 142.

Hainan, 148.
Hakkas, 142.
Hamberg, 142.

Han Dynasty, 3.
Han River, 14, 166, 167.
Hanbury, Miss E., 171, 175.
Hanchung, 153, 167, 169, 170.
Hang Chow, 137.
Hankow, 14, 143, 145-147, 164-166.
Hanlin College, 129.
Hanyang, 14, 147.
Harris, Dr. L. E., 199, 207.
Hart, Sir Robert, 52.
Hart, Dr. Virgil, 155.
Heaven and Earth Tablet, 121.
Hemp, 37.
Hides, 37.
Hien Yuen, 101.
Hill, David, 166, 167.
Historic China, 12.
History of Christian Missions in China, 133.
Hobson, Dr., 141.
Ho-cheo, 34.
Hodgkin, Dr. H. T., 207.
   ,, Elizabeth, 207.
Hongkong, 10, 51, 52, 142.
   ,, Bishop of, 225.
Horsburgh, J., 156.
Hosie, Consul-General, 12, 31, 86.
Hospitals, A.M.E., 154.
   ,, F.F.M.A., 199, 207, 208.
   ,, L.M.S., 141, 147.
House boats, 16, 17.
Hsia Dynasty, 3.
Hsiao T'ung Ch'ang, 200.
Hsien (county), 12, 50, 127, 168, 170.
Hsin T'an, 25, 26.
Huc, Abbé, 133, 134.
Hunan, 113, 146, 147, 149.
Hung Wau, 37.
Hupeh, 14, 24, 32, 146, 147.
Hunt, E. M., 184.
Hwang Ho, 2.
Ichang, 15, 16, 18, 21, 22.
Imperial College, 150.
   ,, Customs, 18, 52, 64.
Imperial Drug Trade, 9.
Imperial Post, 64.
India, 7.
Industry, 67.
Infancy, 82.
Infanticide, 81.
Innocent, Mr., 150.
Inquirers, 186, 193, 194, 209-222, 227, 229.
Inwood, Charles, 157.
Iron Work, 48.
Irrigation, 34.
Isle of St. Johns, 134.

Japan, 10.
Japanese, 49.
Jinrickshas, 14.
John, Griffith, 145, 146, 153, 160, 166, 238.
Junks, 16.

Kalgan, 149.
K'ang Hsi, 5, 111.
K'ang Sao Fu, 199, 210, 218.
Kan-suh, 32, 38, 148, 149, 151, 158.
Kao, 116.
Kiao Chou, 10.
Kia-ting, 33, 154, 155, 156.
King, Dr. George, 161.
Kiukiang, 15.
Klaproth, 52.
Koester, 142.
Kokonor, 32.
Kwang Hsü, 10, 58.
Kwang-tung, 134, 137.
Kwan-hsien, 34.
Kwan Shing, 101.
Kwan-yuan, 34, 156.
Kwan Yin Koa, 197, 200, 220.
Kwei-chau, 32, 38, 154, 156.
Kublai Khan, 4, 134.
Ku-cheng, 143.
Kuling, 15.
Kung kwans, 47, 48.

Lacquered Goods, 47, 88.
Lamps, 46.
Language, 109.
Lao Tsz, 3, 98.
Lawsuits, 215.
Lechler, 142.
Legge, Dr., 114, 142, 160.
Li Chwan, 23.
Life Boats, 185.
Lin Commissioner, 7.
Li Sao San, 209, 213, 214, 217, 220.
Literati, 49, 83, 233.
Literature, 6, 113.
Little, Mr. A. J., 23.
Little, Mrs. A. J., 159.
Lockhart, Dr. Wm., 141, 142.
London Missionary Society, 137, 141, 142, 145-147, 150, 154, 165, 166, 173.
Lu, 119.
Lu-cheo, 34, 156.
Lui-chiang, 34.
Lu Han Railway, 15.
Lung Hu, 101.

Macao, 141.
McCarthy, John, 153.
McClatchie, Thomas, 143.

Mackenzie, Dr., 147, 150.
Madison, James, 138.
Malacca, 140, 142.
Manchuria, 148-150, 159.
Manchus, 4, 12, 46.
Mandarins, 12, 45.
Marco Polo, 43.
Margary, Mr., 161.
Markets, 84.
Marriage, 80, 125.
Marriages, F.F.M.A. Missionaries, 240.
Martin, Dr., 3, 7, 11, 105, 150.
Mason, Isaac, 176, 180, 182, 191, 208, 211, 220.
Mason, Esther L., 182, 204, 205, 208.
Mateer, Dr. C. W., 150.
Medhurst, W. H., 140, 142.
Medical Missions, 141, 143, 147.
Medicines, 37, 51.
Meeting-house, 155, 177, 179, 223.
Mei Chi Hsiu, 200, 205.
Memorial Arches, 96.
Mencius, 3, 96, 114, 116, 117, 118, 121.
Merchants, 78.
Metempsychosis, 106.
Mien-cheo, 34, 169.
Milne, William, 140.
Military, 49, 180.
Military Academies, 45.
Min, 34.
Ming Dynasty, 4, 37.
Ming Ti, 3, 102.
Mi-T'an, 23.
Mohammedanism, 108.
Mollman, Mr., 153.
Monasteries, 105.
Money, 4, 49, 52.
Mongolia, 148.
Mongols, 4.
Monthly Meeting, 204.
Morrison, Robert, 137-140.
Museums, 233.
Music, 71, 193.
Musk, 37.

Nanking, 5, 6, 14, 16.
Native Church Missionary Society, 143.
Native Helpers, 190, 226.
Native Helpers, Training of, 200, 204, 225, 229.
Nestorian Church, 133.
Nestorian Tablet, 133.
Nevius, Dr., 150.
Newman, H. S., 162.
New Year Feast, 88, 90, 125.
Nicholson, Mr. J. W., 159.

Index.

Nicoll, Mr., 153.
Nicoll, Mrs., 153, 154.
Ningpo, 7, 142, 143.
Nirvana, 105.
Niu Kan, 22.
Nuns, 102.

Opium, 7, 8, 9, 33, 37, 69, 86.
„ Refuges, 87.
Oracles, 96.
Orphanages, 72.

Pao-ning, 34, 156, 168, 169, 171, 173.
Pao-ting, Fu, 149.
Paper, 3.
Paper Money, 52, 53.
Parker, Dr. Peter, 141.
Parliament of Religions, 98.
Parry, Dr., 215.
Pawnshop, 68.
Peking, 2, 8, 36, 134, 149, 150, 158.
Peking Gazette, 4.
Pei Ho, 149.
Pigtails, 5, 77, 78, 82.
Pillar of Heaven, 22.
Pioneer, 23, 185.
Police, 14, 48.
Politeness, 29, 66.
Polygamy, 96.
Polytheism, 96.
Population, 12.
Porcelain, 15.
Portuguese, 51.
Postal System, 63.
Pottery, 15, 51, 86.
Poverty, 41, 72, 84, 88.
Priests, 101, 102.
Prefectural College, 50.
Presbyterian, American, 142, 143, 150, 153.
„ Irish, 150.
„ Scotch, 150.
Printing, 4.
„ Presses, 156.
Promissory Notes, 52.
Provincial College, 50.
Public Schools, 49.
Punch and Judy, 84.
P'ung Ch'i Hsien, 200, 230.

Railways, 15, 50.
Rapids, 25-28.
Red Basin, 32.
Reform, 10, 182.
Reform Edicts, 182.
Repository, 141.
Rex Christus, 160.
Rhenish Mission, 142.
Ricci, Matthew, 134, 135.

Richard, Dr. Timothy, 151.
Richthofen, Baron F. von, 44.
Riots, 157-159, 166, 173, 175, 183, 189.
Roads, 35, 72.
Roberts, Lr., 150.
Roger, Michael, 134, 135.
Roller Point, 27.
Roman Catholics, 6, 134-136, 139, 153, 164, 184, 189, 193.
Rowntree, Joshua, 9.
Royal Commission Report, 7.
Russia, 10, 159.

Sacred Edict, 6, 48.
Salt, 33, 34.
Sanatorium, 177, 178.
Schools, 49, 83, 98, 122-126, 130-132, 173, 179, 181-183, 189, 190, 193, 197, 199, 204-206, 208, 225-230.
School for Missionaries' Children, 184.
Scholars, 78.
Scottish Bible Society, 156.
Se Hung Hsien, 191-194, 197, 204, 206.
Shao Hsing, 143.
Shanghai, 7, 13, 14, 15, 51, 52, 142.
Shan-Si, 149, 150. [143.
Sha-sï, 15.
Shan-tung, 149, 150.
Sharp, Isaac, 178, 193.
Shen-si, 32, 38, 149, 150, 158, 164.
Shu King, 109.
Shun, 2, 76.
Shu-ting, 35.
Sie, 168.
Silk, 33, 37, 47, 51, 86, 169.
Silver Ware, 86.
Si-Ngan, 133, 167.
Smith, Dr. A. H., 65, 106, 160.
Smith, George, 143.
Smoking, 79, 175.
Social Life of the Chinese, 53, 77.
Society for Diffusion of Useful Knowledge, 141.
Soldiers, 48.
Son of Heaven, 12.
Southall, C. N., 170, 171, 173, 174, 179, 180.
Southall, M., 174, 180, 182, 208.
Spring and Autumn Annals, 114, 119.
Spiritualism, 96.
Statistics, 160, 241, 242.
Streets, 85, 86.
Street Preaching Halls, 177, 179, 180, 224, 230.
Stronach, A., 142.
Stronach, J., 142.
Stubb, John, 136. [207.
Student Volunteer Missionary Union,

Suicide, 96, 106.
Sui-fu, 34, 154, 156.
Sui Hsiang, 22, 185.
Sui-ling, 32, 62, 105, 207, 227, 229, 230.
Sung, 4, 57.
Sung P'an, 159.
Surnames, 81.
Swatow, 142.
Sz-Chwan, 2, 4, 12, 13, 16, 24, 31. 32, 35, 36, 61, 153-159, 164-169, 171, 175, 216, 227, 228.

Ta Chien Fu, 154.
Ta Choo Hsien, 184, 189, 226.
Tael, 62.
T'ai Ho Chen, 34, 36, 191-194, 220.
T'ai P'ing Rebellion, 6.
Taku forts, 8.
Ta-li-fu, 148.
T'ang, 4.
Taoism, 3, 93, 98, 101, 102, 107, 108.
Tartars, 2, 4, 46.
Tartary, 134.
Taylor, J. Hudson, 148, 149, 157, 161, 163.
Teachers, 83, 121.
Tea Shops, 48, 86.
Telegraphs, 14.
Telephone, 14.
Temples, 42, 47, 96, 101, 102.
Teng Chow, 150.
Theatres, 71, 84.
The East and the West, 11.
The Friend, 162.
The Heart of Sz-Ch'wan, 18.
The Middle Kingdom, 141.
The Yangtse Valley and Beyond, 136.
Three Character Classic, 124.
Tibet, 32, 38, 154.
Tientsin, 8, 149, 150.
Times, 49.
Tonquin, 158.
T'o Chiang, 34.
Trackers, 17, 18, 27.
Tracts, 110, 204.
Tract Societies, 158.
Trade, 37, 47, 51.
Translation of Chinese Classics, 114.
Treaty of Chefoo, 163.
    „   Tientsin, 8.
Tsen Seu, 114.
Tsï Liu Chin, 34.
Tsi-cheo, 34.
Tung Chow, 149.
T'ung Ch'wan, 33, 34, 50, 62, 168-173, 182, 186, 191, 192, 197, 198,

T'ung Ch'wan (*con*.), 200, 204-209, 212, 219, 222, 227-229.
T'ung Liang, 89, 224.
Universities, 132, 150.
Usury, 68.
Vardon, E. B., 182, 208.
Vardon, M., 174, 180, 182, 208.
Viceroys, 12, 159, 170.
Wages, 88.
Wan-hsien, 36, 156, 222.
War with England, 7, 8.
 „   „ Japan, 10.
 „   „ Russo-Japanese, 150.
Water ways, 34, 51.
Wax, 33, 37.
Weddings, 68, 79, 81.
Wei Hai Wei, 10.
Wells Williams, S., 141.
Wen Ti, 101.
Wen Wang, 118.
Wesleyans, 167.
West China Advisory Board, 158.
West China Missionary News, 158.
West China Tract Society, 158.
Western Learning, 49, 120, 131, 234.
Wigham, Leonard, 112, 181, 182, 225.
Wigham, C. N., 170, 171, 173, 174, 179, 180.
Wilson, Robert, 145.
Wilson, Dr. W. (F.F.M.A.), 26, 203.
Wilson, Dr. W. (C.I.M.), 167-170.
Wind Box Gorge, 24.
Wool, 37, 51.
Wrecks, 185, 193.
Wuchang, 14, 143, 147.
Wu Shan, 23, 24.
Wylie, Mr. A., 52, 153.

Xavier, 134.

Ya Cheo, 154.
Yang Tao Ch'i, 191, 206.
Yangtse Kiang, 2, 14, 15, 42, 169, 178.
Yao, 2.
Yeh T'an, 25, 26, 28.
Yen T'ing Hsien, 199, 209.
Yin and Yang, 101.
Yuan Shih Kai, 49.
Yü Ch'i K'ou, 200.
Yuen Dynasty, 4.
Yuen Ta Ch'en, 209, 214, 217, 220; 222.
Yu Lung Chen, 197, 210, 211, 213, 215, 217-219, 221, 222.
Yu Man Tsz, 157, 184, 189, 194.
Yunnan, 32, 38, 154, 156, 158, 161.

3 2044 050 951 763

The borrower must return this item on or before the last date stamped below. If another user places a recall for this item, the borrower will be notified of the need for an earlier return.

*Non-receipt of overdue notices does **not** exempt the borrower from overdue fines.*

Harvard College Widener Library
Cambridge, MA 02138   617-495-2413

WIDENER
DEC 1 1 2005
AUG 0 8 2005
CANCELLED

Please handle with care.
Thank you for helping to preserve library collections at Harvard.

CONSERVED
RSS 7/2003
HARVARD COLLEGE
LIBRARY

3 2044 050 951 763

The borrower must return this item on or before the last date stamped below. If another user places a recall for this item, the borrower will be notified of the need for an earlier return.

*Non-receipt of overdue notices does **not** exempt the borrower from overdue fines.*

Harvard College Widener Library
Cambridge, MA 02138   617-495-2413

WIDENER
DEC 1 1 2005
AUG 0 8 2005
CANCELLED

Please handle with care.
Thank you for helping to preserve library collections at Harvard.

3 2044 050 951 763

The borrower must return this item on or before the last date stamped below. If another user places a recall for this item, the borrower will be notified of the need for an earlier return.

*Non-receipt of overdue notices does **not** exempt the borrower from overdue fines.*

Harvard College Widener Library
Cambridge, MA 02138   617-495-2413

WIDENER
WIDENER
DEC 1 1 2005
AUG 0 8 2005
CANCELLED
BOOK DUE

Please handle with care.
Thank you for helping to preserve library collections at Harvard.

CONSERVED
RSS 7/2003
HARVARD COLLEGE
LIBRARY

The borrower must return this item on or before the last date stamped below. If another user places a recall for this item, the borrower will be notified of the need for an earlier return.

*Non-receipt of overdue notices does **not** exempt the borrower from overdue fines.*

Harvard College Widener Library
Cambridge, MA 02138   617-495-2413

Please handle with care.
Thank you for helping to preserve library collections at Harvard.

3 2044 050 951 763

The borrower must return this item on or before the last date stamped below. If another user places a recall for this item, the borrower will be notified of the need for an earlier return.

*Non-receipt of overdue notices does **not** exempt the borrower from overdue fines.*

Harvard College Widener Library
Cambridge, MA 02138   617-495-2413

WIDENER
DEC 1 1 2005
AUG 0 8 2005
CANCELLED

Please handle with care.
Thank you for helping to preserve library collections at Harvard.

CONSERVED
RSS 7/2003
HARVARD COLLEGE LIBRARY

3 2044 050 951 763

The borrower must return this item on or before the last date stamped below. If another user places a recall for this item, the borrower will be notified of the need for an earlier return.

*Non-receipt of overdue notices does **not** exempt the borrower from overdue fines.*

Harvard College Widener Library
Cambridge, MA 02138   617-495-2413

WIDENER
DEC 1 2005
AUG 0 8 2005
CANCELLED

Please handle with care.
Thank you for helping to preserve library collections at Harvard.

CONSERVED
RSS 7/2003
HARVARD COLLEGE
LIBRARY

3 2044 050 951 763

The borrower must return this item on or before the last date stamped below. If another user places a recall for this item, the borrower will be notified of the need for an earlier return.

Non-receipt of overdue notices does not exempt the borrower from overdue fines.

Harvard College Widener Library
Cambridge, MA 02138   617-495-2413

WIDENER
DEC 1 1 2005
AUG 0 8 2005
CANCELLED

Please handle with care.
Thank you for helping to preserve library collections at Harvard.

CONSERVED
PSS 7/7 6.3
HARVARD COLLEGE
LIBRARY

3 2044 050 951 763

The borrower must return this item on or before the last date stamped below. If another user places a recall for this item, the borrower will be notified of the need for an earlier return.

*Non-receipt of overdue notices does **not** exempt the borrower from overdue fines.*

Harvard College Widener Library
Cambridge, MA 02138   617-495-2413

WIDENER
DEC 1 1 2005
AUG 0 8 2005
CANCELLED

Please handle with care.
Thank you for helping to preserve library collections at Harvard.

CONSERVED
RSS 7/7 003
HARVARD COLLEGE LIBRARY

3 2044 050 951 763

The borrower must return this item on or before the last date stamped below. If another user places a recall for this item, the borrower will be notified of the need for an earlier return.

Non-receipt of overdue notices does not exempt the borrower from overdue fines.

Harvard College Widener Library
Cambridge, MA 02138   617-495-2413

WIDENER
DEC 1 1 2005
AUG 0 8 2005
CANCELLED

Please handle with care.
Thank you for helping to preserve library collections at Harvard.

CONSERVED
HARVARD COLLEGE LIBRARY

3 2044 050 951 763

The borrower must return this item on or before the last date stamped below. If another user places a recall for this item, the borrower will be notified of the need for an earlier return.

Non-receipt of overdue notices does not exempt the borrower from overdue fines.

Harvard College Widener Library
Cambridge, MA 02138   617-495-2413

WIDENER
DEC 1 1 2005
AUG 0 8 2005
CANCELLED

Please handle with care.
Thank you for helping to preserve library collections at Harvard.

CONSERVED
RSS 7/7 c.3
HARVARD COLLEGE
LIBRARY

3 2044 050 951 763

The borrower must return this item on or before the last date stamped below. If another user places a recall for this item, the borrower will be notified of the need for an earlier return.

Non-receipt of overdue notices does not exempt the borrower from overdue fines.

Harvard College Widener Library
Cambridge, MA 02138   617-495-2413

WIDENER
DEC 1 1 2005
AUG 0 8 2005
CANCELLED

Please handle with care.
Thank you for helping to preserve library collections at Harvard.

CONSERVED
RSS 7/2003
HARVARD COLLEGE
LIBRARY

3 2044 050 951 763

The borrower must return this item on or before the last date stamped below. If another user places a recall for this item, the borrower will be notified of the need for an earlier return.

*Non-receipt of overdue notices does **not** exempt the borrower from overdue fines.*

Harvard College Widener Library
Cambridge, MA 02138   617-495-2413

WIDENER
DEC 1 1 2005
AUG 0 8 2005
CANCELLED

Please handle with care.
Thank you for helping to preserve
library collections at Harvard.

CONSERVED
PSS 7/2003
HARVARD COLLEGE
LIBRARY

3 2044 050 951 763

The borrower must return this item on or before the last date stamped below. If another user places a recall for this item, the borrower will be notified of the need for an earlier return.

*Non-receipt of overdue notices does **not** exempt the borrower from overdue fines.*

Harvard College Widener Library
Cambridge, MA 02138   617-495-2413

WIDENER
DEC 1 2005
AUG 0 8 2005
CANCELLED

Please handle with care.
Thank you for helping to preserve library collections at Harvard.

CONSERVED
HARVARD COLLEGE LIBRARY

3 2044 050 951 763

The borrower must return this item on or before the last date stamped below. If another user places a recall for this item, the borrower will be notified of the need for an earlier return.

*Non-receipt of overdue notices does **not** exempt the borrower from overdue fines.*

Harvard College Widener Library
Cambridge, MA 02138   617-495-2413

WIDENER
DEC 1 1 2005
AUG 0 8 2005
CANCELLED

Please handle with care.
Thank you for helping to preserve
library collections at Harvard.

CONSERVED
RSS 7/7/03
HARVARD COLLEGE
LIBRARY